A MATTER
of the HEART

Anurag Behar is one of India's leading educationists and social-sector leaders. For over twenty years, he has led efforts to improve education in India—from the grassroots level to national policies. A deep commitment to building a just, equitable, and humane society motivates his work.

Anurag derives his understanding of India's realities from spending almost half the year, every year, in some of India's most remote regions, with some of its most vulnerable communities. Bringing his expertise and experience to bear, he was key to drafting India's National Education Policy 2020.

Anurag is the Chief Executive Officer of the Azim Premji Foundation, one of the world's biggest philanthropic institutions. He was the founding Vice Chancellor of the Azim Premji University. In an earlier life, he has led a successful global business in precision engineering.

He is a regular columnist for *Mint, Hindustan Times* and other publications.

ANURAG BEHAR

A MATTER *of the* HEART

EDUCATION IN INDIA

WESTLAND
NON·FICTION

First published by Westland Non-Fiction, an imprint of Westland Books, a division of Nasadiya Technologies Private Limited, in 2023

No. 269/2B, First Floor, 'Irai Arul', Vimalraj Street, Nethaji Nagar, Allappakkam Main Road, Maduravoyal, Chennai 600095

Westland, the Westland logo, Westland Non-Fiction and the Westland Non-Fiction logo are the trademarks of Nasadiya Technologies Private Limited, or its affiliates.

ISBN: 9789395073691

10 9 8 7 6 5 4 3 2 1

Typeset by SÜRYA, New Delhi

Printed at Nutech Print Services - India

Contents

PART THREE: UNDER THE BANYAN TREE

Preface

In June 2010, I moved to the Azim Premji Foundation, from Wipro. A month before that, I started writing a column in *Mint*. The paper was relatively new, having started in 2007. In these twelve years, I have missed a few columns but not many. This book is a collection of carefully chosen selections from those 250-odd pieces. The care and thought are all that of Giri and Mala, not in the slightest mine. Left to me, this book would never have been.

All of what I have written is from my experiences in my role at the Foundation. Even those pieces that seem distant from these experiences, seem so because they deviate from the field of education. But that is a mere matter of form. My work in education has become much more than that for me. It is my connection to the harsh and uplifting reality of this world. It is my immersion into this country of mine. It is a bond of solidarity with countless, each a privilege. So, it is actually the reverse: when I write about education, often though not always, I try to write about something else.

The pieces are of uneven quality. But that doesn't bother me much, because one must improve over time. Galling are those pieces, where a sentiment or insight, said or unsaid, by the many that I meet in the course of the twenty-five-odd weeks that I travel in the field every year, has been shallowed or diluted by my poor writing craft.

I am a manager, not a writer. So, this craft of writing, I have only worked on the side. I have wanted my writing to move people. Not to explain or argue a point but to speak to their hearts. Kabuliwala or the tragedy of Karna have made me more of what I am than all of my engineering education. If even a micro-fraction of that resonance, my writing can find with a few, I am satisfied. And will go on.

Move people—to feel and believe. That public education and public goods matter. Teachers and schools can change the world. We must not live with the injustice and inequity around us. Good people can change the world, even if bit by bit. There are more good people than we imagine; perhaps in us too. Truth and goodness matter, even now. Trying matters, the good fight matters, because that is the only way the arc of history bends, even if we are not there at the bend. Empathy matters more than most else; for the heart of the matter is that it is a matter of the heart, as my father would say. And being ziddi, with all this, matters more than all else.

PART ONE

LIGHT IN AUGUST

Light in August

Kanivekoppalu is a small village in the Pandavapura taluk of Karnataka's Mandya district. To reach it, you have to turn off the Bangalore–Mysore highway around 10 km from Mandya, and drive northwest for 19 km more.

The daylight was fading when we reached this village of 1,475 people, and we went straight to our destination—the sole government school that, with six teachers for 142 students, has a better pupil–teacher ratio than the national average of thirty-nine, and even the thirty prescribed by the Right to Education Act. This really is middle India: fed by the waters of the Cauvery dammed at Krishna Raj Sagar, it is not an agricultural wasteland. Around 40 per cent of the families depend on quarries, the rest on agriculture. Only 110 of the 310 families in the village live below the poverty line.

As a result of our visit, the teachers, headmaster and students were still at the school at 6 p.m. Earlier, when our colleagues had fixed the meeting, we had wondered why they had insisted on that time. They had said that the whole school could turn up only in the evening. We had not understood. After we were lovingly fed chou-chou bath, we dutifully inspected the school. The office doubled up as the music room and trebled up as the library, and also housed the public address system. There were four classrooms. Inspection complete, we were ushered into one of them.

The light outside was dying. The guests (us) were seated facing a classroom full of standard school benches. In ten minutes, the room was full with around seventy parents, the teachers and us. The master of ceremonies was a confident young teacher who was clearly a good public speaker. He introduced us to the members of the school development and monitoring committee (SDMC) and to a bunch of quarrymen and farmers whose children studied in the school.

By then it was completely dark outside. In the light of a petromax, speeches were made. One of them pointed out with pride that there was a girls' toilet under construction. Another vowed to ensure that they get one more teacher. There was a jovial, polite and firm demand for computers.

Then, one man started explaining why he had shifted his child to this school from the convent (meaning private) school slightly away from the village. A lady at the back, who knew the story, thought his explanation woefully insufficient. So, she got up, and as she spoke, her eyes welled up with emotion. There were many strands to her story, but it boiled down to two things: One, the man shifted his child as students in this school learnt better because the teachers cared. Second, she said, '*This* is our school.'

Indeed, it sank into me with each passing moment that these people were there that night because it was their school as much as it was their children's. That, despite it being a government school. I understood why my colleagues had said that the whole school could turn up only in the evening: the village community was as much a part of the school as the teachers.

In the colourful history of Karnataka politics, I hope there will be a page for how, in 2002, the then education minister, H. Vishwanath, used all his political guile to introduce SDMCs in the state. He did so against strong opposition from practically every quarter, because almost every set of local stakeholders had a vested interest in not having a transparent, democratic oversight of schools by the local community. People closely involved in this drama say he did it because he had come to believe that SDMC was really the only institutional method to continually try to improve education in the remotest of our villages. This is one of the good political deeds, more or less erased from our collective memory. That doesn't matter though, because the effect of that deed is visible where it should be.

Its effect was there in Kanivekoppalu, working with extraordinary intensity. It doesn't work as well everywhere in Karnataka (and other states which have done similar things), but often it does. The central question of education reform in India is: how do you make it happen? The policies are not so bad, the science of education is good enough, there are some committed and competent officials and, though most won't believe it, teachers are reasonably paid.

There is progress on many fronts. Still, I wonder why it seems so impossible to pull it all together—pedagogy, management, assessment, accountability, outcomes and so on. India's physical, economic and sociocultural terrain is central to that question. That is what makes it too difficult, makes everyone too far away and dwarfs all grand notions, including that of the state, often to nothingness.

In a nation of 1.3 million schools, mostly in places where electricity finds it difficult to reach, no reform can penetrate unless owned locally. That is the magic glue that can bind everything together at the 1.3 million ends of the chain. It's not easy to do this magic, but it's possible. In Kanivekoppalu, on that dark August night, I saw light.

9 September 2010

Path to Perdition

A bullet through the heart of Michael O'Dwyer killed him. This was on 13 March 1940 in London, twenty-one years after the massacre in Jallianwala Bagh, which O'Dwyer had called 'correct action'. Vengeance has rarely been served colder. For firing that bullet, Udham Singh was tried and then executed on 31 July 1940, passing into the folklore of martyrdom in India.

Violent as his action was, in the court of the people of India, it was also justice delivered, which the British judicial system had brazenly refused to do. Perhaps that is the source of the cathartic effect of his action on the country then, persisting through the decades till now.

Despite this, it seems strange that a then newly formed district was named 'Udham Singh Nagar' in what was Uttar Pradesh in 1995. At least till the electoral calculations were accounted for. The population of the new district was (and is) 66 per cent Hindu, 22 per cent Muslim and 10 per cent Sikh. The cynical practicality of politics had no qualms in attempting to use an Indian hero to activate one community.

One late winter evening, just a week short of seventy-nine years to that fateful day in London, the Sampark Kranti Express deposited me at Rudrapur station, the headquarters of Udham Singh Nagar district. The overbridge between platforms 1 and 2 has steep steps. I have often helped carry bags across for those I have felt for, so I picked up the bag of an elderly lady. She was visiting her son, who was in the army on the western border somewhere. That brief walk together was sufficient for her to tell me that 'there is vengeance in the air and it's never good'. Her grandson took the bag from me, and they were on their way.

The next morning was cold for March, and misty. We drove to Khatima and then some distance further. The public (government) primary school of Tedhaghat was on the main road. As I entered Class V, I heard a boy say, '*Sabki apni raay hoti hai, sabko sunna chaahiye*' (Everyone has different views and they must be heard). How could an eleven-year-old say such a sage thing? The answer to that question was clear as I sat for the next ninety minutes with the children and their teacher Renu Upadhyay.

In the first few minutes, it was apparent that with respect to the school subjects, this group was where it should be, maybe even ahead. However, their communication, capacity to think and sensibilities were remarkable. We conversed about whether demons could be good. Then they explained why it was important to work collaboratively. They wrote three stories for me, working in groups, within ten minutes. Then we talked about sources of water and more. All of their parents were daily wage earners.

Like many other highly effective teachers, Upadhyay doesn't see herself as doing anything special. She says she is doing what she should; she is just doing her job. She is so immersed in her role that every nuance of the complex role of a teacher has become a part of her life. She can't parse these out. Just the way that elite marathon runners routinely run more than 40 km in two and a half hours but would find it hard to explain what makes it possible, aside from complete dedication. Which is what Upadhyay has.

As we were leaving, she gave us a poem that a child had written after Pulwama. '*Unke bhi ghar mein hai koi, unke bhi hain sapne kai; phir bhi woh rehte nidarr*' (There is someone in their homes too, and they too have many dreams, but still, they remain fearless), it read, referring to soldiers. The poem was wistful, with not a trace of vengeance. However, that wasn't the case in the rest of Udham Singh Nagar. From Khatima in the east to Kashipur in the west, through that cold week, vengeance did seem to be mixed in the mist. Belligerent sloganeering by a group of teachers in the precincts of a school, demanding instant retribution, was just one bizarre instance.

In another school, I witnessed a 'group discussion' on Pulwama. The first few moments captured the gist: *'Eent ka jawaab patthar; nestaanabood karenge'* (Retaliate with double force; complete annihilation). These bright, confident children were indoctrinated with canned speeches. Eulogising Udham Singh in schools or naming districts after him is not consecration of retribution. He is an actor in the narrative of India's struggle for independence. But extolling war and demanding vengeance in schools is reprehensible. This is antithetical to every idea of good education, undermines all our constitutional values and violates the most elementary of responsibilities of schools. There is a thin line between such schools and the madrasas that train the Taliban. I have no idea how many teachers and schools are infected, but even one is one too many.

I just couldn't let it go. After a while I asked the children, 'What will happen if we hit each other? Again and again?' They thought about it and one of them said 'We will break each other's bones.' A ten-year-old girl kept looking at me, then in a while, with astonishing insight, she said, *'Shaheed to dono taraf honge, aisa nahi karna chahiye'* (There will be martyrs on both sides, we should not do this).

There may be a few more exceptional children like her. But most will follow their teachers, if they lead them down this path to perdition. This is not the India that Bhagat Singh or Udham Singh gave their life for. This is not the India that we have promised ourselves.

14 March 2019

What Education Needs

He finished by saying, 'Thank you for listening to me, for so long and so patiently.'

His name is Lal Saheb. For my sake he was speaking in Hindi, but would mix in Kannada words with ease where he didn't know the Hindi one. The top of his shorts was tied in a knot to hold them up, worn like only a twelve-year-old who doesn't have many shorts can.

He was standing behind his exhibit on the table, with an audience of ten to twelve people in front. Knowing that I had come all the way from Bengaluru, I was the focus of his attention. He started by informing me that his exhibit was about types of soils, and then he started quizzing me. His smile grew as my very limited understanding of soils became apparent. Before it became embarrassing, he stopped the questions and started talking. He explained how soils are formed, their characteristics and implications, agricultural usage and so on. He engaged me in a conversation, making sure I was getting it. Later, my colleague Rudresh, who understands soils, told me that the boy knew all this better than him. The bravura performance lasted ten minutes, and the sun was on my face all through, from the gap in the shamiana.

The November sun can be as harsh as in March in that area; we were in Halagera, a village about 25 km from Yadgir. There were about 250 children manning about 110 exhibits, all made by them. There were another 650 children participating, along with 125 teachers. This was a Baal Mela. Thirty-five government primary and upper-primary schools from thirty-five villages were involved. The exhibits were across a wide range of curricular topics, from trigonometry to photosynthesis. There were working models, charts, puzzles and games. None would have required more than Rs 20 to make; most were made from everyday knick-knacks.

Preparation for the Mela had begun two months ago. A core group of teachers and some other people coordinated the effort across the schools. In the schools, the teachers and students worked on selecting topics, researching them, conceptualising the exhibits and then making them.

This process went through iterations of various kinds in each school. The schools were learning, as the excitement was building up. The event itself was a big fair, a Mela. It was hosted by the village community, whose members were running around making the arrangements. The lunch was prepared by the community people in massive utensils on huge chulhas, built for the event. Five villages from around were supporting them. It was bigger than the biggest wedding celebration in those villages. People from all around had come to see the Mela. Inside the shamianas, the children were engrossed in explaining their exhibits to other children, to teachers and to the hundreds that had showed up from the thirty-five villages.

There was a range in the depth of understanding that the children demonstrated, but none were spewing merely memorised stuff. All were deeply engaged and confident. As I went around, some children would falter at some level in explaining the concepts of the exhibits. Three times when this happened, the boy with the knotted shorts showed up, and went ahead explaining the concept with ease. His name could well have been Lal Badshah. While the Badshah possessed exceptional energy and a startling range of deep understanding, I observed at least thirty other children with remarkable thoughtfulness and confidence. And all the children and teachers present were fully involved.

The previous day, I had visited another Baal Mela. It was in Kurekanal. This involved over 250 children from eleven schools. Unlike the Mela at Halagera, this one had a focus area. All the exhibits were about geography. The arrangements, the preparation, the involvement of the community were the same as in Halagera. This process is common across all such Melas that are held; this year, there have been thirty-four Baal Melas in different villages across the Yadgir district, involving more than 400 schools.

Things like this can just remain exciting social events; it's the process that ensures that it has real educational meaning. The Mela and the exhibit is just the final step, it's the way the teachers and students collaborate and the ownership of the event that makes it an effective pedagogical approach.

It also requires a deliberate effort to connect the preparation to other things that happen in the school, in the classroom and outside; an overall integration within the curriculum in the school. It is also a powerful mechanism of teachers' professional development, when integrated with other relevant mechanisms such as workshops, peer learning networks, etc. Needless to say, it energises the local community around education. So that we don't miss most of the iceberg: to get to this point in Yadgir district, it has taken ten years of painstaking, sustained work by scores of people to build and nurture the process.

Good things can happen in education, if we accept its complexity, rather than looking for shortcuts and silver bullets.

10 December 2014

Tales of Heroism from Gulbarga

One morning in Gulbarga, Mahadev and Jagannath insisted that we visit a school with them. This village wasn't far from the city, about 7 km from the outskirts. When we go to a school in a car, we usually park some distance away. A car can be a matter of great curiosity amongst the kids, and cause a disturbance, which we try to avoid. As we reached the village, the students were still on their way to school. Two of them met us and asked us where we wanted to go. On learning that we were headed for their school, they took charge and led us. They seemed unusually confident for twelve-year-olds, and also seemed unusually cheerful for kids on their way to school. The building of the school was even more unusual. Having been to hundreds of government schools, I had never seen one like that before. It was constructed on columns, raising it above the ground level, as though on stilts. One could almost walk under the school. It had a series of classrooms, side by side, with all doors opening to a common narrow verandah, from where steps led to the ground level. The two children handed us over to one of their teachers, who took us to the head teacher's office.

It was a small room. Soon, the head teacher, Prameela Bai, and all the other teachers, Asha Hegde, Indumati, Jyoti and Sunanda, trooped in. The students had been given some assignments as the teachers wanted to chat with us. While we were adjusting to the cramped seating, which had no place for another person, Shobha strode in. Some people have a presence. She remained standing at the door with a half-smile, and said that she was the anganwadi worker, and not a teacher. Someone corrected her, saying that she was the anganwadi teacher; she brushed it aside.

In the government employee hierarchy, an anganwadi worker is way below schoolteachers, let alone the head teacher.

Shobha's demeanour and the response of the teachers to her did not conform in any way to that hierarchy. She was clearly an integral part of that team. Then, Prameela Bai said Shobha was the founder of the school, and with that she began narrating its story.

Eight years ago, the government primary school was started in the village by Asha Hegde who remained the sole teacher for the first three years. At the same time an anganwadi was also started, and Shobha was recruited as the anganwadi worker; she was from the same village. The two shared a makeshift temporary structure. They also became partners in all the struggles, small and big. The village panchayat was to allocate land for the school, which it kept putting off. No one would admit it, but this disinterest seemed to be driven by deep-rooted socio-political processes. Caste was dominant in local politics, and the school was largely attended by children of the local tribal community. It was what is called in that area a thanda school, a school set up near the tribal habitation.

The blow-by-blow account of those first few years can be a natural screenplay for a Shyam Benegal film. If I could, I would cast Smita Patil as Shobha and Nutan as Asha. The two women battled for three years, Shobha leading the charge, marshalling whatever she could. In the end, the panchayat relented and gave them land. But the land that they gave was directly in a water channel, which would flood in the monsoon. They took what they got, and then worked within the education department for a design for the school that would tackle the torrential water flow during the monsoon. That is how the school on stilts came about. A simple but effective design, the heavy water flow just passes beneath the school. After the school building came up, the student numbers grew, Prameela Bai was appointed as the head teacher and more teachers joined.

We spent some time in the classes, witnessing interesting pedagogical practices and the engaged children. It was a functioning and happy school. At the heart of it seemed a rare deep camaraderie that was there amongst the teachers. Three-sided conversations give glimpses.

Prameela Bai told me, 'I do nothing much; my teachers are excellent.' Asha's affection and respect for Shobha was evident, she was also very clear it was the head teacher who made everything click.

While we were leaving, Shobha said, 'I was an eighth pass; Asha got me to do tenth, then twelfth and then a degree; she made me what I am.'

A school's purpose is educational, but it is fundamentally a social institution. So, any school has to overcome multiple internal and external social challenges to function. This is another reason why the role of a teacher is so complex, which we non-teachers often fail to recognise. There are thousands of schools, such as this one in Sharana Sirasagi Thanda, with their own quiet stories, which when listened to, tell tales of everyday heroism.

17 September 2014

Big Small Steps

My childhood friend Kabir would have been thrilled to be there. The talk was about how to use the school building for pedagogical purposes, that is, for teaching and learning. Kabir is an architect who specialises in developing and using the premises of a school as an integral part of education. There was discussion about how doors can be used to explain angles and how the woodwork and tiles can be used for learning the concept of area. This discussion would be unusual in most schools. And this was the government school in Khamaria, in rural Chhattisgarh.

Khamaria is about 17 km from Dhamtari, the district headquarters, which is 75 km from Raipur. It's a small village, 12 km off the main road, with about 975 inhabitants—mostly farming families with very small land holdings. The plains of Chhattisgarh are never cold; the January afternoon was pleasant. We were sitting on the floor, but for the head teacher and a village elder. I weighed whether it was because they wanted a befitting higher status or because of the difficulty of sitting on the floor, and realised that it was the latter.

The discussion was unusual in the extreme, not only because of where it was happening, but also because of who was involved. It was with a few women from the village whose children were studying in the school and some representatives of the village community. There were seven women and six men. Along with the head teacher, two of the teachers were there as well. There were four of us visitors. We were told that a few months ago, the villagers had rented a tractor-trolley. Some twenty of them had climbed in, along with the schoolteachers, and had gone to visit the government primary schools in Gahnasiar and Doongripara, about 75 km away. They went because they had heard from one of the teachers, who had been there before, that these were excellent schools. They spent the entire day there, and learnt many practical things about good schools. Ever since then, they had been working together to implement the practices that they had seen. The ideas about using the building for teaching came from that visit.

This intensity of community engagement in a school is unusual. They described how it had developed. Clearly the head teacher had played a big role. In his assessment, the turning point was when a few years ago, the community (cajoled by him) decided that only women would be members of the school management committee (SMC). The transformation that decision brought about was captured symbolically in something quite simple. When the SMC comprised mostly men, a meeting scheduled at 3 p.m. would start at 6 p.m., if at all. With the change in the gender mix, a meeting scheduled at 3 p.m. has full quorum by 2.45 p.m. While this story was being told, the men were smiling. At the end, one of them added that it was natural that an SMC with women would work better, because the mothers were far more invested in their children and their well-being. By this time, anecdotes about the school and its history were free-flowing. It was repeatedly pointed out that the elder sitting on the chair had himself done the woodwork of the school, some twenty-five years ago.

We heard of an intriguing practice at the school—any child who is absent, even for a day, writes a nice letter. This is not a leave application. It describes in detail what she did while not in school and what she learnt from that. She then reads out the letter in the morning assembly.

Later, we read through some of these letters. As the conversation unfolded, we learnt that the teacher in charge of the primary section had refused a promotion because he wanted to stay and help take things forward, and so had moved to the upper-primary section as a teacher. This quiet man sitting in the corner seemed to be the force behind many of these novel practices. One day, he had asked two of the women there to get into a class and talk about values. His reasoning was, who better than mothers to talk about values. The two women eventually used folk tales for the class.

As you walk around the school, you see many things that can improve. But they look trivial, dominated by the spirit of the school and the community, striving for improvement. How does this spirit get fostered? There is no mechanical formula or recipe. We won't even search for one, once we accept education to be the complex social process it is. We are aware of some minimal conditions required—a few motivated teachers, basic support from the system and a sense of public good; with that we need to have a go everywhere. We also need to recognise the big small steps in the Khamarias of this country rather than berating them in meeting rooms and newspaper columns.

5 March 2014

Fun with History?

It was in the early 1980s that I read E.H. Carr's *What is History?* While I didn't understand it much, the book was still important for me. The basic idea that there could be different histories was a relief. It helped reconcile the multiple narratives that I would hear. One of them was about how the small princely state of Sarangarh had an inalienable right not to join the Indian union, but how it was bullied in 1948 and had to join. The story's most riveting episode was the climactic face-off with Sardar Patel. I would hear these things in the heat of the summer vacation in Sarangarh. Then, I would return to Bhopal and the nationalistic texts of the history books in my Kendriya Vidyalaya. The books painted a diametrically opposite narrative of the events of 1948. There was, of course, not even a mention of the story that was central to the identity of Sarangarh.

There were many other such omissions, competing histories and muddied waters in the histories that we heard of and read; for example, about the various dargahs in Bhopal, the origins of the Bhopal Lake, the occupation of the Gond lands. So, Carr did me a great favour. Later, while still at school, I watched Rashomon and started reading Latin American magical realism. It was this, with the backdrop of Carr, that let me really enjoy history.

I have watched with interest and admiration as NCERT steadily improves the history books that it publishes. The books are very good, and they draw from the very thoughtful National Curriculum Framework, 2005 (NCF). Many of the people involved with these improvements were there at an annual meetings of our friends, partners and other invitees working in education. It's perhaps described better as a retreat; we call it 'the forum'. We usually hold it at Bengaluru's Centre for Learning, which is perhaps one of the very best schools in this country.

The theme of the forum in December 2010 was history. It was a fascinating three days of discussion with some of the most insightful people working on history and history education. It was also an explanation of how and why history education has moved in a progressive direction at the curricular level. However, these improvements have left most of our schools, their textbooks and approaches untouched. History in our schools continues to be a dreary list of dates and varnished mono-narratives. Children are right to detest the history they are made to study.

My daughter is methodical and organised. In February 2011, two months after the elevating forum on history, she methodically made me go through with her a series of gender discriminatory narratives in the history portion of her social studies textbook. She was eleven then, and so she used a simpler phrase, 'girl-hating'.

In Bengaluru or in the village schools that I am so often in, I have found history the quickest litmus test for the kind of education that is really happening in a school. History brings to life the entire range of politics, prejudices and possibilities of education, in a few sentences and moments. So, I was very intrigued when, on a dry, warm winter afternoon in Surpur two months ago, the gathered cluster resource persons (CRP) said they wanted to talk about history. Cluster Resource Persons are government schoolteachers, placed in a role in which they are supposed to provide academic support to a group of eight to twelve schools. This system is there across most states in the country.

Surpur is in Yadgir district, which figures in all lists of Karnataka's most disadvantaged districts. There were twelve CRPs and they had a ninety-minute discussion. Most of it would have warmed the hearts of the people gathered at the forum in December 2010. They started by talking about the methods of history, and the importance of different sources of history. They were most intense about the importance of the local history of Surpur, its alternative narratives and how the curriculum actually enables the integration of local history in the classroom, despite it not being available in textbooks. Then, they drifted to how geography has shaped Surpur's history, and the interlinkages of what are often considered completely distinct subjects in schools. We ended with the discomfort they felt about recent history, because of its politics being still alive. The possibilities in history, which we stunt, seem to be blooming in the twelve CRPs in Surpur. I am confident that the schools they work with will also discover how to wander around in the labyrinths of man through the doors of history.

Learning and teaching history can be an exciting adventure, full of surprises. Instead, we often reduce it to a monotonous drill, or worse still, a tool of propaganda. The group at Surpur showed the good that's possible, with thoughtfulness and the use of imagination. But then, all this is true of education overall.

22 January 2014

Surpur ke Sholay

It was in Kembavi that it started.

A discussion by a group of teachers had just got over at the teacher learning centre (TLC) and some of them were complaining about the sole computer not working reliably. I was amused to hear that their real interest in the computer was to do with the standard movie-making software. Some of them had been trying to make movies, edit them and give voice-overs on the computer. They were all government schoolteachers from around Kembavi. After one round of complaining was over, I asked, 'Can you not use this film-making for your students?' This incident happened in January.

Kembavi is 30 km from Surpur, the taluk (administrative subdivision) headquarters; the district is Yadgir, in north-east Karnataka (NEK). This area is no different from the disadvantaged parts of Chhattisgarh, Odisha or Rajasthan. For most whose impressions of Karnataka are formed by the glitz of Bengaluru or languorous estates in Coorg, NEK will seem like another country; these districts are among the most deprived in the country on lists that assess human and social development indices.

I returned to Surpur in June. In the heat, the landscape there is menacing. Hills of rocks all around, you seem to be in one of the scorching scenes of *Sholay*. I was taken to the first floor of the Government Urdu Elementary School. One room in the school is used as the Surpur TLC. The school itself was stuck on one of the rocky hills. One old haveli joined with another old building attached to two new rooms made up the school. Getting in required us to go through a maze of low doors, down a short flight of stairs and up another.

The TLC room was darkened. It was ready for a movie show. It was full of teachers and some of my colleagues. My friend and colleague, Umashankar, who had been with me through the trip, had kept this secret well; actually, for the past six months. He sat next to me, gurgling with laughter and happiness as the events of the next ninety minutes unfolded. I was told that they had taken up the challenge that I had thrown at them in January, and had made films for children, and that's what they were going to show me. To pick up one statement in one meeting as a challenge takes a certain character and sensibility. They showed me five films. Each of the films made by them was directly related to something in the curriculum that they were teaching at school. Each was four- to five-minutes long, shot on a small, cheap digital camera of the TLC and edited on the computer there. The films' topics ranged from water scarcity to pottery and to different modes of travel. It even included a short, animated story.

The films were of excellent quality. Well-thought-through scripts, excellent shots, appropriate voice-over and music, almost professional editing; it was hard to believe they were made by a bunch of government elementary schoolteachers living in villages and towns around Surpur. They were very excited. They had become film-makers, who have an almost mythical status in our country. Each one of them narrated how the films were helping them in the class. It used to take two forty-five-minute periods to teach the transport lesson; with the film, it was being done more effectively in just one period. The intricacy of pottery, from collection of the mud to baking, was there for all to see. By comparing ponds in a few villages, the causes of water scarcity had come alive. And so on. After the show was over, they discussed their plans of involving more teachers and also children, and then we parted.

The films in themselves were good, but their effect on the

teachers was far more dramatic. It had given them a sense of confidence that is far more valuable. They had taken charge of the curriculum in a way which usually only remains as a wish of educationists. It is one of the most effective capacity-development exercises that I have seen for teachers. As an aside, it is also one of the few truly effective uses of technology that I have seen in the reality of our country, enhancing real education rather than stunting it. But let's not start distributing digital cameras. All this (and much more) has happened only with the sustained institutional space created by TLC—that is the heart of the issue. Our system with its institutional rigidities, super-centralised structures and an approach that treats teachers (and others) as irrelevant cogs in the wheel breeds indifference. A TLC subverts this situation, creating a local and vibrant community of intellectual exchange and social support, while still being very much a part of the system. But it does take long; in the case of Surpur, it has taken eight years of work to get here. There are no shortcuts in the journey to improving education.

11 July 2012

Gangs of Malpura

The room was 20 ft by 30 ft. There were about forty of us in the room: thirty-four government schoolteachers and six of us observers, all sitting on the ground on dhurries. The flaming flatland outside, with only clumps of thorny babool in sight, was at 44 degrees Celsius; the inside felt more like 50. The fans stood still, with no power. I was bathed in sweat, no one else was. They were all used to these conditions, living in villages and towns around Malpura.

This town with a population of about 30,000 is one of the block headquarters in the district of Tonk, south of Jaipur. The group had collected at 10 a.m. coming from villages and towns around the block, some as far away as 50 km. Working in six smaller groups, they started with the distribution of a reading on how to use microscopes, and what wonders could be discovered through them.

Each group had a basic microscope, glass slides, slicers, dyes and material to make slides from, like potato, capsicum and dirty water. After fifteen minutes of reading, the room broke into a frenzy of activity: cutting and slicing the vegetables, dyeing them, moving the microscope to where there was adequate light. Scrambling to see the slides, and to show with pride to others, when a good one was made. Drawing what they saw, and comparing it with the diagrams in the reading. Identifying the different cells and structures, or the microbes floating in the dirty water.

I was dragged from group to group to witness the wonders of their slides. The heat had drenched me; I was amazed at how they seemed cool and comfortable, with that level of energetic activity, in that oven-like room. The meeting was scheduled from 10 a.m. to 12 noon. They refused to stop.

They had to be dragged away from their activity at 12.45 p.m. They settled down with difficulty in a circle. Goel and Pathak, two of the teachers from their midst, took charge of the proceedings. They facilitated an outstanding debriefing session. The goal was to articulate what they had learnt, and how they would use it in their classrooms.

In thirty minutes of intense discussion, they came up with twelve points, some specific ('dyes have to be fresh') and some fundamental ('collaboration leads to better learning in activities'). Having gone there all the way from Bangalore, I was given the opportunity to chat with them for fifteen minutes. That ended the session at 1.30 p.m., having started at 10 a.m., without even a tea break. They collected their bags and went out in the scorching sun to ride their two-wheelers back to their homes, with the temperature at 46 degrees Celsius.

This group is one of the two voluntary teacher forums in the block of Malpura. It was formed in 2009, initially organised by my colleague Devendra, and over time with increasing organising ownership of the teachers. The two groups have about 150 government schoolteachers in all. The block of Malpura has about 800 teachers in total. The teachers attend these sessions voluntarily; there is no order from the government or an official. They attend it on their time, not school hours.

The session that I have described was on a holiday. With their homes quite far away, and poor public transport, they brave the conditions and spend their own money on petrol for their two-wheelers. They get no credit, no money and no external reward for being a part of this forum. The only question that I asked them was: 'Why do you come here, on a holiday, spending your own money, in this heat, when no one has asked you to and there is no reward for it?' And, they do this twice a month. One of the privileges of my job is that I get to meet such people every few days, across the country. The answer that I heard in Malpura for my question is very much the answer that I hear across the country: 'We come here because we want to learn, to teach better, so that our students learn better.' As simple as that.

There are fifteen such forums that we are involved with across two districts in Rajasthan, with 800 teacher members—that makes it about 15 per cent of the government-teacher population in those two districts. Across the country, we are involved with scores of such groups, and there are probably many more facilitated by other organisations, including government agencies. There is enough goodness in people (that's what teachers are), in enough numbers, to be at the core of sustained improvement in education. Change is fired by institutional structures with some support, on a sustained basis; structures that support intellectual exchange and capacity development, while fostering a sense of connectedness and being valued. Let's extend this hand of support to these good women and men, instead of reviling them. They are the reason for hope, however long and tough the journey.

27 June 2012

Mystery of Nagala

We walked into the government primary school at Nagala, 15 km from Rudrapur in Uttarakhand, at 8.30 a.m. There was no one to receive us. We entered the first classroom that we saw. There were forty-three children. They were all engrossed in their work. There was no teacher in the class.

As Anant and I entered, the children looked at us curiously and started an excited conversation—from telling us about their artwork to reciting their favourite poem and story, and many things in between. For the last ten minutes, I sat down in their midst, on the floor, as Anant recited a poem at their request.

The class retained the difficult balance between noise and silence; abuzz with curiosity and excitement. There was a minor scuffle between two children, which was sorted out very quickly by the intervention of their neighbours. Then we told them that we had to go. Nothing could have prepared me for their reaction. The kids jumped on me and there was a heap of children on top of me, like a football team's celebration after a stunning goal. They didn't want me to go. They allowed me to leave only after innumerable arguments; the one explanation that seemed to convince them was that my daughter and son were awaiting me in Bangalore. Those last five minutes were a loud fracas. It caught the attention of the teacher, wherever he was, and so he had come to the class. He was standing at the door, watching with amusement.

That's how I first met their teacher, Pradeep Pande. Soon I met the other teachers in the school, Ravi Mohan and Vinay Prabha. The principal of the school, Manju Bisht, was away on a short training. Together, this group runs this remarkable school.

The nature of the school is reflected partially in my experience there. The children are confident and curious. They are 'self-disciplined' in the most positive sense of that word. They learn and do good work, often on their own. And they are happy. It's the kind of situation that we would like to see in all our (government and private) schools, but most often don't. This school has the same constraints and frugal resources as a million other government schools. Its children come from the same disadvantaged, underprivileged groups. What, then, is the force propelling the mystery of the school at Nagala, which makes it so different?

We walked through the school. We saw the kitchen with a novel design for the chulahs, which packs the firewood outside the kitchen, leaving more space for movement and less fumes inside. This redesign was within the budget for the kitchen. When the government budget gave them money for two classrooms a few years ago, they persuaded the block officials to let them make a hall instead. It needs imagination and initiative, to get these seemingly small changes done in the government system. It needed more than that, to do some of the other things that they have done in the school. They persuaded a local businessman to sponsor the salary of an additional teacher for a year. We saw the waterlogged backyard, across which the village community had built a raised brick path to reach the toilets. A construction contractor gave them the material for the steel gate to the school.

They described some of their academic issues and pedagogical methods. These were as creative and as practical as all their other actions. They are thoughtful, sensitive and sensible teachers—what we hope to see in all our classrooms. Their abilities and tenacity were really at the heart of the remarkable classroom that we had encountered earlier—which was learning without a teacher. They had devised the system and the culture, so each class could run for some time on its own, because between three teachers they had to handle 300 children.

The answer to the mystery of the school at Nagala is in plain sight. It's the group that runs the school. It works in the same government school system, but the constraints and apathy of the system has never stopped the group. It persistently looks for spaces to manoeuvre within the system. It seeks and gets support within the government and the community. We need continuing and massive systemic improvements in education, but we must not underestimate the importance and power of individuals taking initiative and changing things, within the space they have. I feel that we, too often and too easily, pass on everything to the 'system', abdicating our responsibility in making change happen.

Kailash, one of my colleagues, one day found Pande shivering with high fever, under a blanket in the school office, the classes merrily going on without teachers. When asked why he was in the school in that state, he said, 'If I am here, the classes go on, so I might as well lie down here, instead of at home.'

We need to reform the education system. But we also need to find and encourage the spirited ones—the people who make all the difference.

14 July 2011

Khalbali hai Khalbali, Toofan hi Toofan aur Ziddi Hum Yahan

She was visible in the glow of the winter dusk, framed by a door. The lone hut stood at the edge of the thick treeline. I stopped on the path, instinctively in front of her. She was eighty, perhaps seventy. Having stopped, I couldn't leave without speaking, but I struggled. What could be small talk that both of us could relate to? She didn't move, waiting.

'It is very cold,' I said.

'It is very cold,' she said.

'Have you eaten?'

'Yes, rice,' she replied.

'Who else is there at home?'

'No one.'

'I don't mean now, but who else is in your family?'

'No one.'

I felt trapped. Leaving then, after those words of hers, was impossible, and proceeding with the conversation, fraught with darkness. I braved it and asked, 'Why are you alone?' Her son had died a long time ago, her husband ten years ago. His family had left her in this village, which is where she grew up. There are no close relatives left in the village. She has no land. 'How do you get by?' I asked. She earns from daily wage labour, when she gets it, at her age. Else, some villager helps her.

'Why don't you take their help to fight for your rights with your husband's family?'

'*Kya faydaa*? [What's the point?],' she said.

'What about the various public welfare schemes?'

'I have tried, but *kya faydaa*?'

'Can we do something? I have friends who live in the nearby town.'

'*Kya faydaa*?'

I have been stabbed with those two words before. By the unforgiving circumstances distilled in them. Of her life. Of our life. In the inferno of humanity that has continued to blaze through 2019.

Unnao provides a faithfully bleak allegory for this conflagration. A young woman is raped. Then, she and her family are openly dragged through a hell of atrocities. Finally, they are crushed by a speeding truck with blanked-out number plates. Another young woman is raped. Then she is set ablaze. Emboldened, another perpetrator in another city, threatens his victim with an 'Unnao-like fate', while elsewhere another young woman is raped and burnt. The four accused are shot dead by the police in an 'encounter'. People celebrate 'instant justice'.

The most powerful man in the world publicly mocks and bullies a child. In a country where 'never again' was a foundational article of faith, a synagogue is attacked, two people killed. Under this shadow, Nazi slogans and death threats are raised in the run-up to an election. Elsewhere, a well-known journalist is cut to pieces inside a diplomatic consulate in a beautiful city that is a cradle of civilisation. The global scientific community pronounces a desperate warning about the future of Earth to deaf ears in power, even as the climate crisis buffets the planet every day.

These are the flames that we see, even when we don't want to. Inside, the fuel is the everyday lives of average people. With insecurities and struggles, helpless and angry, and trying, wanting, but never there. All the while, there are enough leaders of perdition inflicting small and big atrocities, tearing at every cleavage of society, lacerating instead of healing and fanning the flames. Truth and goodness are both up for grabs. Perhaps it has always been so, but illuminated by the fire that engulfs us, it is clearer.

'*Kya faydaa ziddi hone ka*? [What's the point in being stubborn, in this world?],' I have been asked. Ziddi is my emblematic metaphor for everything that you need to fight the good fight, win or lose. I, too, have wondered. Did the Mahatma think *kya faydaa* in the end, with the country engulfed in a sectarian blaze? Or did the Buddha say the same to himself, passing away amid the ruins of what he had built, wrought by violence all around, including the carnage of his own Shakya clan? How about Yugantar himself? Did he feel *kya faydaa* as he lay dying amid the fratricidal end of the Yadavas, and the earth scorched by Kurukshetra?

There was a moment at the edge of that abyss. Without my saying so, 13,000 km away, my son knew. He texted me, 'I will do something. I don't know what, but I will. I will.' Those who care and love, know that distance and time are immaterial. That is a promise to carry on with, and to live by.

In that cold, dark evening, from within the treeline, a sixteen-year-old boy emerged. He said, '*Chalo, dadi* [Let's go, grandmother]'. She was ready to go. I asked her who he was.

She said, 'He is the boy.'

'But who is he?'

'He is the boy.'

'Is he your relative?'

'No, but he takes care of me.'

The boy was amused. I asked him, 'Are you related to her?' 'No,' he said, 'but she is all alone. So, I have to do something. I do and I will.' He held her hand and they walked together, into the light.

The arc of history has no natural bend. If it has to bend

towards the just and the good, we have to try, and keep at it. The Mahatma, the Buddha and Yugantar all tried, and so here we are. We are not them. We are infinitesimal, but so have most others been in history, and the cumulative weight has mattered. As 2019 passes, we know that it matters even more. You must be ziddi, because then I can be. For the good fight and maybe more. You must be ziddi, because that is enough for me to carry on with and to live by. And I will be ziddi, for you. We will make it matter—that is the faydaa.

19 December 2019

Vibrant Classrooms and
Narcissism of Small Differences

Puducherry has systematically gone about starting pre-primary classes in all its government primary schools. Anyone you ask there, they point to this levelling of the playing field as a key reason for enrolment increases in these schools, and the drop on that metric in private schools. Most public-school teachers across the country point at the lack of pre-primary classes in their schools as a severe handicap, and a structural impediment that deflects students to private schools, at the very beginning of schooling, which is where they then continue.

Many teachers in Puducherry, of their own initiative, have expanded the play-based and non-didactic pedagogical approach of pre-primary classes to primary classes. Both these matters, on which action is visible in Puducherry, pre-empts the draft National Education Policy 2019 (NEP).

Gomathy was teaching Class III at the Savarirayalu Government Primary School in Puducherry. The students were involved in the addition of three- and four-digit numbers, working in five groups of five students each. Each group had some locally made (or very low-cost) pedagogical aids to help with the exercise. Observation made it clear that each group had a mix of students based on their comfort with the exercise. Gomathy ensured that students who were at ease with the problems did not dominate the proceedings and helped others who were struggling.

Energy was flowing in the class, with kids racing to their teacher for more problem sheets after finishing one. Gomathy explained how the school's teachers had collectively decided to adopt a 'cohort–teacher' approach, meaning the same teacher teaches a cohort of students all subjects as they progress from class to class, till they move out from primary school. This system is very useful in the early classes, when the basis of learning is primarily the relationship of trust and care between students and teachers. Learning from experience, they had tweaked this system to ensure that no cohort of students is put at a disadvantage by the cohort–teacher's limitations. Those who have difficulty in teaching a subject, for example, maths at the level of Classes IV–V, are supported (or replaced) by other teachers who are comfortable in that subject.

Such vibrant, adequately resourced classrooms, with engaged teachers who have an empathetic relationship with their students are an integral part of the NEP's vision. So is the importance of empowerment of schools to take key educational decisions. It also highlights the centrality of the role of teachers, of their working together and the importance of 'professional learning communities' of teachers.

Gomathy surprised me when she told me that she had translated Chapter 14 (National Research Foundation) of the NEP into Tamil. Her initiative and competence are not limited to school classrooms. She was a part of a collective civil society exercise to translate the entire 484 pages of the NEP into Tamil. Later in the evening, at a consultation meeting on the NEP, I saw the result of this remarkable effort—neatly printed Tamil versions of the Policy. About forty people were involved in this effort, most of them public schoolteachers.

Over the course of the next three days, I was in three such meetings across the country, attended mostly by teachers and activists for public education. These were lively discussions. There were several clarifications, many constructive suggestions, a few disagreements and a widespread acknowledgement of the much-needed transformations of Indian education that the NEP lays out.

With hundreds of such points of feedback, the NEP in its final form will surely be significantly improved.

In sharp contrast to such constructive engagement is the reaction of some educationists. Many have read non-existent sections and intentions into the draft. As an example, many have seen the horrors of commercialisation and privatisation writ in the NEP, despite the painstaking effort of the committee to underline the importance of public education. Others are exhibiting narcissism of small differences. Both sets are being irresponsible to the very causes that they have fought for most of their lives. Because most of these causes, fought and advocated by almost everyone committed to a vibrant public education system, including these educationists, are integral to the NEP.

Such educationists also seem to be losing sight of the fundamental nature of public policymaking—always an exercise in negotiation and balance between contending perspectives. Education in our country is a tricky battlefield. Any policy initiative that manages to stick to basic principles and succeeds in avoiding egregious mistakes or surrendering to fringe interests is definitely a success. The Kasturirangan committee has done more; while avoiding such mistakes with remarkable diligence, it has actually created a blueprint for what most in education have for decades wished for.

The final word goes to one of the wisest and most competent of public administrators in the country, who wryly commented at the end of a consultation meeting with a large group of powerful people in education, 'If so many people with deep vested interests are dead against the NEP, it must be absolutely the right thing to do; let's implement it immediately.'

Until our public intellectuals of whatever hue, liberal, left, centrist or right leaning, are more thoughtful about the reality of policymaking, are alive to the political moment and are intellectually non-partisan, policymakers will continue to be very suspicious of experts. And that is not good for society in the long run.

18 July 2019

Stranger in My Own Land

In the past five years, I have spent about 100 days each year in the field. These are places where we work, across districts in Uttarakhand, Rajasthan, Madhya Pradesh, Chhattisgarh, Telangana, Karnataka and Puducherry. I have been visiting these places for eight years, but it is in the last five that there has been a regular rhythm.

This rhythm covers forty-seven districts at least once a year. Our team members are in over 175 small towns. I try to but am not able to go to all these towns every year. Infrequently, I do travel to other parts of India and, more regularly, to Delhi and the US, all of which is in addition to my travelling in the field.

Everywhere in the field, I do the same things: spend time with our team, visit public (government) schools, talk to children, meet teachers individually and in groups, observe some workshops, chat with people from communities where the schools are located, meet people from other social sector organisations and, once in a while, government officials, and also pick up threads of conversations with drivers, dhabawalas and waiters, from where we left off the previous year. All this is not only in the district headquarters, which is usually the largest town around, but in villages and small towns spread across that district.

In many of these places, the dogs and I are familiar with each other. Wherever I am, I run in the mornings on the roads or paths. Every such running route has dogs. The aggressive and spiteful ones, I have identified. But, as I have learnt, most are just nice and friendly. If you slow down the pace or stop, their affection wags their tails.

These repeated visits develop bonds with the places, not just the dogs, nurturing acquaintances into relationships and regularly opening windows into life, which can happen only by chance for a one-time visitor. Clearly, this is one of the great privileges of my role, to be able to experience India with this intimacy.

A teacher brings dal–chawal–subzi from home for me at her school, in the searing heat of Mudgal. She had met me a year before and remembers that I can't eat spicy food. Up, high in the mountains in Kumaon, plain dal–roti is ready for me in another school, along with the mid-day meal for children. They also remember my preference. Lakshmi's children have grown in these years, while her small dhaba between Barkot and Uttarkashi at the Giloti bend acts like a home kitchen for me. And my colleagues, too, never forget.

I couldn't function in this country of spice without the care that I get, often at the cost of much inconvenience to those who bestow this care on me. Most of them have no reason to care, other than that they just care without reason. The human substrate is deep in this country of spice.

How do you make a living when drought has started in January? How many days of wages can you skip to take your mother to the hospital which is 100 km away? What do you do with guards who won't let you enter the forest to get firewood, court orders be damned? Questions like these seem unanswerable to me. But people live through these and more every day, and on very little, in all these places.

Never will I ever forget what the teacher from Dei told me, '*Yahan to sab kuch chalne lagta hai* [We make everything work here].' She was talking about stubs of chalk. Too small to hold, but she uses them till they crumble between her thumb and finger. Everything has value here, never to be thrown away. Used in ways that are hard to imagine, till they can't. Because everything is scarce. Though that is not a complaint heard, let alone a refrain. It is just another dimension of life. Every time I am back in this other India of mine, I spend each rupee even more carefully.

These are different worlds, that of my 100 days, and the rest—not separated worlds, but like the shores and the depths of the ocean. The depths of the ocean is most of India. Those who are on the shores know not of the depths, unless they make an effort. Many have come from those very depths, but have now cut themselves off, and exorcised their memories.

Most economic and political power resides in these shores, which I encounter frequently in the other 200 days. Too few of these purveyors of power—academics, administrators, policymakers, business people, journalists, professionals and more—make the effort to experience this vast and real India. But they offer opinions and, worse, take decisions that affect those whose lives they have no clue about. Politicians make more of an effort, since their trade depends on it.

We are strangers in our own land. Those who take the effort to discover this land may or may not help change things, but they themselves certainly change. How can they not, engulfed by people who are unrelenting in the face of all odds, yet caring without reason? Every visit to this India changes me. Usually bit by bit, sometimes dramatically. Every such day, I am more grateful for the limitless privileges of my life and more aware of the limits of my abilities. And each such day, the limitless power of the human spirit pours energy and hope.

You may not have to travel 100 days like me; it may just be across the street in Bengaluru or Delhi.

Try leaving the shores for the depths of this ocean of human spirit.

28 February 2019

An Average Week in a School

The school was painted canary yellow. I haven't seen another school of that colour. It was perched at one end of the village far away from the houses, where the steep slope began. The village of 1,000 people was on a mountain top higher than most, with the endless Kumaon on all sides. Almora was visible about 30 km away. The startling yellow, and its dramatic perch, probably makes the school visible from very long distances, like a lighthouse. The village is called Satyun.

The colour of that school was the only out-of-the-ordinary thing that I saw and heard last week in Kumaon in Uttarakhand. It was a normal week, spent in villages and small towns, meeting teachers and other government-school functionaries. In three days, across five meetings, I would have heard 150-odd of them. All the people who attended the meetings were there of their own volition and everyone knew that the purpose of the gathering was to discuss how to improve their schools.

There aren't enough teachers in remote villages. Each teacher has to handle multiple grades, a very difficult task. The government must reallocate or recruit for those villages; it's clearly their most important responsibility once they have opened the schools. Many of the schools have very few children, scores of them with less than ten; they should be consolidated with nearby schools. However, shutting down any school is a big political issue. The government should not have gone about implementing the policy of 'a school within a kilometre of each habitation' thoughtlessly, especially in the hills, where the terrain makes the notion of a kilometre an underappreciated problem.

The children in government schools are from the most

disadvantaged backgrounds. Their parents also don't have the time to provide any support, struggling with multiple marginal occupations to make a living. All this makes teaching at these schools far more difficult than at private schools. Aside from the promise of English, having teachers for every grade and good uniforms, private schools don't do more. In fact, the quality of education in these schools is not as good as in government schools; this is known first-hand because most government schoolteachers send their children to private schools.

There is an urgent need for good training and mentoring for the teachers. The new curricular approach is difficult to handle; they find themselves inadequate to deal with it. They cannot understand how the Right to Education mandated 'continuous comprehensive evaluation' (CCE) can work. These are voices that echo everywhere in such meetings across the country. All the points made are valid, and these are issues that cannot be resolved by the people present at such meetings; they need the 'system' to address them. It must be remembered that these are people who want to improve things and are saying all this with good intent. There are other kinds of voices as well.

The yellow school's head teacher is Neeta Pant, and its cluster resource person is Sanjay Joshi. As we chatted with them, we saw many students prancing into the school, touch Neeta's feet and rush out. They were older students, not of that school. We learnt that they were all ex-students of the yellow school, who had joined the nearby secondary school. Their love for the old school and the head teacher is such that they met her before going to their own school, almost every morning. The general air of cheerfulness in that school gives a hint of where this love originates.

The school has the usual two-classroom building, with a small room for the teachers, a verandah at the front, a kitchen on the side and a largish ground in the front. It published its own eight-page newsletter with pieces by students and other persons related to the school. The children were intensely engaged, as were the teachers. Neeta and Sanjay were planning academic improvements for the next session; they were also planning to introduce English. I asked them about the startling colour of the school. They said, 'Well, we just went ahead, did it, no one stopped us.' That's their general attitude: let's do what is required, what we think is good. No one stops us and we certainly can't wait for the entire system to improve. This line was repeated by fifteen other people in those five meetings—often as a response to points made that the 'system' needs to change.

The 'system' needs to change: culturally, institutionally and in many more ways, fundamentally. Efforts of individuals on the ground are not sufficient to change the system. But they are absolutely necessary: to move forward, to improve what we can and to keep hope alive. There are enough such people in this country to keep the faith. Which is why last week was just an average week, meeting people who are not hanging around waiting for the system to change, but are trying to change it themselves.

29 May 2013

Is There a Reason for Hope?

The last 70 km to Barmer, driving from Sirohi, was through the desert. This is not the romantic sand dunes of our imagination, but a landscape of clumpy shrubs across sandy undulating plains, with the occasional hillock. I cannot recollect even one village that we crossed. The stretch was sparsely dotted with the dhanis—clusters of a few houses—too small to be even called a hamlet. The winter evening and the setting sun made this hard landscape beautiful. But even the beauty couldn't hide the demands of living here.

Pleasantly incongruous were the schools. Every 5–6 km, we would cross the neat building of a government school. Their stone walls and faint pink cladding made them look cheerful. Each had a nice compound, with its own playfield. In that 70-km stretch, there was nothing else—just the dhanis and the schools. For me that is reason for hope: schools are there, where there isn't much else.

In three days as I drove around south-western Rajasthan, I would have seen seventy-five schools. All government schools, all with one or two teachers. Only two of them were not working. The rest were open, children and teachers at work. By any standards of human development, this region would be classified as among the most disadvantaged and difficult in the country. But schools are there and they function. Why am I writing about hope? Three reasons: one, despite our education system being in shambles, there is indeed reason for hope; two, this hope energises, and places in context, our strengths and weaknesses; three, my wife has been telling me, 'Your columns have become depressing.' The fact is that our education system is depressing, but we cannot lose hope.

Let me recount some more reasons for hope from this short trip in Rajasthan. There are good, committed and thinking people at all levels in the government education system. I met three of them in the haveli that serves as the office of the district education officer (DEO) in Rajsamand.

They were the DEO, the head of the district Rashtriya Madhyamik Shiksha Abhiyan and the assistant project officer for the Sarva Shiksha Abhiyan—they were full of ideas and curiosity, not what most people expect of government education officers. Their sensitivity to the issues of adolescent girls and the inequity that they face was remarkable. They were intensely focused on how to improve their schools, despite the 30 per cent shortage of teachers that they face.

The next day I met Shankar Lal Bunkar, the headmaster of the government upper-primary school in Malipura. His school has a certain order that most schools will be envious of. He engages with the local communities in a way that he gets them to own the school. One sarpanch (village head) from a nearby village was surprised by the quality of furniture in the school; Bunkar had to explain to him that he got people of another village to sponsor the furniture. He didn't crib about anything.

Like any good leader, he makes the best of his circumstances by seizing the initiative and being positive.

We have been working in two districts in Rajasthan for five years—Sirohi and Tonk. The two districts have seventeen voluntary teacher learning forums. The teachers meet on Sundays or sometimes after school hours. The discussions are on academic issues, on how to be better teachers.

Scores of these teachers attend capacity-building workshops, which stretch over long weekends, completely voluntarily. The two districts have about 8,000 teachers, and 800 of them are involved with these voluntary forums. Eight hundred of the much-maligned government schoolteachers showing up on Sundays—completely voluntarily—to improve education. What else do you need for hope?

From the DEO at Rajsamand to these teachers, there are many good men and women in the system. There are enough of them to make one believe that things will improve over time. I met two of these good men in the government primary school in Aabela.

Govind Meghwal and Kanti Lal Meena are teachers in their mid-thirties. One of the walls in their school has a neat chart with all the achievements of the schools listed—the 'learning excellence' award that was bestowed on the school, the inter-district English competition won by a Class V girl, the district-level athletic meets' prizes and many more. These two teachers are so good that they often function as resource persons (facilitators) in our workshops. I asked them my standard question: 'So why do you do all this, what drives you?' They sort of completed each other's sentences as they said, 'The government pays us a good salary, so we must do our job. And when we try to teach better— we ourselves learn. And our conscience, it tells us that we must do our best, these kids are in our hands.' It's an answer that I have heard so often from so many people that I am very hopeful: improvement in school education could take a long time, but it will happen.

8 February 2012

A Big Village in India

There is a pond in a big village. It is neither big nor small; just enough for it to be the centre of life. Lotuses covers half of the water surface. A stone tile-clad platform hugs part of the northern edge. Rising 20 feet above the water, it is 150 feet long and 30 feet wide. Six magnificent trees shade its full expanse. One can miss the temple at one end, since it is barely 3 feet high, with a similar length and width. No magnificent demonstration of their deities' glory is required if the devotees are sure of their faith.

I sat on the parapet looking into the platform, as the rising sun cleared the October mist from the now golden pond. Twenty-three children and their two teachers were busy in four groups. The youngest lot from classes III and IV were trying to keep pace with the teacher, who would move every minute, creating arithmetic puzzles with pebbles or chalk on the stone. The second teacher was moving among the other groups. The one with the children from classes VII and VIII required no attention. They were reading their diaries to each other. The patchy English grammar neither stalled the flow of their language, nor clouded their sentiments. The two groups with kids from classes V and VI wrote stories and then worked on some maths problems. After a while, I left the pondside and went to one of the other five such classes-in-the-mohalla being run by the thirteen teachers of that school since June.

During April and May, they visited the village every day, providing rations and other necessities to scores of families, not only to those of their students. Soon, it was clear that no one in the country had any idea when schools may be allowed to reopen. Meanwhile, the crisis in the village was stark, with its manifold ramifications. Many of the older children were starting to join the labour force, for example. Unwilling to watch helplessly as the lives of their students unravelled, they decided to do what they knew how to do.

Restarting the school without actually opening it was their solution. They divided themselves into pairs and started regular classes in six spots for children from the vicinity. Two hours for children from classes I and II, and two and a half hours for those from classes III to VIII, six days a week. Children from within a neighbourhood were anyhow usually together, so there was no increase in the risk of a COVID-19 infection. All the classes were held in the open, with everyone wearing masks. They have been at it without a break from the first week of June.

'Why are you doing this?' I asked. They responded: First, if we let education stop for months on end, not only are our students missing those months, but they will lose a lot more. Perhaps just drop out. Second, education is not only about maths and language. We are responsible for the well-being of these children, today and tomorrow. And even more so in this hour of crisis. Third, this is the only way we know how to mobilise this community—to tackle the pandemic. We are a part of them, so we must do our best.

Over the past months, across this country, I have seen hundreds of such teachers, and have heard of thousands more. Silently doing what is desperately needed. Knowing online education is a chimera—even for the most basic matters of learning, leave aside the other goals of education and of a school.

Dedicated teachers have run such classes under trees, on mountain slopes, in dusty courtyards, in temples and in mosques. Some states took progressive steps to systematically organise neighbourhood classes. Karnataka was one of these states—with its Vidyagama programme—which was unfortunately aborted because of a misguided campaign opposing it. Teachers go on across the country—knowing that such real human engagement with their students is critical. For education, and also as an anchor for lives roiled by the forces unleashed by the pandemic.

Towards the end of the day, in that big village, we sat down with a few of the teachers, students and alumni of the school. They enacted the street plays on the pandemic that they have been conducting for the community. They described the rallies they organise, and other things they do, to mobilise the community to contain the pandemic.

After they were done, they wanted to ask me some questions. Still ponds have churned the quest for wisdom across cultures and time. Walden made Thoreau speak for nature. Yudhishthira chose Nakula to live, after answering the 125 questions of the Yaksha on the edge of those waters. Choosing our own Nakula is beyond most of us, though we must try. The least I could do was try to answer their Yaksha-like questions.

Why are human beings here? What should be the purpose of our lives? How do we ensure that we do not deviate from that purpose? What can give true happiness? Why is there so much strife in this world? What are virtues? Why?

Honesty works best, with children. They were satisfied when I said that these are questions that have been in search of answers for thousands of years. And that I can only share what I feel; they will have to discover their own answers. Unmissable is the role of teachers in what those children are becoming. No wonder even a once-in-a-century pandemic has not been able to stop them.

5 November 2020

PART TWO

WHAT IS PUBLIC,
IN PUBLIC EDUCATION?

What Is Public, in Public Education?

What is public about public education? Schools that are funded largely by tax revenues generated by the State and run by the State, through any of its bodies, are called public schools. Such a system of public schools is what constitutes public education. This commonly shared understanding of public education is usually quite adequate. However, this notion deserves a closer scrutiny, with the expectations from education soaring, and delivery falling way short.

So, what is this 'public' in public education? At its core it is about being equally available to all. It is also about people coming together to further public good through education. So, the word 'public' has at least two aspects: for whom—equally for all; and for what and why—for public good. With these meanings of 'public' it becomes apparent that the State may be well-suited to conduct such education.

Nevertheless, state education is a mechanism and not always the same thing as public education. Let's consider an extreme situation: in a totalitarian state, the State school system indoctrinates students to support the regime and its grip on power. This is State education, but not public education, because it is not for the good of the public.

Viewed from this perspective, the importance of public education, particularly for a democracy, starts becoming clearer. To build and keep a democracy, a society needs the capacities and commitments that arise from public education, which serve a dual entwined purpose of socialisation—for all people to become citizens and for all citizens to become equal and empowered. If curriculum were to change to suit the idiosyncratic needs of certain groups, or bend to ideology ignoring truth, public education will no longer remain public, since it will no longer further the public good.

Another kind of undermining happens insidiously, energised by notions like, 'education for the economy', 'education for employability', and so on. These sentiments in themselves are unexceptionable. Corrosion happens when these reflect an implicit or explicit intent to give primacy to the economic aims of education over all else.

Economic aims are important to public education. For citizens to be equal and empowered, economic well-being, and developing capacities for that, is important. But narrowing expectations, curricula and practices to serve economic aims as the top priority gnaws away at public education. It makes education serve the market and its dominant groups—not the public good.

Let's now go to the matter that is more often discussed: the matter of public and private schools and whether private schools can deliver public education.

In theory, a public-spirited private school can mirror public education, if it follows a curriculum that is designed for the public good, and it is equally available to all, irrespective of their socio-economic status. The second condition cannot be met by private schools if they intend to recover their costs from the students, which would immediately exclude the economically disadvantaged. This has led to the notion of publicly funded private schools, which can then purportedly deliver public education.

Undoubtedly, we can find several public-spirited private schools. But most private schools are profit-minded, not public-spirited. For entrepreneurs, a school is just another enterprise. This is natural, particularly when education by its very nature gives asymmetric power to schools over parents and students.

Too many schools abuse this power to cut every cost and increase every revenue stream, education be damned. All this is done while paying lip service to good education. Such schools certainly do not provide equal access to all. Aside from economic barriers, they create significant social barriers of exclusivity. Only if we close our eyes, ears and minds can we deny this reality of private schools in India.

On the matter of 'learning levels', as evidence has mounted, it is clear now that private schools do not have better educational outcomes than public schools, when compared on equal terms. This is not unique to India but is a global phenomenon. So, increasing the number of private schools, including by the support of state funding, has led to no improvement in learning at the education system level, but only to greater inequalities.

This should not be surprising at all and can be completely anticipated, if we keep sight of the fundamentals, and do not get swayed by market fundamentalism. And one of those fundamentals is that private entities establish and run schools, with few notable exceptions, for private purposes—profit, prestige and political influence—while wearing a thin veil of commitment to public good. Entities that are neither established nor run for public good cannot miraculously produce public good, against their basic intent. Private schools cannot deliver true public education.

So, a public education system can only be on the basis of a system of State schools. While a State schooling system may not always provide public education, public education cannot happen without a sound State schooling system. So, every nation interested in democracy and the public good needs a public education system funded and run by the State with clarity of purpose. It is true that states routinely fail to do this effectively. That is a powerful argument for strengthening and improving the

State schools, not for handing over education to private providers. This is critical, since public education is foundational to all efforts for developing a good society and a vibrant democracy.

21 November 2019

Every Ordinary Public Schoolteacher's Wish List for 2018

Here is 'Every ordinary public schoolteacher's wish list for 2018'. The list does *not* contain the very specific kind of wishes that most teachers have about their individual students—which range from the desire that a student becomes more attentive, to another learning maths better, and often includes matters like improvement in a child's health and in the home environment of another. The wish list that follows is written in the voice of a teacher, as I have heard it often:

Dear Mr Officer,

1. Please do not ask me to go out of the school on 'official duty'. If I am out of school, I cannot teach. Even if I am asked to go out of school for ten days in a year, it means about 5 per cent of the teaching days are lost. It is impossible to compensate for this loss. It forces me to rush through the syllabus.

2. Could you please stop the boring and ineffective training programmes that you organise? It is clear to me that I need to learn a lot to be able to teach better. I need to deepen my understanding of the content of the subjects, its related pedagogical approaches and other matters, such as why children behave the way they do. Could you offer, maybe, a bouquet of opportunities from which I can choose, depending on what I need to learn, rather than being forced to sit through something that is either irrelevant or which I already know? Also, wherever you organise these programmes, please do ensure that there are clean toilets on the premises.

3. The trainers should only be the best among the teachers. And they should have been prepared well.

4. There are many teachers who are very good. I would like to get to know them, to learn from them and to seek support when required. It would also be useful to observe how they teach. It would be very helpful if these opportunities are created systematically, rather than leaving it to individuals.

5. Don't make me teach maths when I haven't studied it beyond Class VIII myself. Recruit and appoint an adequate number of teachers for each grade and each subject in each school. Many states have eliminated corruption completely in teacher recruitment—learn from them.

6. Don't make the syllabus so content-heavy that it doesn't leave any time to get the children to understand, connect and apply; this is true especially in an administrative culture which is focused solely on covering the syllabus. All aspects of the curriculum should fully reflect the good and progressive curriculum envisioned in the National Curricular Framework, 2005. For this, the exams will have to be changed, the textbooks improved dramatically and the syllabus redone.

7. Textbooks, notebooks, uniforms and other things should reach us at the school a few days before the start of the session. Do break the long-held tradition of all these things arriving at the school months after the school session has started.

8. Convince the finance minister, and whoever else needs to be convinced, to increase the money that we get for the mid-day meals for the children. For many of these children, this is the most important meal of the day. The allocation for this has not increased in ten years. With the food inflation, can any of us cook today with the same expenditure as ten years ago?

9. Do something sustained to develop engagement of the local community in the school through the school management committee (SMC). I also need to learn how to work with the SMC more effectively, and this would be helped by a peer support network of teachers and head teachers.

10. No more tests and exams. We have more than enough of these in some name or guise. Continually assessing children's learning is not going to improve anything. Instead, could you help us make the continuous comprehensive evaluation that we already undertake more effective.

11. Have courage and fire the truant teachers. You are not able to do that; instead, all teachers are painted with the same black brush. Don't make us suffer for your weakness.

12. Don't keep asking for data that should be available with you. Invest in information and technology and develop a good management information system. Reduce our administrative overload.

13. Nothing substantial needs to be done to motivate us. Only two things will help: One, don't keep blaming us for all the ills of the system. Two, treat us with the respect that is due to any other human being. We are not expecting any special status for being 'developers of the society' (which we are). But do treat us like an equal human being. Not as the lowest rung in a massive bureaucratic machine, often blamed, mostly ignored and regularly mistreated.

14. We want our students to become confident, independent thinkers, humane and responsible. What matters most for this is the culture that we set in our school and classroom, and our own behaviour. Such a culture can be developed in a school only if the administrative culture of the system is empowering, trusting and enabling.

15. Please don't start new programmes every year and keep shifting priorities. We have had enough of flavours of the month and year, and pet projects of high officials. Some states have managed to do this and everything else that I have listed. Please do learn from them.

And last but not the least, please don't ask me to 'innovate'. A teacher by definition has to innovate every day. You can't see this unless you come and sit with us in the class. So, please, please, focus on the fundamentals and let us focus on the same.

Wish you a very happy New Year!

18 January 2018

House of Education

Coorg is beautiful. It is a five-hour drive from Bengaluru. A friend bought land there to build a house—a getaway for long weekends, and perhaps their retirement home. A year after he started building, he wanted advice on solar panels. We talked a bit before I realised that the house was far from complete. The foundation was still being worked upon. In one part of the land, they had run into soggy soil, and in another part, large boulders, a couple of metres deep. He said he was using this time to plan other things for the house.

About a year later, he introduced me to a building management system (BMS) start-up. They were using his house as a show-site for a mini-BMS, and he was very impressed by their approach.

When I met these people, I realised that they had spent a considerable amount of time with him planning the BMS. Since it was to be a show-site, they were ready to install the system free of charge, as soon as the house was ready. This seemed some time away, since the foundation was being worked upon.

Over the next year, I heard of his wife's painstaking efforts on selecting the right source for the Mangalore tiles. That was only one of the many things that they seemed to be thinking through in great detail. The matters ranged from waterproofing for Coorg's weather to material for the doors. Aside from the BMS start-up, they had the help and advice of many good people. My friend is such a nice guy, and helps everyone so selflessly, that people were merely reciprocating.

We bumped into each other a couple of months ago. He was excited about how a GIS- (Geographic Information System) based system would be helping to design a precision-blasting protocol for the boulders. He was also very happy with the progress that he had made in sorting out every detail of the house. 'It will be a great place,' he said. 'You must go and spend a few weekends there.'

It seems some time away, since the foundation is still being worked upon. It has now been five years. The bane of analogies is that if stretched, they break down. So, we will use my friend's house as a limited analogy. What we do with education is much like what my friend has been doing with his house. He should have blasted the boulders or built a deep-pile foundation. Instead, he worked on everything else—often helped by well-intentioned experts, who offered their help. And he did not have the mental discipline to focus on the foundation, despite its obvious importance. The soggy soil and the boulders are still there, while he has designed the system to measure the heat balance of the house.

There will be no house or good education without a sound foundation. We ignore this, likewise, in education. Often distracted by other matters or misled by our prejudices and lack of understanding or deterred by the enormity of the task at the foundation.

The foundation of good education is a good teacher. A sound curriculum and empowering culture enable the teacher. Instead of working on making this a reality, a large part of the work done in education is on other matters. Some that is merely distracting and some that is counterproductive.

Here is a partial list of such things: transfer of teachers and officials; more and more assessment of children, using ICT (information and communication technology) as a solve-all; using RCT (randomised control trials) to discover the obvious and advocate the myopic; 'accountability' of teachers and schools; overbearing regulation and its data requirements; advocating privatisation of delivery; and mechanical formulistic pedagogical approaches. Many more could be added to the list—instead, let us consider why such things capture the attention of those working in education, pulling effort away from the foundational issues.

First, some do not even think of teachers as foundational to good education. They would do their best to reduce and eliminate the role of the teacher. Second, some find the matter of the teacher so complex and daunting that they would rather not attempt anything on it, but work on things that are easier. Third, credible experts from various fields advise and help them to work on matters and methods important to these experts, but peripheral to education. The experts have their own hammer, and so education is another nail. Fourth, there is a desire for quick and visible results.

Working with and for teachers is too long-cycle an effort for them. Fifth, there is inadequate understanding of the teacher's role and capacities required, and so there is a misunderstanding of what it takes to develop these capacities and enable the role. Sixth, there is a deep blindness to the social-human nature of education, with a tendency to reduce it to a mechanical and/or industrial system. Often it is a combination of these factors and some more.

The situation in education is worse than my friend's house. There are very good teachers. But as a system, we have not invested in the capacity of our teachers. We have undermined their role and importance, and vilified them continually, leading to their disengagement and demotivation. If we really want to improve the education system, we cannot merely tweak the superficial. Preparing, developing and empowering our teachers is foundational. Soggy soil or massive boulders notwithstanding, unless we build a solid foundation undistracted and unfazed, our education system is going nowhere.

23 November 2017

Education Is Always Political

Galileo was pronounced 'vehemently suspect of heresy' by the Church in 1632 and lived the last nine years of his life under house arrest, for his espousal of heliocentrism. Curiously, Copernican heliocentrism had been used by Pope Gregory himself in 1582 to alter his eponymous calendar. This schizophrenic behaviour of the Church can be substantially explained by its assessment that Galileo's espousal questioned the authority of the Church to decide what was true.

This blow at the basis of the then political order had to be crushed—while Copernican calculations as a tool to change the calendar were perfectly acceptable. Most certainly, such heretical ideas had no place in schools and universities; the Church controlled that well. In fact, over the next two centuries, the Protestant and the Catholic churches and their institutions often vied for the claim of being more geocentric than the other. It's only by the nineteenth century that geocentrism withered away from the curriculum in schools.

Let's not fool ourselves that such things are memories of an 'unscientific' past. As one example, all world maps that schools use (and Google uses) are wrong, and they feed Eurocentrism. The subtle nudge is in the choice of placing Europe at the centre of the world, but what is egregiously wrong is the relative proportions of the countries and continents. The geographies of 'the North'—Europe and North America—are represented ludicrously bigger than they are; the 48 million sq. km of 'the North' is shown to be bigger than the 94 million sq. km of 'the South'. Open a map and look at these remarkable distortions: in reality, South America is about twice the size of Europe but shown to be equal, Greenland looks bigger than China but is actually one-fourth, and the Nordic countries look bigger than India but are actually one-third. Even matters of the physical world are learnt and taught in schools often on the basis of political values and choices. These may be very deliberate choices, like the Church on heliocentrism or unthinking espousal, as in the case of the Eurocentrism in the maps.

Let's take another example from economics. Textbooks in economics from the 1960s and '70s in India would be full of the virtues of central planning and arcane details of the Mahalanobis model, which seems very strange today. Equally strange are today's economics textbooks, which are influenced by market fundamentalism and dominated by the idealised, rationality individualism–equilibrium nexus, which exists only in these books; this stuff is as disconnected from reality as was the planning model.

For example, what must we know in economics to say we know economics is a substantially political issue and not a purely epistemic one? The content of education in any society is politically influenced. This political influence operates at both levels: to accept what is 'true knowledge' (for instance, the planning model versus market theory) and to choose 'worthwhile knowledge' that finds place in the curriculum from the universal set of 'knowledge'.

I have deliberately taken examples from areas which are not usually referred to when discussing how politics determines the content of education, while in certain subjects and areas, this issue is well known—say, in the content of history and sociology, in the treatment of matters of gender and caste.

The processes and practices of education are as political as the content. What is the language of the medium of instruction? Who all do we include in education? If we want universal equitable education, how do we make it happen? Do we think 'merit' takes precedence over affirmative action? Do the pedagogical approaches adequately factor in the diversity in the class?

Every one of these questions, and many more which determine education, are political in nature. Even more political than the content and processes of education are the aims of education.

Education that aims to develop autonomous, critical thinking individuals and to help develop a just and democratic society is sharply political. And as sharply political would be education that aims to develop individuals who are not questioning but conforming to some existing order. In fact, the aims of education shape the processes and content of education, including significantly determining their political tilt.

Views from the extremes, both the left and the right, regarding the recent happenings in some university campuses, have been unsurprising. Ugly, unethical politics anywhere must be condemned. But what has been surprising is a view stated by some which amounts to 'there must be no politics in educational institutions'. This view reflects either a very naïve understanding of education or an insidiously political (even if unconscious) choice. And that choice is for education to aim to develop people who do not engage with the most important issues around them, do not question and do not think for themselves. This amounts to deep politics in education of a kind that must be rejected. We need education that energises our democracy and builds the India envisioned in the Constitution by developing the abilities of students to think and contribute as autonomous individuals; this education is certainly political. One way or the other, all education is political.

17 March 2016

Divided by Caste

The huge display was the most prominent thing in the school. It was painted on the wall with a black background and white lettering in Hindi. It had the profile of the school, with the numbers and some details of the students and the teachers. The school was a typical government upper-primary school, about 20 km from a large town. The first chart had student numbers in each grade and a breakdown within each grade by gender. The second chart had a breakdown of each grade by caste. There were four caste categories mentioned: Scheduled Castes, Scheduled Tribes, Other Backward Classes and Normal. The fourth category is not a translation mistake by me; the word used in the chart in Hindi was 'samaanya'. The word is commonly used in Hindi and its common meaning is 'normal'. The antonym of the word is 'asamaanya', meaning 'abnormal'. This kind of labelling of the categories suggests that three of the caste categories were abnormal; anyone reading the chart would be left with that sense.

Why would a school want to communicate every day to its students that they belong to different castes, and top it off with the cruel (and false) act of reminding many of them that they belonged to abnormal castes? The school has not made the display of its own; the state department of education wants the display in every school, and it has determined the format, including the words. This matter of normal and abnormal caste was only one of the egregious aspects of the display. Here are some of the others: the teachers' caste was also written, and with the same kind of descriptors. The standard and not-so-subtle marker of gender discrimination was there, with a column for 'husband or father's name', with no mention of wife or mother.

The teachers were classified as 'trained' or 'untrained', which refers to whether they have completed a diploma (or bachelor's) in education or not, and is in no way the same thing as trained and untrained. In any case, why would you want to proclaim to the whole world every day that some specific teachers are untrained, creating another kind of caste hierarchy? If it is such a big and real issue (which it is), do not recruit such teachers, but having recruited, do not belittle them every moment. There is no doubt that the state departments of education and the school need this kind of data for many reasons, most importantly to help with specific actions for disadvantaged groups. But there is no reason to display the data in these formats and with this language, for all to see, all the time. It can also be justifiably argued that this kind of stuff merely reflects the reality outside the school, that is, of deeply ingrained caste hierarchies, and of gender. But that is no argument for a display of this nature. The display is an in-your-face blow against the very aims of education that the school is supposed to serve.

Let me quote from the preface of the National Curriculum Framework, 2005: 'Seeking guidance from the Constitutional vision of India as a secular, egalitarian and pluralistic society, founded on the values of social justice and equality, certain broad aims of education have been identified in this document. These include independence of thought and action, sensitivity to others' well-being and feelings, learning to respond to new situations in a flexible and creative manner, predisposition towards participation in democratic processes, and the ability to work towards and contribute to economic processes and social change.'

This kind of a display, with minor variations, one can see across schools in many states. And the display is only one kind of an artefact or practice in our schools that works against the very aims of education that we have decided for ourselves. It's not only classroom pedagogy that makes education happen in schools; the practices and relationships in the school matter as much.

This is something I have written about often. The progressive and egalitarian vision of education in our policy documents fail in practice, limited by the prejudices of the administration, local functionaries and the teachers. And this phenomenon is not restricted to government schools.

Having said all this, I am hopeful that we will make progress on all these fronts. The reason that I am hopeful is that we have made significant progress in government schools in the past few decades. While we are familiar with the glaring deficiencies of our schooling system, we often miss that we have made more progress in schools on matters of inclusion and justice than any other part of our welfare state system. If you are in any kind of a socio-economically disadvantaged group, getting access to anything that the state provides—healthcare, judicial services, the public distribution system or even basic safety—is a nightmare. However, today no child anywhere in the country, irrespective of caste, gender, religion or economic status, is denied access to schools in any way. And that's progress, in this country of ours.

16 September 2015

In 2019, The Department of Public Instruction (DPI) issued directions to heads of all schools that the caste and the religion of teachers should not be displayed on the school notice board.

The Swedish Education Experiment

When I started visiting Sweden and Finland, I learnt very quickly that the Finns don't take very kindly to their country being called a Scandinavian country, which is a mistake outsiders often make. Finland is a Nordic country. The Nordic (meaning northern) identity is primarily geographical, including Finland, Iceland and Greenland, in addition to the Scandinavian countries.

Scandinavia is a cultural–linguistic region, with substantially Germanic roots. It includes Denmark, Norway and Sweden. But to outsiders, the Nordic region seems to be culturally integrated. This is not surprising, since the differences amongst the Nordic countries are far less than between us and them. This impression has been strengthened by the uniform success of the Nordic countries, on almost all social and economic parameters.

The success has been driven by their broadly similar nature of national governance and polity, a mix of deep commitment to democracy, social security and public goods, with a market-friendly environment for business—the famed welfare-market state. However, if you are within that region, the differences are distinct. Especially if you are in Finland; the 800-year rule of Sweden over the country is never far from anyone's mind.

I visited the two countries thirty to thirty-five times, spending cumulatively more than a year there. I fell in love with the two places. It also gave me an insider's view of the relative differences. Amongst other things, Swedes were relatively keener on experimenting, trying new things; Finns prefer to stay focused on fundamentals. These are relative but distinct differences. Some of the key turns in the history of school education in these two countries and their divergences have been partly influenced by these differences.

In the early 1990s, Sweden introduced policies in school education, which were based on a set of ideas founded on a greater role for market mechanisms in schools. Independent private schools (including for-profit) were allowed, and these received public funding. It was intended to introduce competition amongst schools, along with more standardised testing. Competition was supposed to offer choice to parents, and drive accountability of schools and teachers, thus driving a virtuous cycle of improvement in the system. This also implied abandonment of the notion of common public schools.

At that time, the Swedish school system was anything but dysfunctional. It was the overall (only relative) shift to the right of the polity combined with the relatively higher tendency to experiment, that triggered changes. Finland stayed focused on its course in education, set in the 1970s.

This included a culture of autonomy for the teacher and school, intense focus and investment on university-based, research-driven teacher education and a commitment to equity through a public education system.

The changes in Sweden didn't influence Finland. As the first decade of the introduction of market mechanisms to schools in Sweden got over, there was general optimism that these changes had made a positive difference in the quality of education. These initial signs of success were picked up by the global education reform industry and touted as another bit of evidence for the supposed central role of market mechanisms in improving school systems. As the years passed, this initial enthusiasm started turning to confusion and despair. The performance of the Swedish school system started unravelling.

In the past ten years, there has been a steady decline in Sweden's performance in the Program for International Student Assessment (PISA), with the latest version showing that the country has gone below the Organisation for Economic Co-operation and Development (OECD) countries' average. PISA is one of the few international comparisons of school systems done periodically, this one by OECD itself. Despite the significant limitations of such studies, they indicate the trend. Even more agonisingly, Sweden is one of the very few countries where quality has declined and inequality has grown in schools.

In the same period, Sweden's Nordic (not Scandinavian) neighbour has continued to be at the top of school performance globally. Finland continues its steady work on the fundamentals, committed to public education. And over the past few years, it has built a steady stream of education tourists, who want to learn from the Finnish marvel in schools. There is nothing unusual in what has played out in Sweden. Comprehensive cross-country research by OECD (not an anti-market body, for sure) concludes that market mechanisms do not help in improving the quality of educational outcomes in school systems.

On the other hand, they do increase inequality. This should not be a surprise, since it is well understood that market mechanisms are ineffective providers of socially important and quasi-public goods such as education. However, education cannot be adequately understood by economic analysis. There is something deeper at work. At its core, education is a humanistic social endeavour. It creates many benefits for individuals, not only economic ones. It is also the foundational process for any society to try and achieve its vision. The idea of a just and equitable India that our Constitution proclaims, needs for its realisation, a strong education system. This cannot happen without a well-functioning, public-school system, which is what we must work for.

12 November 2014

Education Requires Research

To improve India's school education, it is critical to improve India's in-service teacher education. I wrote about this on 24 July. Good in-service education will deliberately work on the entire range of capacities that teachers need to play their complex roles. Some of these are developed through research. It's because of this that everyone in education is expected to do research. This does not necessarily involve complex projects, it needn't be published and it's not essential that it generate new knowledge. Its importance is as a method of learning. It's the mindset developed by doing research which is critical for the educator to play her role effectively.

This is important for the teacher, as well for the teacher educator and most others in school education. The reasons are quite simple. Education involves the ability to respond with depth and flexibility to highly varying and dynamic situations, which arise from many sources, like differences across children, the same child behaving differently over time, or varying and changing social contexts. Such responses demand a capacity to observe, hypothesise, analyse, search for related things, synthesise, conclude, apply it to practice and to learn from all this.

Much of this needs to happen naturally and informally in the daily life of the educator. In other words, it requires a research mindset. Another phrase used for this way of working is 'reflective practice'. But somehow, research is drawn out of the reach of the 'ordinary person', which is the typical self-image of most in school education. It's perceived to be the preserve of the intellectuals (some self-professed, others genuine) and scholars. Its methods and approaches create unfathomable mysteries. The rules of the game of research seem such that it's hard to even start playing. These perceptions intimidate most people in schools.

Over the past eighteen months, there has been an effort to demystify research, in a few districts of north-east Karnataka (NEK). This region is among the more disadvantaged in the country. My friend and colleague Umashanker Periodi, who played a central role in this demystification effort, initiated it with a master stroke of repositioning. He started by using the phrase 'Barefoot Research', and not using the word 'research' on its own. The mere addition of the word 'barefoot' brought research out of the citadel of the Academy. It seemed to the average schoolteacher, that anything that was barefoot was certainly within her reach. It was in her natural arena, so to say. 'Let's try doing barefoot research', was the word that spread through all formal and informal channels. Examples and possibilities were discussed repeatedly in workshops, training sessions, monthly meetings, etc. This started in June 2013. In January 2014, the announcement for the Barefoot Research Conference, called Sahamanthana, to be held in July 2014, was made across these districts. Sahamanthana means churning together. Supporting the formal invitation for research papers was the methodical background process of encouraging and helping teachers, principals and other education functionaries to get down to a specific research project and to develop it.

The conference was held in Shahpur, a town in Yadgir district. The conference was hosted jointly by the Department of School Education, the College of Agricultural Sciences (Shahpur) and the Azim Premji University. Many civil society organisations and higher education institutions were also active collaborators. Eighty papers were presented. The themes of the papers ranged from teacher professional development, community engagement in schools, classroom practices to policy issues related to the

NEK region. Here is a sample of some of the research papers: 'A journey of development of Gaddada Narayana Thanda (tribal community) School', 'A study on Teachers Learning Centre', 'Starting a Pre-Primary School in a Government Primary School' and 'A study on "folk literature as a tool" in language learning'. There were over 800 participants across the three days of the conference. There were teachers, principals, cluster and block resource people, college teachers, members of NGOs and so on. The sense of excitement was infectious and invigorating. There was a sense of having grappled with and overcome an important challenge.

A government official from Bengaluru observed that people in Bengaluru would find it impossible to believe that a research conference like this could happen anywhere, let alone in NEK. Another said 'it was a spiritual experience'.

People in school education in those districts are looking forward to next year's Sahamanthana. Some of the research papers presented have valuable ground-level insights. But the real value of this effort has been in the way it has helped start the process of developing certain capacities of those involved. It has also created a buzz around research, helping in demystifying it. Given the complexities of the role of any educator, simplistic capacity-development (continuing professional development) methods are ineffective. It's hard to design, execute and sustain complex interventions like Sahamanthana, but such challenges have to be taken up, if we want our education to improve.

6 August 2014

Improving Teacher Education

About five minutes into the conversation with the block education officer (BEO), I realised we were using the same phrase, 'trainee teachers', to talk about two entirely different things. I had assumed that the reference was to teachers who had joined recently, and were in a training period. We were discussing the poor quality of a particular training session; the BEO suggested that we need not be bothered, since it was trainee teachers who were participating. This seemed callous, till I realised what he meant. He was referring to a group of teachers in his block who had been identified by him to attend all trainings. Whatever the training, it was the same group that was nominated to participate. This was the BEO's way of managing conflicting demands.

There were many kinds of trainings organised for teachers; the BEO had to make sure that there were participants for all, with minimal disruption in the functioning of schools. Most teachers were completely disinterested in these training sessions. Identifying a group of teachers, who for their own reasons were willing to attend training after training, had solved many of his problems. They were his 'trainee teachers'.

This method of managing may seem cynical, till the BEO's reasons are understood. At the root was his accurate assessment that most of the training being organised was ineffective. Also, neither he nor the teachers felt any influence over what was being done. The curriculum, the methods, the duration and timing, everything was decided at the state capital, and he had to comply.

He had repeatedly seen the poor quality of what eventually happened. He had figured out a solution, within his degrees of freedom. What the BEO did need not be condoned, but can be understood. One just needs to talk to government schoolteachers, who have had an overdose of poor training in the past decade.

The Sarva Shiksha Abhiyan (SSA), the flagship school education initiative across the country, itself had twenty days of training budgeted every year for all elementary schoolteachers. This was very good. But driven by its highly centralised design, inadequate facilitators, mechanised methods and many other issues, this training had become a farce in most states, with only a few notable exceptions. In the past two years, the actions to manage the central fiscal deficit had resulted in a funds crunch on the ground, including in education. Since everyone agreed that it was ineffective, the SSA teacher training was one of the first spending heads to get large cuts across states; the training durations have now come down to three to five days per year.

The sorry state of continuing professional development of teachers in India is rivalled by India's teacher preparation (called 'pre-service teacher education') system, about which I wrote on 9 July (see the next piece). Continuing professional development is important in itself, for complex roles such as that of a teacher. However, in the specific case of teachers in India, it is even more important. That is because our pre-service teacher education leaves new teachers largely unprepared to play their roles. Not only does this lead to poor educational outcomes for students, but also disengages and demotivates the teachers, as they find themselves unable to cope with their roles. This is a vicious spiral beginning at the start of the teacher's career.

There is no substitute to building a robust pre-service teacher-education system, one which must replace the existing dysfunctional one. When India gets this done, it will significantly help in resolving the issue of the capacity of new teachers joining the schooling system. However, that will not help the existing 6.5 million teachers in our schools, who have been prepared as teachers through the existing weak teacher preparation system; while some teachers are effective despite this, a large majority needs support and professional development. Otherwise, educational outcomes in our schools will continue to languish for decades to come.

Some necessary conditions for improving in-service (continuing) professional development of teachers are clear. It can't be envisioned as 'training', with its ensuing narrowness; it must be 'education', which is deep and broad. The efforts must not be disjointed, but based on a continuing curriculum, informed equally by the teachers' reality as by the fundamental vision of education. Most importantly, lecture-driven sessions just won't do; many modes must be thoughtfully sewn together. Some examples of these modes are mentored-at-work projects, exposure visits, guided reading, peer support and learning research projects. There must also be a cultural shift, with empowerment of the teacher and people near the teacher to chart her developmental path. The institutional structure to make all this happen exists, in the form of the 600-odd District Institutes of Education and Training. Making them vibrant can be the basis for a transformation of our in-service teacher education. And that is perhaps the most important lever of change if we want to improve India's educational outcomes in the next ten years.

23 July 2014

India Needs a New Teacher Education System

What does it take to be a teacher and so how can someone be 'prepared' to become a teacher? This question continues to be one of the most important ones in school education. Over the past century, views of policymakers and the public on education have evolved, across the world. Roughly speaking, they have become more inclusive, ambitious and comprehensive; including in the ambit of its aims, the development of the individual and of the society. Education has come to be seen as a right of all children, no longer remaining the privilege of a few. The understanding of child development and of the complex impact of social processes on education have also evolved. The knowledge base in most disciplines has exploded, accompanied by changes in the very nature of these disciplines. In brief, education has become richer in its aims, method and content. This rich education, from its most basic aspect to its most exalted, is to be brought to reality in the classroom by the teacher for each child.

Let's note a few illustrations of the demands this puts on the teacher. The typical teacher will handle a group of children consisting of cohorts of multiple ages. Large numbers of these students live with great socio-economic disadvantage, with no educational support at home. The teacher has to get the students to learn reading with comprehension, maths with application and science in relationship to their environment. And this learning is about conceptual clarity, the ability to reason and to think independently. We also want education to develop democratic values in the child. The fact that human relationships are at the core of teaching demands high degree of social and emotional capacities from the teacher. Let's stop here for the time being, because this much is enough to emphasise the size and complexity of the teachers' role.

In India, the person who is supposed to bring this rich education to the primary school classroom undergoes two years of teacher training after finishing Class XII, and they are then supposed to have been prepared as teachers. For secondary schoolteachers, it is a ten-month programme after an undergraduate degree. We will look briefly at both: this poor design, and its implementation which is even worse, but let's get a more immediate sense of the total misalignment of this design of teacher preparation with what we think education should be.

Imagine your eighteen-year-old daughter or son, or any of the young kids that you encounter, shouldering this role after two years of training. It would immediately strike you that not only is two years too short a period for them to learn the content of the subjects that they will teach, the related pedagogical approaches and relevant issues of child development, etc., but also that at this age, these young people are unlikely to have the required social maturity. Some of you may relate to another example. Imagine if our engineering education was such that students underwent a two-year programme after Class XII, and were then qualified as engineers. These engineers would then be expected to do fundamental engineering work, maybe on chip design, on materials, on automobile engineering. What this will do to the engineering industry in this country is clear enough. A teacher has a far more complex job than an engineer, though for various reasons gets paid much less.

Why then has India designed a teacher education system which is so obviously disconnected from what we want from education? There are many reasons; a basic one is perhaps our common shared (unexamined) misunderstanding that 'anybody can teach'. The more direct reason is that the design of teacher education has not kept pace with the changes in our views of education. Most countries with good schooling systems have four- to five-year programmes of teacher preparation compared to our one or two years.

Let me also point out that the duration is only one aspect of the weakness of our programmes. The overall curriculum for teacher education and its institutional structures are both archaic. The implementation of these poorly envisioned programmes is even worse. Too many of the 16,000-odd teacher education colleges are commercial entities that 'sell' degrees with no interest in education. This corruption of our teacher education system, as it happened over the past twenty-odd years, can put to shame even the biggest of the scams that we have experienced.

Over the past two years, driven by the Supreme Court-appointed Justice Verma Commission, a beginning has been made to relook at this crumbling, almost non-existent foundation of our schooling system. Most of its recommendations had been suggested earlier by many others, to no avail. What is needed is the political will to actually implement them, battling the inertia and the vested commercial interests, and to raise public expenditure in teacher education.

Till we build a new teacher education system, our schools will not improve; most other things that we do are like trying to desperately contain the symptoms, while ignoring the life-threatening infection as it rages on.

9 July 2014

Making the Wicked Wickeder

In the corner of a room, or in a hole in the wall, let us put a computer. And let children have free access to it. Or better still, give each child a laptop, rugged and loaded with excellent content. Unleashing the power of a child's curiosity and self-learning, these enable dramatic improvement in education. They can reduce or eliminate our need of teachers, of other learning resources and of practically everything else that makes for a school.

Many readers would call out the preceding paragraph for what it is—a piece of magical thinking. But such initiatives have been widely touted and embraced as solutions to all problems in school education by a vast number of seemingly smart people with otherwise sound judgement.

This piece is not focused on the very limited usefulness of information and communication technology (ICT) in education, enthusiasm for which continues, though it's thankfully moving towards sanity, forced by overwhelming evidence from across the world. For example, the global report of the Organisation for Economic Co-operation and Development (OECD), *Students, Computers and Learning: Making the Connection; 2015*, concludes that 'the results … show no appreciable improvements in student achievement in reading, mathematics or science in the countries that had invested heavily in ICT for education. And perhaps the most disappointing finding of the report is that technology is of little help in bridging the skills between advantaged and disadvantaged students.'

But let us return to other forms of magical thinking in education. Install a video camera in a classroom, so that everything that goes on can be recorded and monitored. This will drive teachers to teach better. Do not employ teachers, but hire them on short-term contracts. Since they are hanging by a thread to their jobs, it will motivate them to perform better.

In psychiatry, magical thinking is a disorder of thought content, specifically about some actions causing specific consequences in some way that defy commonly understood laws of casualty. To cut through this disorder, let us request all perpetrators to apply these three magical thoughts to themselves:

1. Will they send their children to schools that have no teachers or very few teachers? These schools have good computers and very few other resources. The children are expected to self-guide and self-discover, and thus educate themselves. The few teachers are minimally present, intervening only occasionally. With this kind of a role, the capacity, motivation and attitudes of teachers are largely irrelevant.

2. Will they have a video camera installed in their own workplaces, so that they themselves can be recorded and monitored? Do the same for their whole office, studio or co-shared workspace. Everyone will perform better.

3. Will they have their employment contracts with generous retirement benefits at age sixty-five (or life tenures in a university) changed to short-term contracts that must be renewed every year? This too will motivate them to perform better. And, most certainly, this excellent and effective practice must then be deployed for all their colleagues, friends, children and spouses.

None of these people will ever do any of this to themselves. The weirdness of this kind of thinking is stark when it's forced into our own lives. But then why is this kind of thinking there at all?

First, it is the appeal of easy and clear solutions. Improving education is the prototypical 'wicked problem'. Grappling mentally with it is difficult, putting anything to practice is even more so and it is always highly frustrating. The easy and clear solution removes the frustrations and difficulties.

It is ineffective in improving education, but is highly effective in helping people feel good; they feel sure, their cognitive load and anxiety are reduced and they have a sense of satisfaction from having found a solution.

Second, such reductive and behaviourist methods, which is what most of these solutions are, can be expressed precisely and understood easily. 'Evidence' can also be gathered easily. Eliminating the complexity of the world of education, such methods offer a clear-eyed view of the path forward. But these are paths to nowhere. Education is complexity defined, being the social-human process that it is, and this is exponentially more so at the system level.

Third, the egregious disregard for things that should be obvious is enabled by a crude mental diminishment of teachers and their roles, a deep sense of personal exceptionalism and a sharply circumscribed circle of empathy and morality. In more direct words: they think that teachers are untrustworthy and their roles are trivial, while they themselves (and their kind) are paragons of virtue and wisdom, and that all such solutions can be implemented so long as it doesn't affect them and their own.

Unfortunately for education and our children, many well-intentioned people with power and influence in this world are afflicted by such magical thinking. The already wicked problem of education becomes even more so with such influence. Like much else, this too has to be battled, and like all of education, this battle is not a grand set piece, but has to be fought every day, bit by bit.

23 October 2019

Teachers Are Central

The late evening drizzle did not dampen the spirit of the teachers. There were forty-five of them, from public (government) schools around Chamba in Uttarakhand, gathered for a dialogue on the draft National Education Policy 2019 (NEP) at our teacher learning centre. At 7 p.m., no one seemed in a mood to end the session, having started at 5 p.m., though many of them had a long ride ahead to home along the winding mountain roads.

During those two hours, the group discussed the NEP, often expressing how its aspects were resonant with their aspirations and hopes. Their worry was how much of it would get implemented. Most of them did mention that given the size and expansive nature of the NEP document, they had read only those topics that were of interest to them. Their one peeve seemed to be that with the introduction of breakfast at school for all students, in addition to the currently available 'mid-day meal', they may have to spend more time supervising the kitchen—though they did acknowledge that breakfast was much needed for their students.

Over the past two and a half months, while the NEP has been up for public comment, I have met many groups of public-school teachers across India. Most reactions have been very similar to that of the group at Chamba. A few peeves, but an overall sense of satisfaction with the NEP. Why are public-school teachers reacting in this manner?

The answer is quite straightforward. The NEP gives the teacher the importance that she or he deserves in education. One key underlying principle of the policy is that education is a social-human process and, therefore, good education requires high-capacity, engaged teachers. This principle manifests itself in specific policy actions on every front; let me list a few of these.

First, how can we expect teachers to remain engaged and motivated if the most basic physical working conditions are inadequate to appalling? If they don't have access to functioning toilets and running water, decent electricity supply and do not even have a small working space for themselves? If we respect the profession of teaching, then it will first reflect in the education system providing them these basic things.

Second, their struggle to get even the most rudimentary of learning resources and material must be put to a stop. All teachers will have adequate learning material to transact the curriculum. This ranges from books and experimental kits to pencils and paper.

Third, teachers must not be given other tasks. They must be allowed to focus on their teaching and on their students. Teachers will not be pulled out for other kinds of work such as surveys, distribution of public services, local elections, etc. Repetitious data demands on the teacher from the system will be eliminated by the intelligent use of information technology.

Fourth, an adequate number of teachers will be appointed. Today, an estimated 2 million teaching jobs are vacant across the country, while we altogether have 9 million teachers. That's a large deficit. Teachers are handling more students than they can, across multiple grades, and often teaching subjects that they have themselves not studied. This will be addressed immediately.

Fifth, teachers must not face discriminatory service conditions. Lakhs of 'para-teachers' across the country perform the same role as other teachers in their schools, but get paid half to one-fourth. All such cadres of teachers will be regularised—given service conditions and compensation equivalent to other teachers, after going through the relevant qualifications where required. Also, compensation and service conditions will be equalised across primary to high school.

Sixth, teachers will be provided support for professional development and growth. This will be based on their own needs and not driven by some centralised, impersonal system. This will entail providing sustained high-quality education and opportunities for peer-learning. It will also mean objective assessment of their work and recognition for good work, enabled by development-oriented supervision. This in turn will be enabled by appropriate capacity development of school leaders and other leaders of the education system.

Seventh, the culture of the education system—including in schools—will be based on trust, and will empower and enable teachers. It will foster creativity and initiative, and curricular innovation. Teachers will be treated as valued professionals, not as the bottom-most rung in the vast government hierarchy. This will reflect in the daily behaviour of the leaders of the education system.

Eighth, the teacher preparation system (B. Ed.), which has about 18,000 teacher education institutions (TEI), will be overhauled to eliminate rampant corruption and dysfunction; TEIs that are nothing more than 'degree-selling-shops' will be shut down. The curricula will be reimagined—appropriate to the complex and critical role that teachers play, and all TEIs will have high-quality teaching-learning material.

All this is music to the ear of teachers, as it should be. And, therefore, the natural question is whether all this will get implemented. My view on that matter is the subject for another column.

29 August 2019

A Fraying Lifeline

Tombstones for the young, without graves. Each a foot tall, clustered closely together. About half carved with black cobras, for the boys who died young. The other half colourful, for the girls who died young. Every phala has such a shrine. Phalas are hamlets of the Bhil in southwestern Rajasthan. The Bhil call these shrines wadis.

Gautam and I drove from Dungarpur to Chittorgarh in four days, crossing the districts of Pratapgarh and Banaswara. We kept crossing phala after phala, with many wadis visible from the road. The same thought occurred to both of us. Even the bigger phalas don't have a population of more than 200–300 people. How could so many young have died? There were just too many tombstones.

This trip was no different from other trips, visiting schools and meeting teachers. On the morning of the second day, the school that we visited was strikingly neat and clean. It had two classrooms, fifty students, two teachers and a large 2 acre playground. The wadi was visible at one edge inside the school compound.

I sat on the floor with the children. Their limbs were thin as sticks, their hair discoloured and brittle. Their meagre frames made them look half their age. Used as I am to seeing deprivation and poor nutrition embodied in public-school children, this school was still extreme. The children spoke Bhili, which I don't understand. But with the smattering of Hindi they spoke, gestures and laughs, we got along fine. And as the class was ending, the teacher asked the children, *'Kaun kaun rota khaa ke aaya hai?* [Who has eaten before coming?]' Only about 20 per cent of the children in the class raised their hands.

It was eleven in the morning, and it was unclear whether the question referred to breakfast that morning, or dinner the previous night. In the best-case scenario, the 80 per cent that had not raised their hands had eaten dinner. Even so, they had eaten nothing since. But it actually seemed that many may not have had dinner the previous night either. Their last meal may well have been the mid-day meal provided by the school the previous day. My colleagues who visit the school often told me that the school's food is as good as possible with the ₹5 per child per day budget that it is given. The school's two teachers and the cook take special care of what to make, often putting in money from their own pockets.

We went to another school about 20 km away in the afternoon. The school had organised a 'Metric Mela'—a fair to explain the concepts related to physical measurement. Outside, the October sun was scorching, but inside, the school was buzzing. Groups of children had set up twelve stalls inside the five classrooms. The stalls had simple apparatus to measure different physical quantities, ranging from length to weight and volume. Gautam's height was beyond the scale that the kids had constructed and led to much merriment. I methodically interrogated the two groups who were weighing vegetables and people. They passed all my arithmetic tests and even the conceptual one about 'least count'. Then they made a bet about my weight. I gave them a ludicrous number of 300 kg and lost. The mela was the result of weeks of effort by the teachers of the school. It was not only a celebration, but an integral element of an effective pedagogical approach.

The children in this school seemed to have the same level of nutritional deprivation as in most disadvantaged parts of the country—very severe, but not as extreme. The teachers told us that the phala nearby had irrigated land and was better off than other phalas in the vicinity. In contrast, the children visiting the mela from other schools stood out. Their emaciated bodies spoke starkly of extreme deprivation, as in the school with the wadi in the playground. But in both cases, hunger was chronic.

How can education happen with an empty stomach every day? Years of deprivation that have led to severe developmental effects, including in the brain. Perilous health and homes that are forever precarious—not because of any less love or sense of community, but just because of dire poverty.

The challenges that teachers in these places face are unfathomable. Because the challenges these children face in life are unfathomable to most of us. We need not have been surprised by the number who died young. The school with a wadi is a poignant metaphor for this life, always on the edge of the precipice of survival. The school's mid-day meal is a lifeline in this world. The ₹5 per child spent on the midday meal may well be the most important public investment and safety net in many parts of the country such as these. Despite its operational inefficiencies and incidents of graft, the mid-day meal scheme does work for about 120 million(?) children across the country. But it is just not enough. What can you feed a child with ₹5, when that is the only real meal she has? The norms on nutrition are clear; the Supreme Court of India has also weighed in on this matter. More money is what is desperately required to make it happen. The current total annual public expenditure on the scheme is about ₹14,000 crore. Doubling that amount will not dent public finances; the amount is just about 3 per cent of the total public expenditure only on education.

We need the will to do this. We have figured out a lifeline for these children. It is thin and fraying, but it is there. All we need to do is strengthen it.

25 October 2018

The Reversal of No-detention
Policy is Regressive

He smelt of failure. He was twelve years old and sat in a corner at the back. The maths teacher would slap him every day. Dread would grip us from before the maths class, but he seemed inured to the pain and humiliation. The smell was familiar from my earlier schools. Not an odour, but resignation and defiance together in his being when in class. He had failed in the exams and had been detained in that class. He did not return to school after the vacation. No one got to know what happened. This was almost forty years ago.

Till the no-detention policy (NDP) of the Right to Free and Compulsory Education Act, 2009 (RTE) came into force, failure and detention were an intimate part of the lives of students. In my twelve years of schooling across five schools, I encountered many children who had failed and had been detained. Much was common between them. All of them were from relatively disadvantaged socio-economic backgrounds. I cannot recollect a single child from a socially privileged or upper-middle-class home. Detention didn't help any of them learn any better in the slightest; it made things worse. Many failed again, and were detained again. Many dropped out of school and most, from our lives.

There was a lot more that was common to them and us. They were nice and naughty, like any of us. They were neither dumber nor sharper, than any of us. And at least two of them had a riotous sense of humour, keeping everyone in splits. But this normal life was eviscerated the moment they entered the class, replaced by failure. It is very likely that you would remember similar children from your days in school. Nice, average children, their lives gutted by exam failure. Are these memories tinted by the immaturity of our childhood minds?

Educational research is thriving globally. As can be expected, much of this research is about 'what' helps or hinders learning of children. Every such 'what' has an astounding number of studies, in rigorously peer-reviewed journals. Helpfully, like in many other fields, in education too there are 'meta-studies' (or meta-analysis) available. These are analytical studies of a wide range of research studies on a particular matter whose results are combined in an attempt to draw systematic conclusions, if there are any.

John Hattie, professor of education at the University of Auckland, has done something that can only be called a meta-meta-study. It is a synthesis of over 800 meta-analyses, which encompass over 52,600 research studies, across the entire range of matters that impact students and their learning—from curriculum and teacher behaviour to student background and school characteristics, and a lot more. His book, *Visible Learning*, is a readable summary of this gargantuan exercise. The careful researcher that he is, Hattie is cautious in stating his conclusions, despite the massive underlying research base. But this evidence is so overwhelming on some matters, that Hattie has to resort to plain speaking, not the caveated language of research.

Let me quote him on detention (alternatively called 'retention') from the book: 'The effects of flunking are immediately traumatic to the children and the retained children do worse academically in the future, with many of them dropping out of school altogether … it would be difficult to find another educational practice on which the evidence is so unequivocally negative.'

Some of the many details of this unequivocal conclusion follow. Among students at similar achievement levels, those who are detained do not learn more than those who are promoted. Over a period of time, those who are promoted learn more. Those who are detained are very likely to drop out of school. Detained children are almost four times more likely to be from disadvantaged backgrounds. The threat of detention is not a motivating force in any way for children to learn.

Detention has deeply damaging social and psychological effects. Clearly, the fault is not in our memories. Rigorous research across decades, across the world, says the same as our memory: detention is completely dysfunctional educationally and deeply corrosive psychologically.

Parliament has recently amended the RTE to effectively cancel the NDP and allow for detention of children in classes III, V and VIII. This amendment enables one of the most regressive actions possible in education. Those who know better have not stood their ground. They have succumbed to a wide coalition which is failing in performing its role and is hell-bent on punishing the children for this failure. Parents, teachers, education administrators, policymakers, politicians, community leaders and more are complicit. The education policy in this country has taken many steps forward in the past few decades. This is one big step back. It has to be fought and reversed.

Let me quote Hattie again: 'The only question of interest relating to retention is why it persists in the face of this damning evidence.' The answer is quite simple. School education is often an intense struggle for many children, especially those from disadvantaged backgrounds. The system fails in addressing the issues of these children and teaching them well. Society seems to need someone to shoulder the blame. Punishing children with no power to protest for the failure of everyone else in the system is just a convenient and cynical transfer of culpability.

2 August 2018

Test Tyranny

The Indian student who leaves high school would have already taken hundreds of tests and examinations. This reality has not changed much in decades. What purpose does this testing serve?

A test can be used to choose a few from a large number, which is what organisations do when deciding whom to recruit. Such a test assesses whether the person who has applied for a role has the required capacities.

However, we know that testing cannot assess all the capacities. In fact, it may not be able to assess the most important ones. This is why testing is often used as a preliminary 'shortlisting' tool, followed by other methods of assessment such as group discussions and interviews and the evaluation of past work. Not even in our wildest imagination will we recruit solely on the basis of a test for our own organisation.

A test can also be used to certify a person. Passing examinations can certify an individual as a professional accountant or a medical practitioner. But such certification often uses more complex assessment, not just standard tests. In another form, the diagnostic test identifies what the person does not know adequately, and therefore needs to spend more time on.

Let us note two other matters related to testing: First, the simplicity and efficiency of tests make them easy to administer. Second, the worst tests can be so narrow that all that they assess is mere rote memorisation. The better tests can do a lot more, assessing complex capacities such as problem-solving and critical thinking.

However, there is often a trade-off between the efficiency of testing and the useful information that it produces. It is possible to design and implement complex tests for individuals and small groups that produce rich information, but the customisation, complexity and the investment of time of good assessors reduce efficiency.

Here is the problem. Very little of the testing in our education system serves the student or his or her learning. It is mostly used to compare, to rank students and to offer or deny further opportunities. Such testing pretends to be objective, but is rarely so. Every one of us who has experienced such testing is acutely aware of its severe limitations and the stress it produces. We will never depend solely or primarily on them for important decisions. Still, the testing of children seems unstoppable.

One of the most egregious tortures that we put children through is the various kinds of college entrance processes. Almost all of these are dependent on testing to select for admission or the results of 'board exams'. The test trauma that afflicts the life of children of this age is well-known.

Unfortunately, it is also equally well entrenched in our society. So, by widespread social sanction, here is what we are saying: While we know the severe limitations of standardised testing, we will use it to make one of the most important decisions in the lives of all our children. And let our children suffer now and consequently.

This kind of testing for college entrance and the 'board exam' is the prototypical example of high-stakes testing. Combine the limited real usefulness of tests with high stakes, and we have the perfect recipe for dysfunctionality that has afflicted our education system for decades, with each child being judged to have passed or failed based on tests.

What could have a higher stake than judging a child to be a failure? The perversity of this system becomes even clearer when one realises that the responsibility of the education system is to make sure each child learns to his or her potential. It is not to label them, declaring some as 'failures'.

The first big step to change this perverse test tyranny was taken by the Right of Children to Free and Compulsory Education Act, 2009 or Right to Education Act, 2009 (RTE). The RTE abolished examinations and the related policy of failing children and detaining them in the same grade, up to Class VIII. Testing was replaced by the much better continuous comprehensive evaluation system (CCE). This system regularly assesses student progress in multiple ways and uses the feedback in the teaching-learning process. It gives a continuous progress record and specific inputs for improving learning. Research evidence across the world suggests that such methods, called formative assessments, tend to improve student learning. Interpreted well, they also inform the teacher what she needs to do to improve her teaching. For once, our education system attempted to turn away from testing that just labelled the child to serve external interests, to assessment that could give useful information to the teacher and student.

But we now have a chorus of demands to abolish CCE and the no-detention policy (NDP). As a result, it appears certain now that the RTE will be amended to enable the reintroduction of examinations in elementary schools (up to Class VIII) and the scrapping of the NDP. If implemented, this takes our educational system a few steps back.

The CCE does everything testing can do and more, with much better consequences. It just doesn't use the reductionist method of sorting and classifying children that testing does. And this is inconvenient to some education administrators, educators and even many parents. Educating each child is their responsibility, but it is far easier to transfer that responsibility to the child and declare her to have passed or failed.

It is quite remarkable that we are willing to return to testing and labelling our children, the limitations and perversity of which we are all aware of. Our children cannot complain. But the damage to their education and the costs inflicted on the nation's future are here to stay.

17 August 2017

Markets Cannot Deliver Healthcare and Education

In the early 1990s, I joined a small team charged with developing a business of providing loans to hospitals, clinics and doctors for the purchase of medical equipment. Within six months, it was apparent that the economics of the hospitals and clinics was fragile. The cost structure of the sector was such that even the most efficient hospital or clinic required a high volume of patients just to break even. And most patients had neither health insurance nor the personal capacity to pay for healthcare services. The entire system worked on the elemental human principle that when your father or daughter gets ill, you do what the doctor says. You figure out how to pay and if that means you have to beg or borrow, then that's what you do.

Eight years in this business gave me a unique view into the private healthcare sector. Most of the owners of the hospitals and clinics, who were often doctors themselves, wanted loans. To convince me that there was no risk in lending to them, they would share their real financials with me, including the details of their revenue stream. Of course, none of this could be found in their statutory filings and financial statements. Revenue stream details meant patient numbers and their certainty.

One cold winter afternoon, in a small town in Punjab, over delicious kebab, a doctor was explaining to me how he would have no trouble repaying the large loan for an MRI system. Since I seemed unconvinced, he called up his hospital and, in his colourful Punjabi, instructed the staff: 'From now till 6 p.m., anyone who comes with a headache and no cold, or a backache, should be referred for an MRI scan to Jalandhar, till you hit eight, because brother here says that eight per day is break-even for the loan repayment.'

The modus operandi could be more or less crude than this, but across the country it was about the same. Testing had little to do with the actual need of the patient. It was instead directly related to the commercial desires of the hospital or clinic. There were other large-scale malpractices too. For example, hospitals and scan centres would give 'referral fees' to outside doctors who would refer a patient for a procedure. This was basically a bribe to prescribe a test procedure irrespective of the clinical condition. In those eight years, I did come across honest doctors and hospitals, but the list was short.

The great economist and Nobel laureate Kenneth Arrow, who died in February 2017, seemed to speak directly to my personal experience through his seminal paper, 'Uncertainty and the Welfare Economics of Medical Care'. Arrow's paper gave a widely accepted framework, which also explained my experience. Some of the matters from this framework, which I witnessed every day and you can see today, are: when healthcare services will be required is uncertain; that is, you don't know when and what illness will strike. It is unclear that a given therapy will lead to a sustained positive outcome, or a cure. You can't shop around and switch doctors like soap. And the doctor has enormously more knowledge than the patient, creating a relationship in which there is a grossly uneven distribution of power.

The implication of all this is quite direct: markets, driven by the profit motive, cannot deliver good healthcare services. Good healthcare needs other social institutions and structures such as public trust, enforceable professional ethical codes, public delivery systems and tight regulations. Unfortunately for our country, none of this seems to be working. Greed and commercialisation have subverted and trumped all ethical codes, regulations and even basic humaneness.

The past fifteen years of my work in education has given me an inside view into a similarly sordid scenario. It is now clear in India and elsewhere that private schools on an average do not deliver better learning outcomes than public schools. Despite this, private school enrolments have grown, and many believe in the false notion that more private schools will help improve education in India.

Education is even more complicated than healthcare. For example, the relationship between actions and outcomes is even more unpredictable. The actual outcomes and gains are visible only after many years. Educational goals are far more complex than therapeutic goals. The education of an individual also has public aims, children can't keep switching schools and schools have much greater power than children and parents. Clearly, education is not a service that can be delivered through a profit-motivated market.

But over time, we have allowed education, like healthcare, to be overrun by commercial motives. Unscrupulous elements polarise the social composition of schools even more, and exploit their power to coerce people into paying for poor education. Superficial markers like uniforms, the promise of 'English medium', frequent testing and rote-based focus on examinations are used to attract fee-paying students.

A weak public school system compounds the problem. Fund-starved governments, by not increasing the allocation to education, are worsening the situation. The real need is to strengthen public education and also encourage truly philanthropic initiatives. This requires substantial reform of policy and regulatory frameworks, and implementation with integrity. India's much vaunted demographic dividend will otherwise turn into a severe social and economic shock.

13 April 2017

Making Teachers Specialists

If you haven't already done it, then try teaching a child who is in classes V to VIII. Pick any topic, say volcanoes. Driven by the child's curiosity and your own desire for her to learn, the conversation will quickly go deeper and broader than the notion of mountains spewing very hot, molten stuff. For example, you will talk about why the stuff is molten; what makes the core of the Earth hot; why we don't have volcanoes all over the Earth; if it has always been like this; what are the other ways rocks are formed. For such a conversation to happen, many conditions must be met—a relationship of trust between you and the child must exist, you need to be observant of the child's emotional state and knowledge levels and be patient.

Let's focus on one condition: You yourself need to understand all these things related to volcanoes; you have to have 'subject knowledge' on volcanoes. If your subject knowledge is deep and broad, and mine is shallow and limited, the child wouldn't learn much from a conversation with me, but could learn from one with you.

Let's call such deep and broad knowledge, good knowledge of the subject. It's easy to appreciate that if we want the child to have good knowledge of any subject, the teacher must have better (deeper and broader) knowledge of the same subject than what we are expecting the child to develop. This is not in any way a contentious issue in education; there is ready agreement on this basic notion. With this background, let's look at India's school education. To be a teacher for classes I to VIII in India, a diploma in education (D. Ed.) is the basic qualification. These norms on qualifications and all other aspects of teacher education are governed by the National Council for Teacher Education (NCTE). The entry to a D. Ed. programme is after passing Class XII. It is a two-year programme, and doesn't have anything to do with subject knowledge of the future teacher. Its curriculum is designed for other educational aspects, like child development, sociological issues of education, pedagogy, etc.

The implication is that by design the teachers who teach students up to Class VIII are expected to have subject knowledge at the level of Class XII. There are many other deep flaws in the design and functioning of our teacher-preparation system, but let's just focus on this one aspect of subject knowledge. Is Class XII-level knowledge good enough to teach up to Class VIII? Is that knowledge adequately better (using the terminology of the example of volcanoes)? While there may not be a complete consensus on this matter, the overwhelming majority in education would say that the minimal subject knowledge requirement to teach up to Class VIII is an undergraduate-level education. It is very hard to find any country that by design keeps the subject knowledge bar as low as us. Most countries expect an undergraduate-level education in subjects, while their specific designs of their teacher-preparation programmes may differ.

Till now, we have only talked about the flaw in the design of the system; now let's look at the reality. We are quite familiar with the very inadequate learning levels of our schools. It's with this low subject knowledge, even by school standards, that many of our elementary schoolteachers operate. It's no surprise that you can find teachers in Class VIII who don't have subject knowledge that you would expect in a Class VI student. You see this reflected everywhere where teachers' subject knowledge is assessed; the percentage of teachers qualifying through the central and state teacher eligibility tests (TETs) is routinely between 2 per cent and 10 per cent. Teachers who teach classes IX to XII are expected to have a bachelor's degree in education and an undergraduate degree in a relevant subject; some teachers in classes I to VIII also have undergraduate degrees.

However, the quality of our undergraduate education is (in my estimate) worse than our school education. So, an undergraduate degree hardly seems to matter. Let me point out three things: One, although the motivation and engagement of teachers is a completely different aspect, it is often affected negatively by a lack of subject knowledge. Two, there are many other capacities that are required other than to have subject knowledge to be an effective teacher. Three, given that we are talking about eight million teachers, for sure there are some teachers who have good subject knowledge, that is, there are large variations around a low mean.

Three things that are in progress must be deepened and expanded to address this situation. Teacher appointments, both in private and public schools, must be contingent on qualifying through (improved) TETs. Investment must be increased in effective in-service support for existing teachers on subject knowledge. The design of teacher preparation must be changed such that all teachers go through a five-year integrated programme on subjects and teacher education. NCTE has already taken steps in this direction and the prime minister has endorsed this idea publicly. However, given the entrenched interests in the 16,000-odd existing teacher education institutions, this will need some doing.

22 July 2015

Drifting to Teaching

Why did you become a teacher? In my many discussions with teachers, I never ask that question, but it does come up often on its own. Rarely does someone tell a story of teaching being her life's calling. Most often they are stories of drifting to teaching. There are four common narratives. The first is that of the young person who has struggled financially to complete schooling. Despite education in government schools being free, there are costs of schooling for a family, which mount with each higher grade. Each day is uncertain; they aspire for the quickest possible economic anchor. For such people, the two-year Diploma in Education (D. Ed.), after Class XII, which qualifies them to be a primary schoolteacher, is a good option. It is perhaps the lowest-cost professional qualification available. Also, it doesn't close other options. So, many find themselves as teachers, having treaded this path of struggle.

The second common narrative is that of the person, who tried many other things but didn't make it, and ended up being a teacher. These are the kind of people who have enough socio-economic capital to aspire for the 'higher' things. They want to be doctors or engineers or government officers; sometime along the way, as options start closing, they complete a Bachelor in Education (B. Ed.) on the side, almost like insurance for the possibility of failure in all their aspirations. When they are tired of trying for all this higher stuff, they try the teacher recruitment process and become teachers.

The third common narrative is usually that of many young women. They complete a B. Ed. or D. Ed., with the idea that after their marriage they want a teaching job. It gives an income, has predictable working conditions and is respectable. It is perceived as a good balance, when the woman wants to be a homemaker and have another job alongside.

The fourth narrative is of a different sort. From the mid-1990s, many states appointed a significant percentage of teachers on short-term contracts, on markedly lower salaries. This was still reasonable for the individual, since these contracts would just keep getting renewed. Anyone who had passed (at minimum) Class XII was considered for such appointments, allowing a wide set to drift in to being a teacher. In the past few years, the numbers of such short-term contractual appointments have reduced across states, and the Right to Education Act, 2009 mandates a teaching qualification for even such appointments.

Let me point out some caveats to these four narratives. For sure there are other narratives; also, these very narratives and their distinctions may not be very neat. These narratives relate to government schoolteachers; most (non-elite) private schoolteachers that I have heard stories from fall within the first three, with the additional twist that they are still waiting and trying to join government schools.

Given some of the basic characteristics of the teaching profession, such as its income and wealth potential, its relatively low status in the social power hierarchy and the locations (in the smallest of places) of the jobs, it isn't surprising that people drift in to teaching rather than choosing it. These basic characteristics are there because school education is a mass endeavour. And it is a mass endeavour because we have a national commitment to good education for all our children; we have eight million teachers in every nook of the country and growing.

John Dewey commented, 'Education is, and forever will be, in the hands of ordinary men and women.' This sentiment emanates from a notion of education, which is deeply rooted in democracy. It is our democracy that demands and drives the commitment to good education for all children. This is what makes it a mass endeavour, which then can only be shouldered by ordinary men and women. This doesn't mean that these ordinary men and women can't be good teachers, and Dewey didn't mean that either. Let's first recognise that the role of a teacher is not ordinary. Teaching is a complex and highly demanding role: cognitively, emotionally and socially. It requires depth in a wide range of capacities, certain dispositions and ethical commitment to be an effective teacher. But the widely prevalent notion of the role of a teacher is opposite of this reality—we have an impoverished notion of teaching, namely that teaching is a very ordinary role.

Thinking of teaching as a special role is central to having effective teachers. This will enable and force certain fundamental things: the quality of professional development—both pre-service teacher education (B. Ed./D. Ed.) and in-service teacher support, a culture of empowerment to energise the creative nature of a teacher's role and ensuring some basics, like corruption-free appointments and not treating teachers as all-purpose labour. If we get all this right, there is no reason why the ordinary people, in whose hands education will be forever, will not perform their special roles well.

4 February 2015

A Culture of Thinking

The vision of India as a manufacturing power calls for an educated workforce of thinkers and problem-solvers ...

Narendra Modi's speech on 15 August was by far the best Independence Day speech by a prime minister in decades. Even his most indefatigable opponents concede that as a piece of communication it was a masterclass, while they may have disagreed with the content or found it inadequate or insincere. Amongst the many memorable phrases in that speech was 'Make in India'. He was attempting to develop a new narrative for manufacturing in India. That part of the speech took me back ten years.

For many years I was responsible for a manufacturing business. Soon after I moved to that role, I figured out three things: our market position in India while dominant was fragile, there were huge opportunities for growth outside India and to protect our Indian position and grow globally we needed to become enormously more competitive.

That is how I started pursuing Manohar, the best engineering mind I knew, to join me in the business. Through the 1990s, he had built and run the highest of high-tech manufacturing facilities, for one of the world's largest multinationals. After he had got to know our business, he asked me, 'Why have you outsourced your thinking?' He was referring to our manufacturing and engineering processes. Over the next few years, we faced the vagaries of the market, faced intense competition within India, and in turn ourselves expanded and gained market share globally. Manohar and many other colleagues played pivotal roles.

While I moved out of the business years ago, the effort

continued. Today, the business is enormously more competitive, stronger and bigger. It's the global leader in an engineering-intensive, precision manufacturing industry. In those years as we battled for competitiveness, the toughest challenge was from South Korean and Japanese companies. We felt that the Japanese and Koreans must be cheating. It took many market skirmishes to accept the reality, that somehow we were missing something fundamental. It also demolished the belief that lower 'labour cost' was key to competitiveness.

That fundamental was Manohar's old question, 'Why have you outsourced your thinking?' Competitiveness springs from out-thinking others continually, not outsourcing thinking. This demand for out-thinking was not only while formulating strategy but at all levels, in every excruciating detail, and hidden in every unnoticeable minutia. Also, it was not about one day of good thinking, but layers and layers of thinking built over years. It was a culture of thinking.

Such a culture of thinking demands everyone to think. From the design of the products, choice of the materials, design of the supply chain and the manufacturing processes to everyday issues of manufacturing, cost and quality—everything demands deep thinking. This was what our Japanese and Korean competitors were good at, and slowly we became good at it as well. Let's take an example. Our welders were no less skilled than the Koreans or Japanese. The issue went beyond skill. Did they understand geometry and use it? Could they figure out how metal parts would expand differentially and why? Could they use different mixes of gases for heating? Could they change process designs?

It was all about curiosity, questioning, analysing, synthesising, problem-solving, creating options and examining critically. This was as true for the welder and machinist, as for the product designer and material specialist. I observed across industries that sustained competitiveness required this culture of thinking. All else was fleeting, including low labour cost. There is always another country which can offer lower labour cost; even more fundamentally, roles that don't require thinking, and work that can be done mechanically, gets automated. This basic restructuring of manufacturing has only accelerated and deepened; the future is going to need thinking workers even more than before.

The prime minister's vision of India as a manufacturing powerhouse calls for the preparation of an educated workforce of thinkers and problem-solvers. So, when I hear talk of how our school education must be changed to become more employability-oriented and focused on specific vocational skills, I am horrified. Such ideas envision developing skilled (for example) welders, rather than thinking people who could be welders. This recipe will neither make people employable nor India a manufacturing powerhouse. Specific vocational training has its place, but not within basic school education. In the past few decades, India has developed a rich and nuanced understanding of the aims of school education. This is reflected in our curricular goals and principles.

For sure the progress in curriculum is not yet reflected in practice in most schools. But that doesn't mean that we are not on the right track. Developing the ability to think is one of the central goals of our school curriculum. This arises from the basic aim of education: to develop a democratic society. In today's hyper-competitive and dynamic marketplace, it is also at the core of employability and economic development. To successfully 'Make in India', we have to educate our youth well. Not just to be skilled workers, but to be smart and thinking individuals. That requires us to stick to first principles—of good education.

3 September 2014

Perils of Innovation

If he had not been a wealthy man, he could have found a role as Arnold's adversary in *The Expendables* or some such super-brawny movie. It looked like he wanted to crush me, which he could have done with his fingertips. He had requested a meeting, wanting to learn about school education in India.

Early in the discussion, he stated his view emphatically that information and communications technology (ICT) was the fountain of innovation for solutions to India's problems in education. On such matters there is no point in mincing words, so I told him this was not correct, at first politely and then, as he refused to listen, more directly. Along with his wealth, he hadn't acquired the ability to listen. So, he raved, louder and louder, about the game-changing impact of smartboards and sundry other tech toys, and how these could reduce dependency on teachers.

Then he started attacking me as a stuck-in-the-mud Luddite, and for being another irritating obstacle to much-needed innovations. Since I was confident that I could outrun him if he did attack me physically, I saw no reason to tolerate this nonsense in my own office. So, I told him that we would end the meeting right then.

Not all discussions on innovation in education have the same drama, but some things are common. Basically, the committed, passionate advocate of the so-called innovation feels frustrated by my refusal to acknowledge the innovation as innovation, let alone a significant one.

Let me take a couple of more examples. There was this deeply committed educationist arguing for curricular innovations.

What he was referring to was the integration of specific streams of vocational education from Class VI. This would include things such as plumbing, masonry, electrical repair, etc. A good economist claimed hiring a local villager at low salary, giving her a short training and using her as a teacher was an innovation that would lead to improved learning levels.

What's common to all these things that are claimed as innovation is that they all have the good intention of improving education from its current state. One could argue that most such things are not innovations because they have been tried before, with limited or no success. While that is true, I think there are two more fundamental issues in claiming such things as innovation in education.

Let's take the first issue, which is quite simple. If you were to get a bunch of experts in education to consider whatever is being attempted, would they find reasonable consensus, informed by the then understanding of education, that it's a good thing to attempt educationally?

This would mean due consideration, for example, of aims of education, pedagogical alternatives, the nature of subjects and the understanding of child development, while also considering the socio-cultural context. It would mean factoring in of the impact of the proposed innovation on the capacity, culture and autonomy of the school. All this would be equally applicable to curriculum and pedagogical practices, as to resourcing, arrangements and structures of school organisation and systems.

On this matter of educational soundness of the three innovations that I have mentioned, a brief summary would be that these things are neither fundamentally good for education nor better alternatives. Many advocates of such innovations themselves would agree with this educational summary. However, they would contend that given various kinds of constraints that our school education and society face, these things must be attempted.

To address this matter of our given constraints, let's look at the related second issue, which is even simpler. Whatever is being touted as an innovation to help improve the current state of education, would you want your children to go to a school that uses it?

Would you want your children to go to a school that thinks that poor teaching can be offset by smartboards? How about your children's school vocationalising education from Class VI? Or using someone from the neighbourhood as a teacher after four weeks of training? The answers to these questions will lead to the common, basic problem with such things. These things are all being proposed such that they will be implemented in schools that serve disadvantaged populations. We will never think of implementing these things in schools serving the upper-middle class. Such things only harden and deepen systemic inequity. Instead of improving what is required to be improved, which are the well-understood fundamentals (teacher education and support, system culture, greater investment, etc.), these are attempts to take shortcuts, the kind which we will never accept for ourselves because these are suboptimal or wrong. At its core, this is injustice.

Education by its very nature demands innovation and creativity, within the classroom and school.

Paradoxically, our organisational culture throttles that creativity, while touting other things as innovation. For anything to be classified as innovation in education, let's put it to two simple tests: is it educationally sound and is it equitable and just?

11 June 2014

Myths of Privatopia

There is a land called Privatopia. There, Leviathan is but a distant memory, of the beast that withered away. It's a clean and healthy land. Children grow up there with great education.

Gleaming roads connect all places. Transport works without a glitch. The water is sweet, germ-free, delivered to every house. Sanitation works perfectly. High-tech hospitals take care of the few who are ill. Peace in the land and its security are maintained by the ever-alert forces. All this has been made possible after the beast was helped to wither away by the dynamic forces of competition and markets were encouraged to take over all these services. The glorious day when other essential services like legislative representation, justice and parenting will also be offered by the efficient forces of markets is not far away.

This caricature of a place without any public systems and services resonates with the ideas of many of my friends on what can solve India's problems, till I get to the last few words. Most of us do live in our own Privatopia. The Indian upper-middle class does not get involved with public systems in any way, unless it's completely unavoidable. There are good reasons to avoid Indian public systems. The simplest of which is that these systems do not deliver what they are supposed to. In addition, their general wastefulness, corruption and brazen disregard for basic human dignity is obvious.

So, the abandonment of public systems by those who have money and power is quite understandable. However, this phenomenon is leading to something deeply insidious to a good society and democracy. The well-off and the influential are not only abandoning public systems, but they are abandoning the very idea of it. A lack of immediate personal stake in these systems, combined with a strangely narrow understanding of economics, leads to hankering for Privatopia. These ideas and their pursuit are hollowing out the foundations of good society. Even those who understand the market-oriented economic theory and why certain goods and services have a character which make them non-deliverable by the market, can't bring themselves to accept that India needs to fix its public systems. They (including senior government officials) continue to think of privatisation and competition as solutions. School education, which is my area of work, is in the front line of this war. India's schooling system is more privatised than any other country in the world, almost by a factor of two, and growing. Only failed states have similar percentage of private schools; failed states by definition have failed public systems and institutions.

Theory, experience and evidence all point in the same direction: that good public schools are the only route to good education at a systemic level. I have earlier written about how well-researched evidence in India busts the myth that private schools perform better than public schools. Let me mention a few experiences from across the world. Diane Ravitch's very readable book *Reign of Error* gives a blow-by-blow account of this war on education and its insidious effect in the US. The Swedish school system is showing worse results and growing inequality after two decades of privatisation. Not many countries have tried this self-defeating strategy of introducing markets in schools.

For a comprehensive global view, let's look at the Programme for International Students Assessment (PISA). This is a cross-country study of school education conducted periodically by the Organisation for Economic Co-operation and Development (OECD). PISA has been accused of making facile international performance comparisons; but despite its limitations, its characterisation of country-wide systems is still useful. PISA is unambiguous about the record of public systems. Let me quote verbatim from the concluding chapter of PISA 2012, which sort of addresses the implications of its research for policy: '... in contrast, some features, most notably the prevalence of private schools and competition for students, have no discernible relationship with student performance, at least at the system level ... thus, after socio-economic status is accounted for, private schools do not perform better than public schools ... although individual parents may derive an advantage for their child from the privileged socio-economic context—and attendant resources—of private schools, school systems as a whole do not seem to benefit from a greater prevalence of private schools or a higher degree of competition among schools.' In simple terms, the comprehensive evidence from sixty-five countries says that competition and market-based mechanisms do not improve school systems; on the other hand, they increase inequity.

India's education will not improve till our public education improves. There is no way out. But forget about trying, the idea itself has been abandoned by most of the Indian elite. The efforts to improve education in India are reflective of a deeper struggle; the struggle to retrieve the idea of public systems, including public education, and then to make them function. We may not be a failed state because of our 'vibrant' democracy, but will fail as a society, if we let our public systems wither away.

25 December 2013

The Ideology of Education

Last year in winter, a widely respected Nobel Prize winner regaled us over three days with stories of what he called policy-based evidence-making and its parent, ideology-based evidence-making.

All the stories were from serious academic research. I was reminded of this last week, when I read many reports in the media, about certain research projects on school education. *Mint* also ran two features related to these projects: 'The conclusive case for school choice' and 'Adding contract teachers to regular ones improves outcomes'. To be fair, these stories in the media were not really reporting ideology-based evidence-making, but its lesser cousin ideology-based evidence-interpretation. We (at the Azim Premji Foundation) should know something about these research projects, which are making all these headlines, since we have been deeply involved in them.

These projects have been collaborative efforts involving multiple agencies. On the ground, we have been in charge, and have run the projects, for the past eight years in five districts of Andhra Pradesh. It has been quite an effort with over forty project staff on an average, for all these years. The reports and details are available on our website. For serious researchers, we are happy to provide access to the base data, since it has a lot more research potential. Let's take the projects one by one. The first project explored one basic question: are private schools doing a better job than government schools or vice versa? That is, is there a difference in the learning levels of children across private and government schools? Now, as I have written many times before in these columns, this seemingly simple question is actually vexed by many complexities, the most important of which is that the socio-economic background of the child has a substantial impact on learning, aside from schooling. What this means is that it is invalid to compare the effects of any two kinds of schools, unless one can be sure that the children in those schools have similar socio-economic backgrounds. This project was designed to make sure that we are able to compare effects on learning across government and private schools on children with similar socio-economic background.

The conclusions of this five-year-long study are unambiguous: once variation in socio-economic background is accounted for, there is no difference in learning outcomes across government and (non-elite) private schools; private schools are not doing a better job of teaching children. This is clearly a big conclusion. It is not necessarily new, since other studies that have controlled for socio-economic factors have come to the same conclusion. However, it is an important addition to counter the commonly held misperception that private schools do a better job than government schools. So, the media reports on this study are misleading. The study doesn't leave even a fig leaf to cover for private school performance, so the market-ideology-driven interpretation can only be, 'Oh, but the private schools deliver the same performance at lower cost.' That point has no justification unless some other fundamental questions are answered, the simplest of which is: why and how do private schools have these lower costs? And without an answer to that question, there is no legitimacy in putting the big conclusion of the study in the background, and side-interpreting the results to suit a certain ideology.

Private schools are able to exist at their cost structure, because they are parasitic on the labour market (and other related things) created by the government schooling system. So, direct cost comparisons are invalid. Let us not even open other critical issues—how fair or exploitative such private school practices are, and most importantly, how both kinds of schools deliver equally poor learning outcomes. In any case, if you want to be faithful to the question and conclusion of this particular study, the headlines should actually read, 'Study demolishes the myth that private schools are better', and not focus on issues it has not explored.

The second project is even simpler, and almost funny. This study has tried to assess the effect of different kinds of interventions in schools, as reflected in improvement in student learning. The interventions ranged from giving grants to schools, incentives to teachers and to groups of teachers and so on. One of the conclusions of the study was that more teachers per school (actually per class and child) leads to better learning. Employment status of the teacher, that is, on contract or permanent, is a related but irrelevant aside, since this status has no differential impact on learning outcomes. So, the correct headline that can be drawn from the study is 'Adding teachers improves learning' and not 'Adding contract teachers to regular ones improves outcomes'.

These long research projects reaffirm the complex challenge of improving our education system. They also indicate that the belief that private schools are a solution to our problems in education is not founded on fact. The fact is that there is no substitute to a good public education system, and we have to build that.

30 October 2013

Education System Should Have Ideal, Not Practical, Goals

A month ago, I wrote about the problems that teachers are having in using continuous comprehensive evaluation (CCE). A friend who read it wrote back to me with two simple questions: If it is so difficult to implement CCE, why does the Right to Education Act, 2009, mandate it for all the schools across the country? In general, isn't it better to try and implement something that is practical, rather than aim for the ideal which is clearly unworkable in the current conditions? A recap on CCE: it is a method of assessment of a child's learning on an ongoing basis and it is used in the class to teach the child better. CCE replaces tests up to Class VIII; it doesn't give any scores or marks. Such an assessment method serves many goals. For example, it helps in improving learning rather than judging children; it focuses on multiple capacities of the child and not on testing rote; and it's non-threatening and so, socio-psychologically better for the child.

There are many hurdles to CCE actually getting implemented. Some of these are: teachers have to handle thirty to forty kids together, across multiple grades; they do not have the time for the subtleties of CCE; teachers lack the capacities required to use something like this effectively; the pedagogical approach in reality in most schools remains rooted in rote. So, then, why try for something like CCE? Why not settle for something more practical? Especially when the implementation has to be across the massive Indian schooling system, which has about 1.5 million schools and over 200 million students. In my view, we must look at education (including its components) as it ought to be. We should derive goals for our education system from this 'ought to be'; let's call these the ideal goals. On the other hand, what I am calling 'practical' are goals that are incremental, seemingly achievable improvements within the current constraints of the average school.

I will list three reasons why our goals have to be ideal, and not practical. The comments that follow are general and use CCE only as an illustration. Examples of other such issues could be: the curriculum of schools, the design of our teacher education system, the culture of school management and so on.

Today, our system does a shoddy job of what actually needs to be practical. To be successful, the planning and its execution to get to any goal must be practical, that is, must take into account realities on the ground, develop relevant strategies, execute with rigour and not compromise on the goals even if the progress is incremental. Our education system (with few notable exceptions) doesn't do all this. It takes any goal, converts it into a set of procedures and documents, and considers its task done. It has an extraordinary ability to take out the spirit of everything, and convert it in to a mechanical tick-the-box approach. To go back to the CCE example, most states seem to believe that it will get done magically across the thousands of schools, with some minor training of teachers, and filling up of some checklists.

The goals must be ideal, but the execution plan must be practical. No great insight in this, but mostly we don't get it. Aiming for the ideal goals on even one aspect of education (for example, assessment) presents an opportunity to improve other aspects. This is because of the integrated nature of education. Assessment, teacher capacity, teacher education, pedagogy, curriculum, school and system management, culture, etc., are all so intricately and organically linked that efforts to change one dimension necessarily means changes in the other dimensions. For real improvement, all must move with some synchronicity, even though perfect coordination may be impossible.

A practical goal by definition arises from an acceptance of the current state of affairs as constraints, whereas an ideal goal is a potential lever to change all aspects of the system. Articulating practical goals for a system only deepens inequity in an already iniquitous structure. This happens because in reality the practical becomes a goal for the disadvantaged; whereas the privileged strive for the ideal as their goal, pushed by both internal and external forces. The well-off schools were doing versions of CCE long before it was mandated. The deep impact of this divergence of goals is manifold because the disadvantaged schools that need support and resources get it with only the practical goals in sight. This has a determining impact on those who need support most, that is, the large majority of our 1.5 million schools. Such choices have cumulative, historical effects and they cannot be unwound. So, a society or nation committed to equity and democracy must decide what education ought to be and then go for it, for the whole system. It's then that the burden of making it happen becomes clearer, and the society has to figure out how to make it happen, obliged to do whatever is required and provide whatever support is needed.

4 September 2013

A Weak Support System

'Mujhe administrative mein kheench lijiye,' I heard this often as a kid. 'Pull me in to the administrative side.' The translation loses the sense of urgency that it conveys in Hindi. My large extended family and their friends were (almost) all in government service. A fair number of them were in education—in some academic role or the other, as teachers in schools and professors in colleges. I heard that phrase from many of them as a plea to people who were 'high up' in administration. The desire to abandon academics was driven by the attraction of 'administrative' power and the reality where academicians were under the thumb of even the lowest member of the administrative hierarchy. That was thirty years ago.

It was a biting cold afternoon in January, in a small town in Kumaon. We had a meeting with the staff of the block resource centre (BRC), the nodal academic support institution for government schools in the block. It was the kind of a meeting that you can expect in any BRC.

There was discussion on apprehensions about the right to education (RTE) and something about inadequate staffing. Quite a bit of it was about how they have no time for their actual roles as senior officials keep pulling them into all kinds of information-gathering and dissemination activities. These range from gathering information about mid-day meals, distributing government orders and collecting data on admissions. As we were leaving, it got even colder. On a bend in the climb uphill, one of them said to us, to no one in particular, *'Mujhe administrative mein le lijiye.'*

Things haven't changed much in all these years. He knew that we did not hold government positions, but thought that people from Bangalore and Dehradun would have some influence in the right places. Hence his plea. Most educational districts have three to eight blocks, which are administrative units. BRCs are academic support institutions for schools in that block. Blocks usually have 100–200 schools, which are divided into 'clusters' of ten to twenty schools. Each cluster has a cluster resource centre (CRC), to provide more immediate, direct academic support to schools.

Academic support means a host of things: professional development of teachers, material development, improvement in assessment, in-school support on difficult issues, among others—basically, all kinds of academic stuff to improve education in the school. This is a comprehensive structure, which has been envisioned and invested into by the government. The CRC and BRC form support ladders in the district and are capped by the District Institute of Education and Training (DIET). The country has created this structure of academic support for schools in the past twenty years. There are over 500 DIETs, a few thousand BRCs and many more thousands of CRCs. Together they account for 30,000–50,000 people.

This large scale and multi-level system is designed for coverage, proximity and depth. It demonstrates that we are willing to invest for improving education. The problem is that this well-designed system doesn't work well—partly because it has the same maladies that are found in other parts of our large bureaucracy. There are some specific reasons as well.

First, as narrated by BRC staff in the town in Kumaon, education administration tends to use these academic people freely for menial and mundane administrative purposes. The system pays no heed to the academic purposes for which the structure has been devised. Second, the roles demand that they should be staffed by academically sound (and interested) individuals. In reality, usually the average teacher is posted in a CRC/BRC. For such a person, it is nearly impossible to play the role of the academic expert for similarly capable teachers. Third, these institutions are not academically empowered. Usually, they act as messengers even on academic issues, with no expectation of applying their own mind. It is not possible to make effective academic interventions in that culture.

While it may take a lot to make this large system vibrant, it is not so difficult to make it reasonably effective. The basic tasks are quite obvious. For starters, recruiting capable individuals from within schools and investing in developing their academic capacity should be a priority.

Second, a culture that recognises the value of academic work and lets teachers get on with it needs to be fostered. Third, within the framework of the curriculum, these institutions need to set their own goals and plans that are responsive to local conditions. They should not be treated as minions within the administrative hierarchy.

Finally, India needs a separate 'academic cadre' to ensure that only those who are interested in such roles join it. Those interested in administrative roles should have no part in it. A fundamental overhaul of the pre-service education system (for example, at the level of training imparted in the Bachelor of Education programme, among others) is perhaps the most urgent need in Indian education today. This will also help the academic support structure to become more effective. In a country of our size and diversity, we will always need a system of academic support for schools. We are committed to it and have created it. We have to make it work.

3 October 2012

What to Teach?

What is worth teaching, learning and exploring is a crucial issue for any educational system and institution. Somehow, this does get decided. This is not just about today, but has been true for thousands of years. Through the history of education, religious bodies have played a pivotal role.

The Church, the Muslim clergy and, if you were to look further back, the Buddhist Sangha have been key stakeholders in education for most of history. What was to be taught, learnt and explored was determined by theological priorities. In practice, this translated into a wide range of institutions. Nalanda and Takshashila were centres of learning with very broad and eclectically determined areas of study, not entirely driven by Buddhist concerns. On the other hand, madrasas in the middle of the last millennium were focused mostly on religious study. Let's jump to the present and ask ourselves this question: how do we today decide what must be the matter of study in our schools and colleges?

The answer seems so obvious that the question doesn't seem worth asking. It seems clear that the government somehow handles this issue. It also seems obvious that the government doesn't decide this in an arbitrary fashion, but gets this done through a group of sensible people, who in turn must be following some thoughtful process. As we go deeper into this issue, it becomes more complex, and also more confusing. It's not so difficult to intuitively understand how this group of sensible people decide, for example, whether to study physics or not; it becomes more difficult to understand how the decision is made that studying biology is more important than studying carpentry, or how much relative importance must be given to studying languages vis-à-vis mathematics. It becomes more complex when you look into the next level of detail, for example, within geography, do you pay more attention to physical geography or to social geography and then what topics to take up in what detail.

It's apparent by now that what seems like a fairly simple question hides many complexities. But we can still take comfort from the fact that the bunch of sensible people charged with this task will somehow do a reasonable job. After all they have probably been chosen because they understand these issues well. Let's not forget that these people were chosen by the government. We should also ask why should it be that the government has the mandate to take this decision, in the first place. The answer seems obvious. Since education is a crucial social good, a definite avenue for developing individuals and society, decisions related to education must somehow be determined by larger social will, factoring in social, economic and cultural concerns.

The government is representative of this social will. There is also a defined process of functioning of the state, for example, what issues can be decided by the executive, what by the legislature. It must be obvious that I am simplifying matters, and brushing away nuances, but we are not missing the broad nature of this thing.

Let's mull over a more controversial and intriguing thought. What would the group of sensible people, acting as agents of the government, which in turn is representative of the will of the people, decide on what should be stated as the origin of the universe, as a matter of study? Is any of us surprised (in India at least) that the origin of the universe is not attributed to divine creation, in standard school curriculum, though that may well be the prevalent belief in the country? So, somehow, in this particular matter (as in many others) the accumulated wisdom of humanity overrides the seeming current 'collective will and belief'. Actually, what gives legitimacy to this override is the expressly articulated vision of our society. This vision is built by us, most concretely represented in our Constitution. The Constitution makes us secular and emphasises scientific temper. Which is where the legitimacy of this (and many such overrides) comes into being. The good thing is that we intuitively understand this in our country.

It's such situations that make it clear that the choice of what to study is not driven primarily by some here-and-now collective desire. It is driven by a methodical and cumulative set of choices which are in consonance with our vision of our society and its individuals. It is also validly drawn from the generally agreed (and accumulated) body of knowledge that humanity currently has. Ordinarily, the group of sensible people do a good job of this and have done so in our country. But once in a while they are overruled by the state (or some wing of it). When this overruling is to protect our constitutional ideals, it has legitimacy. However, when it is driven by political expediency, it has little or no legitimacy. The guardians of our Constitution and its ideals have decided to drop a cartoon from a textbook, and are considering banishing all cartoons from all curricula; does this override have the legitimacy of the constitutional vision, or is it an act of populist, political expediency?

16 May 2012

The Making of a Rote Nation

What we want from our children is better 'marks' in exams. That's the wish of an overwhelming majority in this country. In reality, we have an examination, not an education, system. In Hindi, the resonance of the two words makes this reality more emphatic, we have a *pareeksha tantra*, not a *shiksha tantra*. The objects of our national obsession—examinations—primarily assess memory and procedural skills. This is true across grades, schools and boards in varying degree. It's equally true for our higher education system. Our examinations reflect our notion of learning. We tend to equate mechanical procedural skills and memorisation with learning. Rote and more rote become the path to learning, 'cracking' exams and, therefore, getting marks.

While most don't give it a second thought, some teachers, principals or parents readily agree in a conversation that this examination obsession is not education. Even if they don't articulate it lucidly, they want children to gain conceptual understanding, to learn to think critically and to analyse, to develop the ability to apply knowledge; to actually 'learn'. But even this minority forgets or ignores this real 'learning' in real life.

In part, that is because even this minority is acutely conscious of the 'social function' of marks and exams. That of 'sorting out': selecting or rejecting for further education, for jobs and social status. The majority is anyhow fixated with this social function. This fixation completely eliminates the real purpose of examinations, which actually is to assess in order to help further (real) learning.

Many of those involved in education are acutely conscious of this deep flaw in our system. Parts of the government system and many private schools have been continually trying to work on this—with only very slow effect. The effect is slow because real improvement is possible only with sustained synergistic work on the fundamentals, that is, when all the intertwined complex elements of education build towards facilitating genuine learning and not rote. This includes: capacity of teachers and school leaders, curriculum, books, classroom environment and pedagogical methods. As work continues on all this, what's surprising is the inadequate attention paid to improving and changing examinations themselves.

Examinations are in a sense a significant point of leverage in the education system. The changes in examinations have a multiplier effect, going well beyond individual-by-individual or school-by-school effect. This is because examinations are in large measure designed and governed 'centrally', for example, by a board or by a district authority. Therefore, changes at the 'central' level can impact a very large number of schools—giving that change a substantial leverage.

Improving examinations does not require magic. It's about changing what the exams assess: moving them from assessing mere memorisation and procedural knowledge to assessing understanding, thinking and application. In collaboration with the Karnataka government, the Azim Premji Foundation did this across 9,000 of (largely) rural government schools for three years—2003–06. While that three-year experience emphasised to us how only changing examinations will not improve education, it also equally emphasised that changing examinations gets the schools to start focusing on what they should focus on instead of rote memorisation. There was indeed a substantial leverage effect. This leverage effect would be even higher, if we were to change the key high-stake exams, for example, the Class X and Class XII exams and various 'entrance' tests.

The Right to Education Act has got it directionally right: focusing on 'comprehensive continuous assessment' (CCA), assessment appropriate for development and the elimination of 'high stakes' from assessment. This is a better approach to assessment compared with 'examinations' only. However, it will take years, if not decades, before we are able to implement CCA across the nation. It requires a level of skill and ability on the part of the teachers and schools, something that even our most privileged schools struggle with, let alone the large majority of our ordinary (both government and private) schools among the 1.6 million. In the meanwhile, we can certainly change examinations to reflect real learning.

Given the social function of exams, it is one area where industry and general population can play a clear role, but don't. Instead, we look at the marks of our children and feel happy or sad, and also look at the marks of potential employees for hiring. We mouth a homily once in a while, but go back to the comfortable, simplifying tyranny of 'marks' in our real lives. We, the 'demand' side, are silently accepting this hollow education, in many ways, and visibly through the acceptance of the current examination system. We also think of a dynamic and innovative India. We think of economic prosperity of our country through high-skill and value-added jobs. We dream of India returning to its rightful place in the world order. These are all castles in the sand: the sand of rote. We are actually building a rote nation.

7 September 2011

Limits of Small Successes

They had worked with seventeen schools. After eighteen months of working with these inner schools, they were seeing improvement with the learning outcomes. With confidence that comes from the conviction of success, the consultant who had led the project was coolly dismissive of the idea that India's scale, diversity and complexity limited the value of his methods.

He was very sincere in pitch, as we sat overlooking the lovely city that he worked in. We enjoyed the breakfast and the view and moved on.

Moving on and ignoring such confident advice is a survival skill in our work. You are inundated every day by solutions, methods and ideas that are 'proven' and would dramatically improve education if implemented at scale. Almost all of this advice is with the best of intentions, and with complete conviction. Usually the conviction, confidence and push are greater, if it's an advocate of the idea, rather than the person who has actually implemented it (the latter usually are far more measured). The advocates are forthright in their admission that ideas implemented at a relatively small scale, in controlled conditions and in one particular context may not be applicable elsewhere and at scale; however, somehow the idea that they are espousing is different, and these limitations do not apply.

We face this with teacher training, curriculum, pedagogy, technology, school management, motivation, 'integrated approaches'—in every facet of education and more. Indeed, there are many worthy examples of small successes for all of these. 'Small' is relative to the scale, diversity and complexity of a district in India, let alone the entire nation. It is also in the context of the socio-economic and political reality of the country, which can be 'controlled' or 'overcome' at a small scale, but overwhelms everything, the minute you leave that bubble.

I think we do a great disservice to the country by not recognising the limits of small successes, and bear its consequent negative impact on two dimensions. First, many a times, fascinated and convinced by some such successes, someone who has the authority to do so has implemented it at scale. The least damage that it does is the waste of money. The more pernicious effect is the disorientation and confusion that it creates in the ranks of teachers, school leaders and education functionaries at the district level and below. Over a period of time, such implementations may happen often enough for these people to substantially lose their professional and disciplinary moorings.

Let's take an example. Some pedagogical methods have been attempted to be implemented at scale and quickly, inspired by some excellent model implemented at just a handful of schools. In the absence of most of the other conditions of where these models were originally implemented (the quality and kind of teacher training, school conditions, assessment methods, class size and uniformity of background of students, teacher qualification and support and so on), these methods have at best been ineffective, and at worst have left teachers feeling lost and helpless, especially because soon enough another such idea comes along.

Besides the disorientation and confusion in the ranks, such implementation at scale creates another problem. It creates the illusion of good work being attempted, distracting the entire system from the fundamental and painstaking work that is really required. In defence of such scaled implementation, the most that can be said is that it usually doesn't make things worse for the child than it already is.

The second dimension of not recognising the limits of small

successes is the issue of significant opportunity lost. There is much to learn from small successes. But that requires method and time to understand the limits. To draw out what can be used in other contexts, including across large systems, and then implement it appropriately. Indeed discovery, exploration and experimentation do happen only at a small scale. What can only be discovered in a test tube and lab requires rigorous method and investment to be developed for use in the world, we know that. We need to do that in education as well.

There is an even more complex issue for which we may have no solution, but the consciousness of which can perhaps be useful. In some domains, 'scaling' is not possible—at least in the way it is understood in industrial domains. These are complex domains, where locality and specificity is everything. This is driven by the basic truth that these domains deal with individual human issues, needing individual attention.

Education and healthcare are two of the most important such domains. However, the reality of dealing with millions of children (or patients) does need a large system. The problem is that we have 'scaled' our system on an industrial model. That's done, but there is no need to continue to 'scale' solutions with an industrial mindset. Quality and equity can be infused only school by school; 'scaling up' should only enable that.

In the meanwhile, we can also try to empathise with the teacher, who is the one who really faces the music of the kids every day, and not yo-yo her from one brilliant idea to another.

2 June 2011

The Gateway and the Chasm

In beautiful Bhopal, where I grew up, most of us spoke Hindustani. Though we thought we were speaking Hindi, all of us aspired to speak Ghalib's Urdu. At my home, the language was Chhattisgarhi. Thanks to the British Library and my father's endless book collection, I was equally at ease with English. There was also a failing effort at school to teach us Sanskrit. What the school did succeed in doing was to build an appreciation for the Sanskritised Hindi of authors like Jaishankar Prasad and, more enduringly, a soft corner for the different 'bolis' (often referred to as 'tongues', but actually fairly distinct languages) of north India.

Later in life, after four years in Tiruchirappalli, I gained a working knowledge of Tamil. This gateway of languages has taken me to a glorious world of diversity and beauty. It has been a privilege to feel the intensity of Ghalib and Sahir, to soak in Kabir's tolerant world, to read Faulkner, to watch Habib Tanvir's *Charandas Chor*, to admire Prasad's *Kamayani*, to catch the jokes at tea stalls on Tamil Nadu's excellent roads and to be heartbroken by Chandradhar Guleri's *Usne Kaha Tha*. This uplifting perspective shaped my thinking about the extraordinary diversity of languages in India, till I found out five years ago that this diversity was actually a linguistic chasm for others— especially an unfortunately large number of children.

It was a village classroom, 30-odd km from Udaipur. A single-room school, with about forty children, between six and nine years old. An earnest teacher was speaking in Hindi as a class full of children stared back blankly. As if he were speaking to a stone wall. We watched in silence till there was a mild altercation between two of the kids. The teacher intervened, speaking animatedly in a version of Mewari. In an instant, the wall vanished, and it was clear that every child got mentally involved with the mild fracas, including the teacher's admonishments.

I went back to Udaipur, to meet my friend Hridaykant Dewan, a man whom I respect enormously, as much for his lifelong commitment to good education, as for his understanding of the issues of education. He explained to me what happened in that classroom. It was just that none of the children understood Hindi. When the teacher spoke in Hindi, which was the official medium of instruction in Rajasthan, they were all disengaged. He had to revert to Mewari to manage the fracas.

As we spoke, the full import of the issue dawned on me. Rajasthan, a state we think of as 'Hindi-speaking', actually speaks many languages. The schooling, however, works through Hindi. A large percentage of children enter the classroom at age six, confronted not only with the bewilderment of a school, but also the incomprehensibility of anything that is being taught—because it's in an unfamiliar language. The teachers, who generally do know the local language, try to bridge this gulf, but they are limited by the curriculum. Many of these students are first-generation schoolgoers. They come from underprivileged backgrounds. Not only do they battle their social baggage, but they also battle this linguistic chasm. This has deep implications, in terms of limiting learning, on the child's social and self-development and on the school's overall progress. It's a complex problem, driven by the limited number of languages used as media of instruction versus the actual languages used by people.

The Government of India has given twenty-two 'languages of the 8th Schedule' the official seal. According to the census of 2001, twenty-nine languages have more than a million native speakers, sixty have more than 1,00,000 and 122 have more than 10,000 native speakers. In my estimate (I would be happy to be corrected), not more than 16 languages are used as media of instruction in schools across different states.

Why is my gateway their chasm? That's because I am a child of middle-class privilege; it's the parental and social support I got that turned diversity into a virtuous cycle of learning and acculturation. Disadvantage (and being underprivileged) works in the reverse direction, fomenting a vicious cycle—the unfamiliar language of schooling weakens the already weak ability of parents and the community to provide learning support.

It is a problem created by structure. In most cases, the teacher is familiar with the child's language. But the system does not see the teacher as a contributor to the curriculum; instead, it tries to develop a curriculum that prioritises common transactional standards over contextual creative processes. Such a curriculum can only have so many variants.

The immediate need is to recognise the child's language as critical, and to empower the teacher's role as the bridge. For this, the only real solution is a sensitive curricular approach with appropriate material, enabled by teacher capacity-building. That's the one hope of turning the linguistic chasm into a glorious gateway for all.

13 January 2011

Limits of ICT in Education

Over a four-year period, we at the Azim Premji Foundation produced the largest single library of digital learning resources (DLR) in India for children. Contained in 125 CDs, these were exciting lessons for children from Classes I to VIII. Made in eighteen languages—including tribal ones—they were designed to be completely integrated in the school curriculum.

We worked with various state governments to use these DLRs in thousands of schools. They ran very well in some places, and not so well in others. This was a big bet, and a lot of investment. It had an even bigger opportunity cost for us—we could have been doing something else in the time that we did this.

After five years, when we took stock at a fundamental level, we realised that the whole thing was at best a qualified failure. Certainly, the children and teachers who used them, loved them. It created excitement and interest in the classroom. But beyond that, there was practically no impact in a sustained, systemic manner on learning. I will just list the issues, without attempting to explain how these worked in a complex interrelated manner.

First, the limited numbers of schools with computers (today, an estimated 14 per cent have at least one) have a very poor uptime. In the studies that we conducted, this was at best 30 per cent, driven both by poor electricity supply and the inability to fix technical glitches. Let's not even discuss internet availability. Second, the school culture, its leadership and the broader system that the school was part of had a determining impact on whether the computer and DLRs were seen (and used) as a new toy, as a piece of furniture or as the crown jewel that needed to be protected. Third, irrespective of the DLR quality, its use for learning was only as good as the teacher in the classroom. With a few exceptional teachers, it became a useful tool. With an ordinary teacher, it was just a means of entertainment. Fourth, the DLR seemed to add no value to the dialogic, discovery-driven process of actual learning—which was completely determined between the children and the teachers. If it did add anything to the standard rote method, it was not noticeable, and it was certainly not needed.

So, with a rational mind and a heavy heart, we abandoned our focus on DLR. Today, we use it in very limited ways in schools, and continue to share it freely with anyone who wants to use it. Now, we think of information and communications technology (ICT) as an important tool on the management side of the education system. We continue to explore its potential, but we believe ICT is important, not fundamental.

If you are an outsider (to our organisation), and an enthusiastic believer in 'ICT can be a big help to Indian education', you may think of many reasons why we ended up with this qualified failure, including (perhaps) poor design and execution of the DLR and the programmes, by us and our partner governments.

We can tell you our view (and that of many independent organisations)—the DLRs were (and are) very good and the programmes were executed well, within the reality of the Indian education system (that is, in most of the rural and semi-urban schools of the 1.4 million in India). Also, consider the fact that organisations usually want to show successes even where there are none. Why would we tout a failure, having given it so much from our side?

The answer is simple. We confess this failure candidly, because we find that innumerable people inside and outside the education system think of technology (always meaning ICT) as something between a panacea and 'the most important solution'. A number of them are in influential positions, and these misconceived notions can have a significantly detrimental effect on the national effort to improve educational quality.

This effort must lie in teacher and school leader capacity-building, in examination reform (away from rote to assessing real learning), improvements in curriculum as well as accountability, governance and management. All this must happen, not just in intentions and policy, but in actual implementation—in a sustained and institutional manner. ICT would have a role in all this, but not the central role.

At its best, the fascination with ICT as a solution distracts from the real issues. At its worst, ICT is suggested as a substitute to solving the real problems; for example, 'Why bother about teachers, when ICT can be the teacher?' This perspective is lethal.

In the past few months, we happened to meet education leaders from Finland and from the province of Ontario in Canada—two regions with outstanding school systems. Across two continents, they said the same thing: 'Not a dollar will we invest in ICT in itself; every dollar that we have will go to teacher and school leader capacity-building.' Like us, through experience, they have learnt the limits of ICT.

16 December 2010

The Focus for Education in 2017

The most important matters in school education, about the nature of education itself and its place in a just and humane society, are not waiting to be discovered. We forget them at our own peril. And if we do, we risk repeating the egregious mistakes of the past. We can also be certain about approaches and issues, which will be worked upon and fought about, this year and the next. So here is a cheat sheet of twenty-five such matters for 2017:

1. The aim of school education is to develop good human beings and a good society, and this is foundational to our democracy.

2. This good society is what we have envisioned in our Constitution. The ultimate arbiter of constitutional values should be the supreme court of public reasoning.

3. There is no substitute for public education in a democracy. We must reaffirm this unequivocally, through our actions.

4. We have a special responsibility towards school education as a society. Educators have a special responsibility in education—social, political, human and epistemic.

5. Education will be political and has to be. Curriculum and textbooks will be the visible battleground, though even more important is the war about aims and actual practices.

6. Education must have economic aims also, to help India develop and help individuals become economically independent. However, these economic aims must be subsidiary to the notion of good society.

7. All children must have the same good education up to Class XII. There must be no 'streaming' into vocational and academic; in fact, all children must be exposed to vocational education.

8. Education focused on narrow skills for jobs will leave individuals helpless, because the economy is changing so rapidly. Education must develop fundamental capacities—independent thinking and problem-solving, for example—so that people can adapt.

9. Private schools do not perform better than public schools, on an average. The dramatic increase in private schooling in the past decade and a half has not improved school education. Privatisation and the markets are no solution to the most essential of social goods.

10. Private schools must not be stifled—but commercialisation must be stopped, else citizens will be fleeced and education damaged.

11. More testing, assessment and ranking lists won't improve the quality of education. Using a thermometer more often (or publicly) doesn't cure a disease. Testing-based accountability of educators is a disaster; it damages the education system at its core.

12. Technology won't solve the problem of improvement of learning. It can help, in the same way that books can, but no more. Starry-eyed fascination with technology will lead to useless investment.

13. Governance and culture of the education system must be empowering.

14. The heart of the matter is the capacity of people in the education system, most importantly that of teachers, including school leaders and other education leaders.

15. Teaching is by far the most complex profession in any society—that must be the organising principle of the system.

16. Our teacher education system (B. Ed.) is by far one of the weakest (and most corrupt) in the world. It needs a complete ground-up rebuild. This will need political capital.

17. We have 8.8 million teachers. This existing teacher base

needs massive investment in effective capacity-development. We also need an adequate number of teachers in all schools.

18. The best teachers cannot compensate for deprivation and poverty at home. Education and learning are deeply determined by the socio-economic conditions of the child. There must be other mechanisms to tackle this very complex issue.

19. We need dramatic improvement in our early childcare system, and also in education for children with disabilities. We also need a lot more secondary and higher-secondary schools across the country.

20. Examinations must be improved to assess real and deep capacities rather than memorisation and procedural skills.

21. The mother tongue is the most effective medium of education in early grades. However, given the reality of the social capital of English, all children must have the opportunity to learn the language.

22. Better infrastructure is essential. The reality on the ground is very different from what is claimed—a large proportion of schools *don't* have adequate water.

23. Overall, much more public investment is required. We must move towards 6–8 per cent of gross domestic product for education. Regional and rural–urban disparities must be addressed.

24. We must make allies for change and improvement—especially the teachers. There are good people everywhere. Trusting and empowering teachers is key. Scapegoating and disrespecting them will take us nowhere.

25. There must be integrity and coherence in education, from aims to culture to structure to practice to the human beings involved.

Education is not an economic service. It is a social-human and moral endeavour; it's about people and their aspirations for the good life. And it is about what we owe each other in a democratic society. To improve it, we need to be stubbornly focused—what I called ziddi in one of my columns (see The Importance of Being Stubborn).

5 January 2017

A Plea to Educators

The National Education Policy 2020 (NEP) approved by the Union cabinet on 29 July 2020 replaces the National Policy on Education, 1986. It is not as though in these intervening thirty-four years educational policies have not been changed or tweaked. But it is indeed after more than three decades that a comprehensive policy has been developed, addressing nearly all aspects of Indian education.

It is useful to keep in mind what the NEP is not. It is not an implementation plan, which must now be developed, both by the Centre and the states. It is also not a law; legislative actions on many counts will be required for its implementation, both by Parliament and state legislatures.

In its essence, the NEP is a coherent framework designed to fulfil the aims and objectives of India's education through the relevant mechanisms, institutions, norms and resources. It is a sixty-six-page document and is based on the 484-page draft National Education Policy (dNEP) developed by the Kasturirangan Committee and submitted to the Centre in May 2019. I was a member of the drafting committee of the dNEP.

Only on a few matters does the NEP deviate substantively from the dNEP. The National Education Commission proposed by the dNEP hasn't found a place in the NEP. But its absence doesn't dilute the spirit or intent of the dNEP. There are a few other matters that I will not mention here. I don't want to fall prey to the 'narcissism of small differences' that I have written about earlier, wherein, despite an agreement to a large extent, vehement energy is misspent on the few disagreements (see Vibrant Classrooms and Narcissism of Small Differences).

Education policy is a profoundly contentious matter. It is invested with the hopes and aspirations of all people. It is a vehicle, process and theatre—for power, politics and ideology, in the deepest sense. It must negotiate with and deliver on all this, while ensuring epistemic soundness as well as educational effectiveness, and do so with limited resources.

So, the widespread positive response to the NEP is remarkable. Even some leaders of political parties in the opposition have felt compelled to commend it. It has been received equally positively by people in education, while a few have opposed it sharply. Since educators can play crucial roles, let me try to persuade everyone in the sector to support the implementation of NEP wholeheartedly, along with providing constructive critique which may improve it. The only ones I would not attempt to persuade are those who are reacting negatively because of their apprehensions of a loss of personal power or setback to commercial interests.

Some may stop their attacks once they accept that this is not an implementation plan, since their peeves are about 'how will all this happen'. Others have their own specific differences with the NEP, which may have influenced their response. They must decide whether opposing the entire policy over a few disagreements is prudent.

Then there are many who are apprehensive of and disappointed by the language of the NEP and its absence of details. The text seems ambiguous and non-committal on many matters. This should only be expected, since the formal written language of any government is by nature cautious. But this could undeniably lead to problems. Not just now, but over the long term. Both inadvertent and motivated interpretations are possible, which may be antithetical to good education. An energetic use of the 'principle of charity' from philosophy may be an effective counter to this. This means drawing the best and the strongest possible interpretation of a text and putting one's might behind implementing that interpretation quickly, thus setting things on a course that would be hard to tamper with later.

There are also some people who are opposing the policy because they are committed to opposing the political party in power at the Centre. Some believe that the text of the NEP is mostly good, but this government will never implement it. Others draw the worst interpretations from the text of the policy because of their opposition to the government. And then there are those who appear to be attacking the NEP without having read it.

Opposing the NEP is an ineffectual political strategy. A powerful political party cannot be harmed by opposing an education policy. Instead, if they also use the 'principle of charity' in their reading of the NEP, they will find many things that they have themselves battled for in education over the decades. For instance, its explicit commitment to strengthen the public education system as the foundation of a vibrant democratic society. And then they, too, could put their might behind implementing those matters well. In other words, if they don't trust the words as they are in the policy, they could call its bluff by trying to make those words reality. Many of them have been deeply committed educators. On the NEP, they need to act as educators, not politicians.

We are at a moment in Indian education that could be seminal. It is for us to make it so. Irrespective of our politics, ideology or differences, if we use the good in the NEP and make it happen, we will change the education system and thus help change India for the better.

13 August 2020

UNDER THE BANYAN TREE

Under the Banyan Tree

The great banyan was shielding them from the sun. It wasn't yet blazing in late March, but it was hot out in the open. The two little girls were swinging and slipping from its dangling roots. Too young to be alone at home while their parents were out earning their daily wage, they had accompanied their siblings to school. They were too young to be even in Class I and so, had a free run of the premises. When I encountered them, they had decided to occupy the chabutra over which the banyan grew. There was a mazaar on one corner of the chabutra which itself was near the entrance at the western edge of the school quadrangle.

Lakshmi and Mary accosted me without interrupting their swinging, interrogating me in tandem. Clinging to the roots, they were at my eye level. Once they were satisfied that I was not a teacher, they challenged me to beat them at their game. As I was climbing up the chabutra, they shouted together, *'Baba ka ghar hai, joote utaar ke aao.'* (It is Baba's house, take off your shoes.)

I slipped off my shoes as a mark of respect, climbed up and played with them for a few minutes, and then wanted to leave. They asked me whether I was leaving because I was thirsty. I said the head teacher was waiting for me, and in unison they said he was a good 'sir'.

At another school I had visited earlier, students of Class VI sized me up within 20 minutes. No child was left out of the banter. When they asked me my name, I said, 'Mohandas Gandhi'. Many started shrieking that the Mahatma was dead. Then I said, 'Narendra Modi,' and they rolled over with laughter. I challenged them, 'Why do you think I am not the Prime Minister?' And so, it went.

'*Aap Mussalman hain?*' one of the kids asked. Others repeated the question, asking me if I was Muslim. Why did they think I was, I asked, and they pointed at my chin, '*Aapki daadhi hai.*' (You have a beard.) My reply that I was indeed one, paused the banter, puzzlement visible on their faces. Then one of them shouted, '*Nahin aap Mussalman nahin ho!*' (No, you can't be Muslim), the assertion echoing around the class. How did they make that conclusion? The response was instantaneous, '*Kyunki aap achche aadmi ho.*' (Because you are a good man.)

In the school with the great banyan, I sat at the back of Class VIII. They were discussing the elections held in the state a few months earlier; not the politics, but the electoral process. There was disagreement on the reason for some constituencies being reserved; the teacher intervened and then stepped back, letting the conversation flow. After a while, the teacher turned to me, and asked me to have a chat with the students.

What, I asked, is the point of democracy? It is the best way to live and govern. Why? Because we are all equal. Are we really equal? Yes, we are; we are all human beings and equally so. Socially and economically, we are not equal today, but democracy will get us there. For example, reserved constituencies are a way to achieve such equality. In fact, democracy is not the best way but the only way.

I pressed them, but why are we equal? That question led to a five-minute conference among the children. Once they concluded, they faced me and declared, '*Kyunki sab insaan andar se achche hote hain.*' (Because all human beings are inherently good.)

'*Mussalman bhi achche hote hain?*' (Are Muslims good too?) I asked. And they laughed loudly. 'Why are you laughing?' I asked. Because it was a ridiculous question, totally ridiculous; '*Mazaar waale baba sabse achche thhe; sab insaan achche hote hain.*' (The

Baba was the best human being. All humans are good.) Then they spoke with pride about the school's parliament, animatedly about caste and gender equity, and thoughtfully about superstitions. I left for the next school.

When I wrote about schools being temples of democracy (see Inspired by Grace), I received two kinds of criticism: first, that many of those who embodied anti-constitutional values were highly educated. Second, that the metaphor of the temple was dangerous, since the word of the school could become gospel, undermining all critical faculties. Temples are among our most potent institutions and cannot be held hostage, neither as a metaphor by fears, nor in reality; but this deserves a detailed response.

The first criticism is a misreading of that piece (or perhaps it lacked clarity). Schools must be temples of democracy, but only a relatively small proportion today are effectively that. Many are the antithesis. No wonder that some of the most educated are the most bigoted. Many are also comically unaware of their own state, wallowing in material success with smug self-belief in their being paragon citizens.

The contrast between the two schools is representative of our education system. We need to make all our schools like the one with the chabutra. Education and its institutions cannot bear the entire burden of developing a vibrant democracy, but their role is significant.

The two little girls lay flat on the chabutra as I was leaving. *'Baba ko namaste kar ke jao,'* (Say namaste to Baba and then go) they commanded, and I obeyed. And then I left. With Lakshmi, Mary and the mazaar under the great banyan—the national tree of the Republic of India—in a real temple of democracy.

9 May 2019

Inspired by Grace

Two little girls named Mary and Lakshmi, and a mazaar protected by a great banyan tree. That tableau in my column (see Under the Banyan Tree) seemed so perfect in all its detail to some that they asked me if I had made it up. Perhaps just the names? Many more asked another question—how do you respond to such deep prejudice? They were referring to children in a school asserting, 'You cannot be a Muslim because you are a good man.'

Working with thousands of schools across the country, occasionally we come face to face with intolerable cruelty. But we encounter discrimination and prejudice more frequently. Overt or covert, mild or harsh, it lurks just beneath the surface. It is there among teachers and the communities surrounding schools. Also, in the culture of schools, which infects children. Every fault line of Indian society lies bare—caste, class, gender and religion. So, what do we do?

First, we recognise this matter as central to our work. The aim of education is to create a just, equitable and humane society, and a vibrant democracy. To fulfil these aims, the cleavages of Indian society must be healed, bridged and eliminated in schools, which then play a significant role in doing the same for society. If our work is in education, developing constitutional values is at its core. Too many individuals and organisations working in education focus narrowly on 'learning levels'. For them, education is about language, maths and other subjects. All that is important, no doubt. But ignoring its civic, social and human aims deprives society of its most important pathway for progress.

Second, to work on this core, we must be where education

happens. This healing can only be done by teachers, which demands work with communities of teachers—with their beliefs, behaviours and perspectives. This requires building relationships of trust. It's impossible to talk to strangers about such innermost feelings. Being an integral part of the communities that you work with is the only way for sustained engagement. Which is why my colleagues live in small towns and villages across this vast country.

Third, our team itself must have consonance on these matters. All of us are from the same society. We too carry the virus of prejudice, in some measure. Diffidence, even more. Therefore, explicit alignment with these values and a commitment to action requires systematic effort. Surely, those who join us to do this kind of work are self-selecting on these values. But experience suggests that while this innateness is important, it requires continuous reaffirmation and support.

Fourth, it requires capacity within our team to deal with these matters. What should we do upon encountering discrimination and prejudice? How does one engage on such matters? What are the philosophical underpinnings? How do we make it real and relatable? Why should anybody change at all? The requirement is of clarity, confidence and tenacity.

Fifth, when and how do we do this work? Training sessions targeted at 'eliminating discrimination' have no chance of success. Integrating dialogue on these matters with daily life is far more effective. For example, in a maths workshop, when a teacher says that girls just can't learn maths, an opportunity arises to confront gender biases. When in a school, children are fed the mid-day meal prioritised along caste lines, that is an opportunity to question this most intransigent of our cleavages. Occasionally, it is possible to engage directly. For example, through developing an understanding of our Constitution. Theatre, music and literature are often very effective in animating and questioning what may not be touched upon by other methods. However, there really is no formula. Approaches and methods for each situation need to be devised, building on these basic blocks. And every instance of discrimination or prejudice must be seized as an opening.

Sixth, confronting prejudice requires courage. Challenging the deepest of beliefs within the communities that you live in and doing so persistently is very hard. Arguing for gender equity is relatively easier, though not necessarily any less complex. Caste and religion are a different matter altogether. These seem to bring out the worst demons of our nature; steadfast valour is needed.

Seventh, the energy for real change comes from empathy. However closed, senseless and bigoted the person in front of you may seem, progress happens only through dialogue. Sincere dialogue is possible only with genuine empathy. Perhaps we need inspiration from the theological notion of grace. Empathetic engagement is the only path to progress. Else you walk into one of the two traps—diminishing the person in front of you, or fleeing from him into cliques of comfort. Both are completely dysfunctional.

Eighth, we do not work on our own. Teachers with the deepest reservoirs of humaneness, unflinching courage and fire to change this world abound in the nooks and corners of this country. We work together because this is our India.

Going back to the first question I was asked. I did not imagine that tableau under the banyan tree. Every detail is real, as real as this India of ours that has made it so.

23 May 2019

Finding Our Mahatma

Where would you find Gandhi in our schools?

A picture of the Mahatma is up on some wall in almost every school that I have visited.

Usually, it is the most faded of all pictures, having been up there the longest. Gandhi is also known to most children. In every classroom that I enter, the first thing that the children ask me is my name. I usually respond with Mohandas Gandhi or Narendra Modi. The ensuing mirth of disbelief is a good ice-breaker and is possible only because the children know of the two individuals in some manner.

Usually, they are aware of a few scattered facts about the Mahatma. He is dead. He was very old. His picture is up on the wall. Often, a couple of children will talk about his having something to do with India's freedom movement. In most high schools, a few students can usually narrate a relatively cogent biography. Many, across classes, can quickly pull out the textbooks that contain him. Where really is Gandhi in our schools?

At 8.30 a.m. on a day close to his 150th birth anniversary, I was greeted in a school by an all-students group song. In Hindi, it would be called a song in veer-ras, a song inspiring valour. It challenged all enemies to a fight to the finish. It promised a fate even direr to enemies within. It swore a relentless pursuit of evildoers to their death. The crashing waters of the Bhagirathi flowing beside the school was like a drumbeat to the song; six to twelve-year-olds consecrated extreme violence on the banks of a river whose myth of origin is about giving peace to 60,000 souls who were condemned by a curse to become ash.

The teachers looked expectantly at me for approbation. The brutal imagery of the song sung by little children was too much to let go. So, I asked Kailash, with whom I had visited this school, what he thought I would do if he boxed me in my face. The children were listening. He said I would hit him back. Then what would he do? I asked. Hit me back harder, he said. The imaginary scuffle quickly escalated to knives and guns, with both of us fatally wounded. Then we restarted the scuffle. What would he do if he boxed me and I didn't hit him back? He would be puzzled, he said, and perhaps hit me again. If I still didn't retaliate? He would stop, he said. The children got it immediately.

We went back to the song and its treatment of enemies and others. There was no need for more prompting. Lucidly, they described how they would deal with even mortal enemies peaceably. A bit of the Mahatma was rediscovered.

That is where he really is. Gandhi is in our children. It is up to us, to our schools, to the teachers in our schools, whether we nurture the Mahatma in our children, or leave him hanging in a faded picture and buried in a dreary textbook. That is what too many schools do. However, there are also those that bring his spirit to life.

Another school, on the banks of the same Bhagirathi, has no room for violence in word or action. The explicit norm of the school, followed by all teachers and students alike, is that disagreement must be resolved through dialogue among the parties involved. It may happen with a neutral mediator present, which is often a student. Displeasure must be expressed in the politest of terms. Since the norms were agreed upon by all in the school three years ago, there has been no real breach.

Somewhere in the jungles of central India, another school screens the Richard Attenborough movie *Gandhi* every October. That is followed by a week of discussion and debate on the life of Gandhi, his methods and his relevance. He is not deified, but examined critically. After the week is over, each class develops a project on 'A Gandhi of Today'. Yet another school, in the arid Deccan plateau, has no referees or umpires for sports. The teams playing nominate scorekeepers from among themselves and each player is a referee for her own actions and behaviour. Disputes are resolved between the nominees of each team. When examinations are held, teachers do not stand as invigilators.

Another school in a small town in the drylands of western India gives all its students an impossible project every year. They must identify a situation of conflict, one in which they themselves may or may not be involved. Then they must resolve this conflict through Gandhian means. Their track record of resolution is low, but the understanding in this school of the importance of means over ends is high.

These are not isolated instances in these schools. The content of discussion in the classes, the approach and methods of teaching and the practices and culture of these schools are all in a tandem attempt to develop values and capacities that are Gandhian. The schools are loath to claim success, but they would proudly proclaim that they are trying. It is a quest for all seasons and all times: how to grow our humanity. If in tribute, on his 150th birth anniversary, schools can begin nurturing Gandhi in our children, we will tap reserves that too often wither away.

Empathy is at the heart of this humanity. Earlier a sceptic, I have become a faithful. If we could all just live in accordance with *vaishnav jan toh tene kahiye je peeda paraayi jaane re* (A devotee of Lord Vishnu is one who knows the pain of others), we also may find our Mahatma.

10 October 2019

What is Your Stand?

The intellectual encountered a teacher. The young man teaches in a Naxalite-hit district. The intellectual is not a self-professed one. The gist of their dialogue follows:

Intellectual: So, what is your ideology?

Teacher: I don't have an ideology, sir. I teach children.

Intellectual: Doesn't that mean that you are so immersed in your ideology that you don't even know? Like fish not knowing what is water. What guides you?

Teacher: I don't know about ideology sir, but I think the Constitution is sufficient to guide me.

Intellectual: But what is your stand? On state repression? On annihilation of tribal life by all sides?

On exploitative and extractive development? You are in a war zone. You must have a stand.

Teacher: Well, sir, my stand is that I will stand here and teach. You can starve me, but I will teach.

You can beat me up, but I will teach. If you kill me, then any way I am gone. So, that is my stand, sir.

The intellectual recognised the presence of a higher power and left. The passing of 2018 and the coming of 2019 is of no significance to the teacher. When the war started is irrelevant to him and its end is nowhere in sight. However, two things he does know. If he were not to teach, whenever that end is to be, it will be pushed out further. And that his teaching may not bring an end to the suffering of the children, but does create the possibility that one day they too will take a stand.

Equality, humaneness and decency have not gained ground across the world in 2018. The dreams of our Constitution are no closer to reality. The little girl from Kathua is forgotten. To take a stand is the best we can do. To recognise that we are in the battlefield of a war with no end in sight. The long arc of history will not bend towards justice unless we keep at it. Institutions, organisations, groups and individuals, all have to be at it.

Like the teacher, there are many at it. Which is why 2018 was no worse than 2017. The war stands in balance. For every inch of gain, there has been an inch of loss. My role gave me the opportunity to meet hundreds of such people last year and perhaps you may have met many more. If we want the arc to bend a little more, to shift the balance in 2019, we can observe the five things that are common to these people who take a stand and keep at it.

First, they are all constructive. Critique, dissent and protest are all necessary, but insufficient to make for a better world. Developing alternatives, opening paths and building without destroying is more necessary. They embrace the grind of getting things done in our messy reality, including failure, frustration and occasional success.

Second, they act in their sphere. Systemic changes are essential. Structurally embedded and historically dominant forces are all around us. Sources of power rarely provide ballast for change, usually acting to preserve what is there. They obsess over none of this. It doesn't faze them. They know how easy it is to freeze with inaction, to feel like a helpless pawn, and fade to inconsequentiality. So, they act in the sphere that they can. For a few, sometimes there is visibility of their actions being a part of a bigger struggle, perhaps inching towards progress. However, for most, a lot of the time, it is just about making a difference in their own immediate small world. That is all right; they keep at it.

Third, they relate to people, forming communities and

coalitions. They see the human being and not an ideology. Hindutvawadi, leftist or mercenary, they will have a cup of chai with everyone.

They accept people in their bewildering complexity, never reducing them to one dimension of their identity. They work with everyone. As they reach out to the human, they usually find one. Then it is not impossible to find common human concerns that can bind a community and build coalitions.

Fourth, they work on the ground. We have deluded ourselves into believing that there is some inexorable momentum towards equality, freedom, justice and more, because of the Constitution. And that we, individual citizens, are entitled to this trajectory of improvement, with no contribution aside from some trenchant critique. Or, at most, our role is to hector all, ensconced in secure jobs, with our intellectual fineries.

However, they know that the Constitution is a promise to be fulfilled. It is only a call to action.

They know that legislation can only set up the guardrails of our democratic dream, which the judiciary can try to insure. They know that we are not entitled to a better world. Changing the hearts and minds of people is the only way, which can only be done on the ground, only one human at a time, and they are at it.

Fifth, they are ziddi. They are unrelenting under all circumstances. Their ziddi spirit cannot be starved or beaten. In wars with no end in sight, this counts. In a world where the good, the right and the truth are all unanchored and unsure, this counts more than anything else.

None of this makes for an uplifting new year column. However, meeting the teacher is uplifting. Go and hunt out a few like him. Even better, become one of them in 2019, swelling the ranks of those who take a stand with their ziddi spirit.

3 January 2019

Cop and Teacher

His greying, closely cropped hair and the white short-sleeved shirt accentuated the strength of his body. We sat across a large table made of wooden planks. It was a sparse room with some steel cupboards. Drenched in sweat, my shirt was clinging to me. That the sun blazes with such intensity in end-September was unknown to me. The sand dunes around were smouldering. The air had 83 per cent humidity. But he looked cool and comfortable. I will not name him, because I want to protect his identity.

He told me that he was a child of the desert, born somewhere beyond those dunes. His family had enough means to be called middle class. He went to school in his village and then the government college in the nearby town. At twenty-two, he got selected in the state police and became a constable. After his training he was posted to a nearby kasba. It was a matter of great prestige in the local community. The power that a policeman wields is experienced every day by the average citizen. And the community is well aware of the steady stream of additional income that policemen receive, they call it upari kamai.

His father was a big influence on him. It was the life that the father led, rather than his words. So the few words that he spoke became life principles for his son. One of these was *'Garib ko kabhi dukh mat dena.'* (Never give grief to the poor and weak.)

In his role as a policeman, these words haunted him every day. The upari kamai for the higher-ups came from richer people. But for the constable and the sub-inspector, it came from the street vendor, the small farmer and the small trader. He tried to stay away from the ways of the system. He saw how policemen preyed on the very citizens they were meant to protect. The culture of the system designed his role to give grief to the poor and the weak.

He lived with this visceral conflict for fifteen years. And then he enrolled for a Bachelor of Education (B. Ed.) programme. Fortunately for him, unlike many other states, the government of Rajasthan had its priorities right and was recruiting teachers. He went through the process and was selected as a teacher six years ago. He quit the police and became a teacher in a public school.

We were sitting in the office room of the school. He narrated his life's story to me while methodically filling forms for a sports tournament in which his students were going to participate. Before that I had spent two hours in the school with the children. I had mentally given an A grade to the school on all three of the dimensions that I informally assess schools on, in such brief interactions.

First, the school was kept with care. It was neat, from the kitchen to the classrooms to the toilet. It maximised the use of its infrastructure and resources with imagination. Second, the children were free in their movement and talked with confidence. There was no fear in their eyes, only curiosity. They were engaged in their work with interest.

Third, they could certainly read and do arithmetic. And this they did with understanding, not mechanically. The students also had a reasonable conceptual grasp of the various matters we talked about.

Achieving all this with students, all of whom lived in deeply disadvantaged circumstances, missing the support and opportunities that economic well-being provides, was remarkable. He said that it was because the four teachers in the school worked as a team. Their goal was that their students must develop in every way.

I asked him to compare his life as a teacher with his life as a policeman. He said that it was very difficult to do that.

As a teacher, every day was an honest day's work. And each such honest day paid for itself, seeing his students learning and develop. He himself learnt new things every day, since he was faced with creative challenges continually while working with children. He wished officers of the department would trust the teachers and support them. In his experience, only 10 per cent of teachers were insincere. The rest would blossom in their work with trust and support.

As I was leaving the school, I told him that I would write about him. He laughed and told me to be careful about what I wrote about the police. And then he added seriously, 'Please don't write ill about them, there are good people in the police also—they also need some encouragement.'

Later that evening, we were 90 km away from his school. In another part of the desert. Fifty-eight teachers sat packed in a room which had trapped the day's heat; the mood wasn't cooler. They were watching *Samvidhaan*, Shyam Benegal's television miniseries on the making of the Indian Constitution. Playing and pausing the series, they were discussing what they saw. Matters such as freedom of expression, reservation and gender equity, which they saw being debated heatedly by members of the constituent assembly, were roiling their emotions even today. Whichever side of the heated debate they were on, every one of them left happy and satisfied, at 7 p.m. Not because they had won, but because they had learnt.

Five of them stopped to chat with me. They repeated the policeman-turned-teacher's words—they needed trust and support, because the teacher's role is creative, complex and challenging. These words are echoed by teachers across the country. I wonder what it will take for the nation to listen to this voice, which is asking for so little in return for all of the nation's future.

12 October 2017

Ambedkar's Teacher

Babasaheb Ambedkar is believed to have said in 1952, 'I owe my whole intellectual life to Prof. John Dewey.' It is likely that he did say this, or something very similar. There is enough in his published writing to validate this sentiment. For instance, in *Annihilation of Caste*, he wrote, 'Prof. John Dewey who was my teacher and to whom I owe so much ...'

Ambedkar has perhaps been our pre-eminent leader-intellectual, and his sentiments should, if nothing, pique our interest in John Dewey. Many would need no introduction to Dewey, and even those who do, are likely to be familiar with the general thrust of his ideas, without knowing the man responsible. John Dewey (1859–1952) was an American philosopher, psychologist, and perhaps best known as a reformer of education. Dewey is one of the central figures associated with the philosophy of pragmatism, with functional psychology and with progressive education. He was a vocal public intellectual, advocating for social reform and liberalism. His prodigious written output has been collected in thirty-seven volumes. Dewey was Ambedkar's teacher at Columbia University, New York, from 1913 to 1916.

Any attempt at summarising the gist of Dewey's ideas would be foolhardy, so let's just have a cursory glimpse of some of the more important ones, which are surely inadequately representative of his whole body of work. The overarching theme of Dewey's work was democracy. For Dewey, democracy is about participation and not only about representation. This participation requires public reasoning and dialogue, within ever-expanding and self-critical communities of inquiry, constantly revising their beliefs based on new evidence. Dewey envisioned democracy as an ethical ideal and not merely a political arrangement, and so saw it extending from politics to the economy and society. He saw education as the foundation of democracy, and as the key process for reforming society.

The aim of education is to develop autonomous, thinking and engaged individuals, and help realise their capacities to the fullest potential, which should be put to use for the greater good. Education is a social process and experience is central to learning. Effective education is possible only with the student as an active participant in the processes and in the curriculum, with adequate weightage for the content and the role of the teacher, and without tipping over into the extremism of child-centrism. Dewey saw the teacher as a professional, and central to the enterprise of education. His educational writing spans an extraordinary range, reflecting not only his great intellect, but also his personal experiences of running schools.

Today in education, we are all Deweyites; we may not even know it, but most of us are.

His ideas are so deeply ingrained in education across the world that even those who would be considered antithetical to core Deweyian ideas—votaries of primacy of vocational education, advocates of conservative education, among others—end up using his ideas simply because they are effective. Considering what Ambedkar himself said, the extent of Dewey's influence over him (and vice versa) needs to be studied seriously; not many attempts have been made.

There is no doubt that more than most people, Ambedkar was his own man. His own searing personal experience, the depth and breadth of his social–political engagement, the well-known shining intellect and more shaped him. But the resonance between Dewey and Ambedkar is hard to miss, even if we had not known of their relationship: the commitment to democracy, not only political but social and economic, the emphasis on participation and not merely representation, the importance of public reasoning and the foundational role of education for democracy and equality.

Dewey was a philosopher, and Ambedkar the leader of a nation and its people. The teacher witnessed his most famous student converting their ideas into real institutional arrangements, for what was then, and remains now, the world's biggest democracy. No wonder that the Constitution of India is liberating, equalising and humanising. So is the curriculum of our schools. There is a deep resonance between our Constitution and education as we have envisioned it. So, in a sense, in education we are all Ambedkarites as much as being Deweyites.

The famous caution of Ambedkar about the Constitution eventually being only as effective as the people who implement it applies equally to education. The gulf between the India of our Constitution and the reality is as wide as the gulf between our curriculum and educational reality. However, this makes our liberating and progressive Constitution and curriculum even more relevant and important. India needs both, and their deep mutual resonance, to become the nation that we have promised ourselves.

Let me end by quoting Ambedkar quoting Dewey: 'Prof. Dewey said … "Every society gets encumbered with what is trivial, with dead wood from the past, and with what is positively perverse [...] As a society becomes more enlightened, it realises that it is responsible not to conserve and transmit the whole of its existing achievements, but only such as to make for a better future society. The school is its chief agency for the accomplishment of this end."'

31 March 2016

A Measure of Life

The teachers and I sat on the floor and chatted. He sat quietly outside the circle, doodling on a small notebook. He was nine years old. He was gentle and caring, but his rage could explode the next moment into a vicious vortex of violence, unmanageable by the teachers. They had figured that the effective way of dealing with him was to let him do exactly what he wanted, and then he would be calm, would try to learn and generally be cooperative. That day four years ago, he had decided that he wanted to sit with us and not in his class, and so it was.

Within weeks of his joining the school, a year before that day, some of its teachers had visited his village to figure out his life story. It wasn't clear whether his mother had died or abandoned the family, but she was not there in his life. He lived in a shack with an elder brother and a drunk father. The fifteen-year-old brother worked as a daily wage labourer, which is what the father would do, too, when sober.

Last month in the same school, I searched for him in a group of eighty-one children from Classes IV–VIII who had gathered to talk with me in one large room. He wasn't there. He had left the school last year, despite every effort from the teachers, as I learnt later. Now, instead of going to a school, every morning he goes out hunting for that day's labour.

No other child in that group of eighty-one lives in such a vacuum of love. They all have their own pleasures and pains and hopes and fears, while the precarity of their lives is what they all have in common with that boy. One crop failure away from ruin, an illness in the family away from starvation and an incident away from the end of their childhood. Poverty and caste shape their lives.

They had been told by someone that I was a 'big officer from Bangalore'. Without any hesitation, they got into a conversation with me. Confident and clear, they had none of the stock-in-trade questions that make for a semblance of a conversation without being one. They asked, 'How did you become such a big officer? What did you do?'

Truth matters with children. What is the true answer to that question? The truth and the whole truth. True without becoming a gospel of individual enterprise or reduction to the fatalism of circumstances, and true in the context of their hard lives. So, I told them about how blessed my life has been. How the people in my life have supported me and cared for me, when close or distant. How I have had a life of privilege. How I have tried—to work hard, to be honest and to care, but that I don't really know how it has all come together. I feel doubly blessed and grateful.

In my unclear response, the children heard the truth. Then they said, 'Tell us of the difficulties that you faced in your life.' The truth about this was much harder to tell. But anything less than that would have been a betrayal of their trust. It also would have been callousness towards their everyday life of difficulties.

I told them about that night in Bhopal between 2 and 3 December 1984 and its aftermath. They had not heard of it before. They tried to comprehend the number of deaths. They related it to a nearby town getting wiped out. They wanted to know everything. What was the factory making that had such poisonous stuff? Why were they allowed to do it? If that poison was in the pesticide, what would happen to the land? What was done with the factory after that night? How can generations be affected by one night? Then, they wanted to know, how I survived. So, I described the effect of wind, water bodies and distances, on how the gas spread. They figured out that methyl-iso-cyanate must be denser than air. They also figured out that those sleeping on the ground would have been at most risk.

What about justice? They asked. Who has been punished? What has been done to help the victims? In our compact of honesty, I told them what has happened in the past thirty-five years. They were very upset. There was disbelief on every face. I searched for a truth to share that would leave them with hope. So, I told them that people are still fighting. For justice and for restitution. They will not give up, even after thirty-five years. They liked that.

It was 4 p.m.; time for the school to close. Children that they are, many ran out of the room screaming. Some gathered around me, asking me to come back. They knew not of Bhopal. But they could think and question. They had a clear notion of justice and fairness, and they cared.

The school is not all of it, but has played a role, as all schools can. A school can be an oasis of many kinds in the life of precarity that millions of our children live. However, it is not any more for that boy who dropped out. The rage that burns his tenderness, how will it run through the course of his life, such as it is?

PS: Abdul Jabbar died last month. He was one of those who fought for thirty-five years for Bhopal. Unflinching in the face of power and apathy—of the state, of money and of people who moved on. Whatever measure of justice he achieved, in addition, he also made the truth that gave hope to kids in a distant school. And to many like me.

5 December 2019

The Continuing Importance of Being Ziddi

Rogue was limping in the morning. He is our garden cat, who was a tiny kitten until February this year. By the afternoon, the limp was gone. And the nagging feeling inside me went away. I never had a bond with animals, until this past year.

It started with four shivering kittens one early October morning in 2016. At 4.30 a.m., I had no one to turn to for advice, and I couldn't turn away. I put a rug on them, and left a plate of milk. When I came back from my run, the milk was gone. And the kittens were chasing each other as only kittens can. They stayed on in the garden. We named them Tinker, Tailor, Soldier and Spy.

That is how I got involved with the life of cats and they got involved in mine. Independent creatures that they are, they would vanish and then return. Our garden was their home.

Then one day Spy died, crushed under a car, on the road outside. That is when I realised the beginning of a bond. Then Soldier died. And Tinker and Tailor never came back. We heard that someone from the neighbourhood had killed them. Why? And with the fire of that rage, the bond was forged.

Two weeks later, in January, we found two more in the garden. We called them Rogue and One.

They grew up from their tininess into lithe, young cats. One vanished in October this year. He used to nibble at my toes. I miss him. Rogue misses him. We grieve together. My mother says that when she was a child, and returned to her neighbourhood after three years, her garden cat came back. It gives me hope; One may come back. They say cats are not like dogs; they don't bond.

You should have asked all six of them how they felt about my son. They can't talk, but I can see.

My life changed in this period. A world opened up that did not exist before. I also started noticing dogs. Many of you know this well. But to me the discovery of their devotion and love was astonishing. Neither of their own volition, nor forced by circumstances, will they leave the ones they love. Ever. We can't say that about us humans.

It was sheer coincidence that I was reading research on animal behaviour. This rigorous research was on cognitive capacities, social behaviour and emotions, of animals ranging from dolphins and octopuses to cats and dogs. As I read more and observed the cats and dogs, it seemed possible that animals are much more human in every way.

I remember a conversation often. A colleague used an often-used, axiomatic statement. Education is about becoming human, so we cannot talk about the education of animals. Her response, from wisdom and greater knowledge of animals, was, 'Don't be so sure.' The comment was not about education itself, but about the assumption of categorical difference between animals and humans.

Most people like us, shaped by modernity and the urban environment, think of animals and human as categorically different. What if they are not?

In this same year, the world has changed even more; the change in my life is nothing. Humans have done a lot to expand the boundaries of what it means to be human. If a repeat child-molester can stand in elections for high public office, get the endorsement of the head of state and lose the race by just about 1 per cent; if the elected president of a nation can boast of having killed a man at sixteen, and it's only one more news item on the ticker tape; if a man can be burnt alive, the video uploaded on

YouTube and there are public protests against the killer being arrested; if Twitter is the command-and-control mechanism for the world's largest nuclear arsenal; if a neo-Nazi party can get 12.6 per cent of the vote in Germany, while triumphantly proclaiming its bigotry; if someone can kill Tinker and Tailor, because they are cute kittens, we certainly have new norms for what it means to be human.

It is all around us. Though gathering for decades, it was unleashed with new force in 2016, bringing out blatantly the deep ruptures in the most fundamental notions of what it means to be human.

While we are bidding goodbye to 2017, 2016 is not ending. And it will not end soon. We are still in the fight of our lives, for the good, the right and the truth—for what it means to be human. Since it is still 2016, I can do no better than to write what I did last year (see The Importance of Being Stubborn)—an exhortation to be ziddi in this fight.

Hope or despair is ours for the making. If we stand away, we let in despair and weakness. If we commit to a shared moral purpose in action, then we strengthen the fight for the good.

When the good, the right and the truth are all unanchored and untethered, being ziddi, unrelenting, under all circumstances counts more than anything else. But being so alone is insufficient. We all must be ziddi together, to really put an end to 2016, and not let another year like that arise.

In the meanwhile, we have demolished the categorical difference between animals and us, if it was ever there. So, I can now modify the axiomatic statement in education. Education can be about becoming a dog. I certainly would rather be a dog, perhaps a ziddi dog, than a human, if this is what it means to be human.

21 December 2017

Dichotomy of Two Cultures

Last week, a friend told me his solution to India's problem of poor learning in schools, a solution that others have also advocated. The essence of this approach is: let's get the very best teachers on video links and in prerecorded formats to all schools, while the teacher in the classroom can play the role of a facilitator, and so we needn't be bothered about her capacity as an educator.

I asked him my standard question for such circumstances, whether he would want his daughter to go to such a school, where a terrific maths teacher is video-streamed in to the classroom (along with hundreds of other similar classrooms) which has a facilitator. This friend has a sense of the nature of good teaching and learning, and knows that these are processes embedded firmly in social relationships, so he backed off from his solution. He remains troubled that there seem to be no neat solutions for the matter of how to improve the teaching-learning process in all classes for all children. He recognises that improving education is a kind of 'wicked problem', but can't accept its implications in terms of the necessarily slow, unclear and socio-politically fraught way forward.

Many people propose a variant of my friend's approach to various social issues. They do it with deep conviction, often ignoring the fundamental social-human nature of such issues, not appreciating that most such issues are wicked problems or are entangled in many. Instead, they think of these as mechanical problems, admittedly complex, that can be solved by a few grand ideas or tools. Such solution approaches have clear and simple models, leading to a belief that it is doable and it will work. These are like technology models; there is definite design with everything having a place and function, input–output variables are known with predictable relationships and the elements are largely controllable.

On 7 May 1959, C.P. Snow delivered his famous Rede Memorial Lecture on *The Two Cultures*, which was later published as a book. Its essence is well-known: 'the intellectual life of Western society is split into two cultures', that of sciences and of humanities; they can't even talk to each other. This is a major obstacle to overall progress and in solving the world's problems. This dichotomised formulation has justifiably had its trenchant critics; still it has had significant influence on public discourse in the past sixty years. When thinking about social issues we seem to implicitly hold our own versions of the two cultures. One is the techno-model view and the other is the social-humanistic one. While a few may hold one and be totally oblivious of the other, when it comes to action, often one or the other approach is advocated with a perfunctory nod to the other.

People in the thick of things, on the ground or even otherwise, have a bias for the social-humanistic approaches. People acting or proposing such action from the (relative) outside go for the techno-model approaches. This inside–outside point of view is not the only determinant of the preference to one of the two cultures, but surely is significant and most identifiable. Such preferences are not surprising. From the inside, the messy, impossible-to-model nature of social issues is obvious, based as they are on human behaviour and social dynamics. From the outside, even if you appreciate that these are fundamentally social and human issues, the realisation is in the abstract and can be 'modelled in or out'.

This matter of two cultures in action has deep and significant implications. A lot more power and money is in the hands of the people who usually (not always) see things from outside, for example, policymakers, bureaucrats, multilateral bodies, grant-making organisations and business people. Inside and outside need not be dichotomised, but it's rarely ambiguous as to where someone stands on this continuum. The power and money behind the techno-model culture is not just because of the inside–outside issue, in India.

We have become exactly the opposite of what Snow described as 'the state of Britain' in his lecture. Our society has overemphasised education in the technical and scientific disciplines for decades, almost to an extent that the humanities and social sciences have to justify their very existence. This has contributed to raising generations of the successful, who are often unquestioningly positivist, reductionist and deterministic. Many of these people, who are not unquestioning and have nuanced thinking, still come down overwhelmingly on the side of techno-models for action, based on what they consider as pragmatic considerations.

The great challenge that faces us is to bring about a consilience of these two cultures. Such a coming together will be effective, if the centrality is ceded to the social humanistic approach, in the social sector. On this matter, some good-intentioned politicians are worth observing; they seem to understand all this naturally, perhaps because their success in their chosen fields rests on such a consilience in action.

Meanwhile, in education, we have to keep battling the ever-new techno-models being tom-tommed, which are actually all the same old, in new clothes.

14 October 2015

Using History to Build a Strong Nation

In the past few months, statements about Indian history have been made, which have generated much controversy. Here is the gist of some of these statements, all of which invoke specific episodes from some of our ancient texts, to demonstrate that India was technologically and scientifically a very advanced civilisation a very long time ago. The births of Drona, Karna and Kauravas have been used as examples for knowledge of genetic sciences and of the technique of developing 'test-tube' babies. The resurrection of Ganesha has been used as an example of plastic surgery. The Pushpak Vimana from Ramayana has been cited as an example of technology for air travel. Some of us have heard such statements in the past also.

As the backdrop for the arguments in this column, we will use two principles. First, we will believe that whatever people are saying is with good intentions and with personal integrity. Second, we will adopt a basic principle from (good) philosophy that any idea must be judged in its best form.

We can now think of two groups of people, amongst those who have been interested or involved in any way with this issue, even if only to the extent of reading newspaper headlines. The first group believes that these statements are expression of historical facts and truths. The second group believes that these statements are false, and mythology is being invoked as history.

There is possibly a third group, that of people who have not made up their mind. In my assessment, the number of such people is so small that we will ignore this group, and even if the numbers are not as small, the arguments here will not change. The basic matter that divides these two groups, that whether these statements are true or false, is not a symmetric matter. The two groups do not have an equal burden of proof.

In the context of the (current) widely shared understanding of human history, these statements are false. That 'widely' is really very wide indeed, including historians of all sorts: rightist, leftist, nationalist, subaltern and all other types. This is not only in India, but across the world. It also includes almost all scholars from every other discipline, and most people who could be called informed or educated. This is why the burden of proof is with the first group. They cannot just make an assertion, and claim it is true. They will have to gather evidence to support these statements, and present them (and the methodology) widely for rational examination, that is, subject it to the test of reason. This can perhaps be best done by historians and other scholars in the first group. Till this has been done adequately, people from the first group need to be acutely aware of how their belief in the truth of these statements will be viewed. The more they reaffirm their beliefs publicly, the more likely they are to lose credibility, in most quarters.

Let's focus on those who are making these statements seriously and with thought. It's quite likely that they would be aware of this asymmetric burden of proof. So then why are these statements being made? Let's leave aside that sub-group which is so self-absorbed that it considers these assertions as self-evident truth, without room for doubt. Why are some serious and thoughtful people making these statements, braving loss of credibility?

There is a complex of reasons, but perhaps the strongest is their deeply felt need to generate a sense of pride in India and Indians. This is one strand of their even deeper desire to see India strong, and to systematically work towards it; building a strong India is the real goal, and the source of their energy. This project of building a strong India has also led to efforts by some to integrate the core ideas of these statements into school education; since they know well that school education is one of the most important processes in shaping a nation. To remind ourselves, I have assumed good intentions and personal integrity on everyone's part as also the notion of judging ideas in their best form (which will apply to this matter of 'strong India' as well).

Amongst many things that are necessary but not sufficient to build a strong India is a culture of reason, of questioning driven by doubt and of openness. Since the modern world is built on a foundation of reason and rationality, this is not a matter of choice; and India becoming strong is in the context of that world.

So, when rationally unexamined ideas, which under the weight of all current evidence are false, are asserted as truth publicly, it weakens India. When such ideas find their way into school education, they corrode the most basic process of building a strong nation, by undermining reason and rationality. For all of us invested in the idea of a strong India, it will be useful to remember that often pride comes before a fall and reason is the foundation of strength.

24 December 2014

Education in the Land of Extremes

That February in 2012, at dusk—one of those sparkling and crisp kinds that you find only in the mountains—we found a room with a rent of Rs 300; the heater was an additional Rs 350. Our bones had been frozen during the afternoon meeting at the Lohaghat Block Resource Centre (BRC), and so we took the heaters unhesitatingly. It's the coldest night I can remember. It felt as though the cold was being collected and poured into our rooms. It was certainly not Scandinavian temperatures, but just the construction of the place, and poor heating; clearly that hotel had been designed as a cold storage. We survived the night. Obsessive as I am, I still went for a run at 6.30 a.m.

I went back to the same BRC last month, in May. It was almost hot. The stink from unclean toilets was incongruent with the creativity of the meeting room. Every inch of the walls was painted with something educationally significant. It was not the usual homilies (Education is the greatest treasure) rolled out from the state capital, unthinkingly on to the walls of schools, but stuff that someone had thought about.

The pièce de résistance was the ceiling painted like the Sistine Chapel. It was an intricate depiction of the solar system, all across the 20 ft by 30 ft ceiling. The large lamp at the centre was the sun. It took me a while to understand what the grid lines were doing there on the solar system. It was a depiction of the time-space continuum; the distortion of the lines to depict gravity is what makes it clear. What a wonder it was, Einstein's time-space continuum on a ceiling in Lohaghat, co-existing with the unsurprising stink from toilets! The meeting itself carried on with this theme of co-existence, of delightful surprises and unsurprising banality. It was a discussion with government schoolteachers, who are a part of the local voluntary forum. These are basically informal teacher learning networks, which meet outside working hours, to develop their own capacities. I have written earlier about these forums, and how in our work we find this spirit of self-improvement and commitment to better education, across the country.

That evening in Lohaghat, the meeting had twenty teachers. Let's take the banal and deplorable first. One man was insistent that a little bit of fear in children was necessary for their learning. He saw that as justification for a little corporal punishment. He found support in one other teacher, who helpfully pointed out that a little bit of corporal punishment must be a little bit, and not of the kind that leaves marks on the child's body. They agreed on that.

There was another lady who claimed that any one of us could go to her school and test for ourselves that all children from Class II onwards could read and write. One of the other teachers wanted to know how she made it happen. She explained she started with letters and then words and then they could write and read. No one could understand how this universally ineffective method worked in her case, and another teacher asked her this pointedly. She just invited us even more loudly to come and test out her students.

One of them went on a long monologue about how the fathers of most children in the villages were alcoholics. The believer in corporal punishment agreed with him. A young teacher protested. He said he found no more drunks in villages than in towns. He had come to the meeting to learn how to teach. He believed that if the children were not learning, it was because of his own limitations; but if this was all these sessions amounted to, he would stop coming. That cracked the hesitation, and out came the interesting stuff.

One of them expressed surprise at the claim that fear helped in teaching. He had his method to make children comfortable in the school. He starts each day playing the harmonium and singing with the students, especially the Class I kids. Another teacher talked about how, in her experience, learning of a language happens much better through whole sentences and words; that children need to understand and relate to the meaning, and that letter recognition can follow. She went into some detail of what she does in her classes.

The corporal punishment duo had drifted into a side conversation. One of the senior teachers was an accomplished diplomat. Without belittling the duo, he nailed the illegality, ineffectiveness and inhumaneness of corporal punishment. At the end, I walked out with the young teacher. He said he would come back for the next meeting. He liked the discussion on language. A land of extremes. Isn't that the phrase we use all too readily about our country? In Lohaghat (and across the country), you have teachers at both ends. They all need support to become better, not derision and neglect.

25 June 2014

Building an Ethical Society

Raag Darbari is the definitive novel about politics and bureaucracy in India. Somewhere in its opening pages, Shrilal Shukla writes: 'Our education system is that bitch on the street which any passerby can kick around.' The novel is full of such asides, each insightful. When we have carped a bit about the ethical wasteland our society seems to have become, we say, 'Schools must teach values, that is the long-term solution.' It's just another one of the kicks, which Shukla laconically observed.

How can schools 'teach' values, when values are absent from most behaviour that a child will see around them in their overall environment? School education (and the child) is integrally a part of the very society that it is supposed to make the child ethical. We lightly pass on the burden of building an ethical society to schools. Ironically, many of the (same) people who expect education to bear this burden also, in general, tend to think of 'employability' as the primary purpose of education. 'Values' is only an aside, an add-on purpose when they are ruminating over the 'lack of values'. This, when the learning of values is far more complex than the learning of all that is generally supposed to constitute employability.

Many people (including me) involved in education will gladly take the impossible burden of trying to build an ethical society through education. No one, though, would contend that this can be done by schools on their own. I use the word 'ethical' with its broadest normative meaning—equitable, just, humane. They would embrace this burden because they think of the primary purpose of education as being the development of the individual and society in the broadest possible manner.

So, let's grapple with the issue of how to do this. Let's assume that we have an agreement on normative (desirable) values for our society. These are based on a liberal interpretation of the values enshrined in our Constitution. Given the state of our nation, we know that this is a big and fragile assumption.

Let me take you to a classroom. A group of kids are sitting at the back and another group in the front. This is not the usual front and back-bencher divide. These groups have a fair distance between them and not much within. At 'mid-day meal' time, the group in the front is given food first, the group at the back waits for its turn patiently. Centuries of waiting for their turn has taught their community to be patient. In this village, treating this community (considered 'lower caste') in this discriminatory manner is normal even today.

The social science textbooks that the same kids read in the classroom will have homilies about equality of man and our constitutional commitment to equity. There are no prizes for guessing what will really shape their beliefs (and behaviour) about equality and equity—the textbook or what they live through in their school.

The gap between the word and the deed is not a malady peculiar to village schools; it's as much there in the metros. Is anyone surprised to see the principal treating teachers like minions and parents like dirt in Delhi? And the same principal will easily give a heartwarming speech about building a sensitive environment in the school. It's obvious that no child will learn values by having a subject called 'value education'. Values are shaped through slow, complex social processes that an individual lives through, not by being 'taught' in a classroom. The social processes and relationships in the school are the key determinants of fostering and shaping values. Thoughtful curriculum, including books, which deeply integrate these values and their implied sensibility in a non-didactic manner have a supportive role.

It is fundamentally about having no gap between the word and deed. About how the students, teachers and principal behave with each other, how their relationships evolve. Do they treat each other with respect, what is considered 'good' form and behaviour, how are differences with community norms resolved? In short, it's the school and classroom culture and its relationship with the outside community that has the greatest influence (in the sphere of school education) on the evolution of the students' values. Shaping school culture is difficult. It can happen only if a concerted and sustained attempt is made. Our national policies and education frameworks have the right direction on this, thus creating a broadly enabling environment.

The crunch really is in how this is translated into practice at every level: the policies of state education management, its implementation and finally the school where it all comes together for the student. The other crunch is in our teacher education system integrating the expectation of the teacher playing a critical role in the overall development of the child. Suffice to say that we are doing a shoddy job on all this and still continue to expect education to solve our problems.

Shuklaji must be smiling knowingly. A good job on all this could give some hope for school education to shape an ethical society. We have to keep at it, since there aren't too many other methods. We have to continue to try to get the islands of schools to turn the tides of the ocean.

21 March 2012

What Do We Do with Our Horses?

The two horses were standing still on the road in the dark winter morning. I returned after an hour-long run, and they had drifted about 50 m. They were still standing still. That was two weeks ago. I went on a week-long trip and returned. They were still there. This was the third time in three years that two horses have appeared on that road near my house.

That afternoon, I went to a house where I had never been before. To meet people I had not met ever. Before I reached the house, my thoughtful host sent me a cautionary text, 'We have three dogs.' When I reached, two of them threw themselves at me. Hugging and nuzzling me, prancing about at the excitement of seeing me. Their names were Bella and Marx. They seemed to have missed me, as I have missed them. But this was the first time I was meeting these dogs.

Instantaneous communion is the capacity of dogs, not mine. But I have opened myself to this experience in the past three years. Beginning with Tinker, Tailor, Soldier and Spy, the four little kittens that adopted our garden. Followed by a bolt of conversation questioning my implicit assumption about categorical differences between humans and animals. And then the first two horses appeared on the road, in this chain of events.

Earlier, animals and I would occupy the same physical space, but their world was closed to me. Because I had kept the doors bolted. It took a week or so before I registered those first two horses. They would drift slowly within a kilometre on the road, but they remained there. They looked old, which they were. Then I went on a trip to Barmer; it was September. Most rural government schools in that area are beautiful. In the vastness of the desert, land is not in short supply. Almost all schools have neatly walled campuses, with the buildings clustered on one side, and the rest of it a sandy expanse of playgrounds. They have carefully tended green patches, usually of neem trees, around the buildings. Scores of schools harvest every drop of rain that falls and use it through the year and reuse every drop they can.

The blaze of September in the desert becomes real only when you experience it. I was drenched in sweat sitting inside a classroom. Through the open door and windows, we could see the school gate right across the sandy playground, about 100 m away, and beyond, up to the high sand dunes. I was sitting at the door to catch the breeze. There was a fourteen-year-old girl sitting near me. It was Class VIII, and they were learning maths.

It was tough going. He was a language teacher compelled to teach maths, since he was the only teacher in the middle school. The grill gate of the school swung open, pushed by a goat. It was followed by five more goats. The six walked slowly across the playground to the corner with the handpump atop the tank with the harvested rainwater. The girl too noticed the goats. In a flash, she was off. With no footwear, she ran across the sand to the handpump. She started pumping the water out and drenched her head in the water. Then she continued and the water drained to a small shallow pool. The goats were waiting, they slurped the water. She had to pump more; the goats were not done. The whole thing took about five minutes, and that is when I realised that she had drenched herself to face the afternoon blaze as she tended to the goats. Through these proceedings, the teacher merely glanced out.

After the class, I asked the girl whether the goats were known to her.

'No,' she said.

'The water is so precious here, you gave so much of it to them.'

'They were thirsty,' she replied.

'But the school will need all the water, wouldn't it?'

'Whatever we have, we can share; if we don't take care of them, who will?'

I returned home and the horses were still there on the road. Now, I saw them through the eyes of the girl who ran to water the thirsty goats. We tried to find a home for them. With increasing desperation. There would surely be someone or some organisation that could take them in? But there was no shelter for two old horses in a city of 10 million people. Then one day, the two vanished. This is what we do to our old horses that have served with devotion and affection, leave them to drift and die.

What kind of a world do we want? Do we abandon the weakest and those who serve, or, do we share what we have and slake their thirst? Do we return the unconditional love and devotion we receive, or do we turn our backs on both love and suffering?

That day near Barmer, after the girl went away, the teacher said, 'Sir, maths *nahin padhaa sakte, toh kam se kam pyaar-mohaabat se jeena toh sikhaa sakte hain.*' (Even if I am not able to teach maths, at least I can try to teach them to live with love and compassion.)

There is much darkness in our world and in the human heart. Schools can help let the light in and help build a world of compassion and empathy. In this world, we care for all thirsty goats, and the love of Bella and Marx is reciprocated in full, across distance and time. And that of humans too. But if schools talk of bullets and revenge, or we interrogate our school children on charges of sedition and worse, we are well on the road to perdition. Those two horses are there on that road, still.

13 February 2020

Education for What?

A ritual that I await in my journey through Indian schools often happens in the evening. The village can usually pause during this time, and we have what is called a 'community interaction'. It's generally a freewheeling chat, with not just parents of students, but just about anyone from the village. One of the common matters of discussion in all such chats is: Why do you send your children to school?

From the verdant basin of the Cauvery to the heights of the Garhwal Himalayas, the answer follows a common refrain: 'For a better life'. Layers of meaning in that phrase have unfolded for me in the course of every such conversation. A stable livelihood that pays more is one part of this complex wish for a better life. But the notion straddles hope of every kind—gaining greater respect and more influence in the community, development of the village, a quest for equity and justice, and sometimes, 'How else can India progress?'

Let me remind you that these are not the tea-fuelled conversations at some university canteen, but in a village school. The hopes of our nation rest more deeply on education than I could have imagined; the hopes of the disadvantaged, even more so. Is it surprising that similar hopes were echoed by US President Barack Obama's recent State of the Union address? Obama spoke at length on education. Emphasising its centrality, he exhorted Americans to take up teaching 'if you want to make a difference in the life of our nation; if you want to make a difference in the life of a child.'

From the village in India to that address, what we are hearing are the expectations from education, as they are today. These societal expectations that guide the purposes of education have not necessarily been the same through human history. They have evolved. John Dewey, the pre-eminent philosopher of education in the twentieth century, called it, in the broadest sense, as the means for 'social continuity of life'. Education happens not only in school, but elsewhere, perhaps everywhere. Over the past two centuries, though, school systems have become the pre-eminent social enterprise (I am using this phrase with its original and literal English meaning, not the fashionable 'social business' one) for education. In this context, Dewey explained curriculum as 'the funded wisdom of the human race'.

So, whether we explicitly recognise it or not, school systems have become the primary organised social enterprise for renewal, improvement and continuity of society—from liberal democracies to theocracies.

Hence, states have acquired an increasingly larger role in education, in schooling.

This has been the context for the rapid growth of schooling through much of the world in the past 150 years. The evolution of liberal, democratic and welfare societies and states has generated the notion of equitable, good schooling (a 'right' in various countries) for all citizens. The role of education (and schooling) as one of the primary social enterprises needed to fulfil society's promises to itself, and convert its hopes into reality, has only grown.

If you were to Google 'systemic change (or reform)', it would prompt you with versions of 'systemic change in education'. Globally, we indeed tend to think most often of systemic change and reform in the context of education. India, China and other developing nations are understandably focused on building, improving and changing their education systems. So is the US— it is indeed one of the nation's central concerns; Obama wants to 'out-innovate, out-educate, out-build' the rest of the world. Turn your ears to places like Finland, Sweden and Canada, with clearly good education, and you will hear the same desire to change and improve their education systems, despite their already high standards.

One cannot think of a nation that is not working on changing and improving its education.

The reason is that every nation is a work-in-progress. It wants to improve, it has hopes and it has fears. Therefore, given the role of education (and schooling) as the primary social enterprise to fulfil society's promises to itself, it's the most natural thing that we would want to improve and change our education systems—to achieve and address all this, and more.

So, when schools in India fall short of even helping our children learn to read and write, we have to see the gulf, rather the ocean, between our own expectations from education and what we actually have. It's the same ocean that is there between the society that we want to be and what we are. And that is why every step on this journey of improving our education is a step towards the just, equitable and humane society that we had promised ourselves on 26 January 1950.

10 February 2011

PART FOUR

OUR NATION,
IN SOME MEASURE

Our Nation, in Some Measure

He was a quiet man. He was also a good and disciplined driver. Fast, when needed, without taking risks, and mindful of the comfort of his passengers. Despite three days of arguments swirling around him on topics from politics to corporal punishment, he never offered an opinion. In that early winter day, we were driving towards another meeting of teachers. The argument was about why people send their children to school. Is it mostly about getting them better livelihood and jobs, or are there other motivations?

It takes an unusually fair and open-minded person to seek validation or otherwise from someone who has not spoken for three days. I would not have done it. The question was directly to him, *'Aap apne bachchon ko school kyon bhejte hain?'* (Why do you send your children to school?)

His response was in character, precise and brief. *'Is duniya mein shiksha ke bina izzat kahan hai?'* (There is no respect in this world without education). All of us knew that one person's view is not the final word. But the clarity of his response put a pause to the argument. My sense of vindication was tempered by my admiration for the act of asking that question and accepting the answer with equanimity.

Before that conversation, I would ask that very question once in a while, when I met parents of students in the schools that I was visiting. After that conversation I started asking it systematically, across the scores of schools that I get to visit in the country. In parallel, some of my colleagues, who are especially good at researching difficult issues in the complex reality of real India, got interested in the same question. The result is the recently published field study *Educational Expectations, Aspirations, and Structural Constraints* (Azim Premji University). Expectations of parents from education for their children were explored through rigorous interviews in the study. Here are some of the key points that have been paraphrased:

More than 96 per cent of the parents said education was important for both boys and girls. Over 30 per cent gave reasons related to employability as the main usefulness of education. However, over 25 per cent of the parents had mainly reasons that conveyed the importance of education for broader social objectives other than employment.

These reasons were quite distinct from their expectation that school education would help their children have better livelihood or jobs. The study has labelled these reasons as 'social purposes', which are of three kinds—reasons that underscored self-worth, reasons that emphasised respect in society and reasons that underlined empowerment. The wide prevalence of the importance of these 'social purposes' is even clearer, when the 'top three' reasons cited by parents are considered. As much as 84 per cent of the parents cited 'social purposes' among their top three reasons, for both girls and boys, whereas employability-related reasons were cited among the top three by 71 per cent for boys and by 52 per cent for girls.

The study mirrors the experiences and intuitions of many of us who work in education—that parents expect a lot more from education than only better livelihood and employment. These expectations are even sharper for the socially disadvantaged. Asking that question systematically now for some time, I have seen multiple layers of human feelings on this matter.

On a dark monsoon afternoon, in a small village somewhere in Chhattisgarh, we were sitting inside a school classroom constructed in 1915. There were about twenty people there, all of whose children were studying in the school. I speak Chhattisgarhi reasonably fluently, which they clearly did not expect from someone from Bengaluru. Perhaps that is a reason we had such a conversation about my question. Here is the gist of what they said.

First, the school is a visible marker of equality and freedom. It had been standing there since 1915, but most of their families had not been able to send children to the school, and some were not allowed to, till a generation ago. The simple act of all children from the village going to the same school is emancipating. Second, caste is a reality that they live with. And they know that education can empower them to loosen the tight grip of caste over their lives. Third, the rules by which this world works are loaded in favour of the educated. They cannot protect their rights, demand their dues and prevent (or reduce) their exploitation unless they are educated. Fourth, how can anyone struggle for a better world, even if they want to, if they are not educated? B.R. Ambedkar was what he was because of education.

Such expectations from education should not surprise us. Reducing education to an instrument for employment, or basic literacy and numeracy, which much of our intellectual and policy discourse tends to, is inadequate, wrong and unjust. That the disadvantaged expect much more from education should be even less of a surprise. The promise of education is empowerment, equality and dignity. So, when education fails, which it does too often in this country, it fails the deepest of aspirations and hopes of our people. If we have to redeem the pledge of our nation, not even substantially, but in some measure, education has to succeed.

14 February 2019

Not by Education Alone

One of the hundreds of dusty small towns in North India, this one is not particularly remote. The nearest airport is a two-and-a-half-hour drive on a four-lane highway. Evenings in March are cool in that region, even if the days are turning hot.

This particular evening was cool too, and even with sixty people sitting on the floor, the small room did not feel stuffy. The animated discussion had to be brought to an end at 7.30 p.m., else it would have continued. Many of the teachers had to travel over 20 km to reach home. It was the weekly evening discussion of the forum of government schoolteachers. This forum is a peer-learning group in which teachers engage voluntarily.

Gender equity was the matter being discussed. The veneer of correctness was thin. Everyone, woman and man, in the two-hour discussion started with only what ought to be said. But the difference between what they felt and what they said was too much. Despite a man and three women holding out till the end with their ideas, the room reached a comforting consensus. Clear affirmation to bringing in total gender equity in some distant future, with a reaffirmation of benign patriarchy for today, satisfied everyone except the small radical group.

Even I felt satisfied—having learnt not to pick red flags like how patriarchy could be benign, instead weighing the progress made within our messy reality. The intense discussion was because these teachers were thinking about matters related to gender in their own milieu. And they were aware of what needs to be changed. This is important. In the absence of teachers having this kind of understanding, education cannot contribute to improving gender equity. For sure, understanding in itself is insufficient, but it is the starting point.

Five hundred metres, to the spot where our car was parked, was a pleasant stroll. A teacher taking the same route home was keeping stride. With a smirk, she said, '*Kehne ke liye to kuch bhi keh dete hain, ghar me betiyon ki ungli kaat dete hain.*' (To make a statement they will say anything, but at home they chop off the fingers of their daughters.) She was referring to the male teachers. I asked her what she meant. She said that in that area, when men think that their daughters are becoming 'belagaam' (out of their control), they chop off their little finger as a warning.

Exaggeration on such matters on both sides, the good and the bad, is routine. My disbelief was apparent, it encountered a smile from her and we parted ways at the car. The hotel I stayed in that night was an hour from the airport. Next morning, a junction on the route to the airport had a traffic snarl. There was a weekly haat in a village. As my car crawled, I saw the colourful wares and the shoppers. A few seconds before my car hit the spot where the snarl eased, my eyes fell on a girl sitting in an auto. She must have been eighteen. She was holding a bag, both hands visible. She had nine fingers. The little finger of her left hand was chopped at the base.

My car surged ahead, her auto raced off into a side lane and my heart stopped. The rage in me had no outlet. A colleague confirmed that he, too, had heard of finger-chopping in that area. But in a country where daughters are routinely killed at birth, as also for their love when they are older, a chopped finger is not even reported.

By the time I landed in Bengaluru, two flights and six hours later, the episode had become another stark reminder of the limits of education. We forget that injustice, inhumaneness or the effects of poverty cannot be fought by education alone. Sure, in the long term, there is no substitute for education's role in developing a good society. But in the here and now, we need education, and more.

In the fourth week of January this year, I was in Bibballi, a village near Sedam, just off the road from Gulbarga to Hyderabad. Three thousand girls had come from all over the Sedam block to participate in the kishori mela. They had worked in their own schools to develop interesting ways of presenting issues related to gender. Colourful poster displays and creative exhibits filled room after room. Lively music and riveting theatre, both were there. From reproductive health and dietary diversity to female infanticide and constitutional commitments to equity, the range of issues tackled left very few unaddressed.

With bricks being broken and dust clouds rising from the stomping of feet, it was the group of karate girls who best captured the spirit of the mela. Excitement, confidence and courage, energised by being together. Collectively, the strength of the 3,000 girls was way more than the sum of their individual strengths.

Schools as fundamental social institutions, present in every village and small town, can systematically play a role in developing this collective spirit and strength, going beyond what is generally considered in the realm of education. That has been the side effect of the effort in Sedam.

Energised by the experience, the teachers and officers present decided to systematically and frequently conduct kishori melas within clusters of schools. Fires of this kind, if lit in the 1.5 million schools across this country, will make it increasingly difficult to chop off the little finger of a little girl. Till then, my heart remains pierced by that little finger.

1 March 2018

Of Motivated Teachers

On a warm summer evening, up in the Kumaon mountains in Pithoragarh, we watched Abbas Kiarostami's film, *Where Is the Friend's Home?* It was an audience of about thirty-five people, most of them government schoolteachers. The cryptic, flashing English subtitles of the movie were not very helpful to the audience, most of whom had only a passing familiarity with the language. And the language of the movie, Persian, was alien to everyone. It did not matter, as we sat riveted for ninety minutes.

No language barrier can stop that movie from speaking to you, and that is the craft of Abbas Kiarostami. Shot on location in a village in Iran, with local, non-professional actors, its production is as deceptively simple as its story. Ahmed, a seven-year-old boy, living in Koker, brings home his friend's notebook from school, by mistake. The teacher has threatened to expel his friend from the school if he doesn't complete his homework in the notebook one more time. Ahmed doesn't know where his friend lives, other than that he lives in the neighbouring village. The movie is Ahmed's search for his friend's home to return his notebook that evening so that he can complete his homework. Ahmed's natural actions by the end become an almost epic quest, fuelled by his compassion and desire to do the right thing, confronted continually by an adult world which is almost always uncomprehending of the child and often unintentionally hostile to him.

No one left when the movie finished. For ninety minutes in the afterglow, the teachers discussed the movie. They talked of whether it was empathy or duty that drove Ahmed, and whether these two motivations are related or totally distinct. His school seemed so familiar that they laughed. There were deeply felt comments on the inability of adults to listen to children, and on the distance between a child's world and that of the adult's, despite occupying the same space-time.

Ahmed's grandfather became the centrepiece of a heated debate on why adults commit wanton violence against children. They talked about the relationship of Ahmed and his parents, empathising with the boy for the lack of support at home, without condemning the parents who are immersed in the daily struggle of life. They found the social context of distant Iran fascinating, with older crafts and livelihoods being marginalised, with rigid gender roles and with a sense of life drifting along to nowhere. The discussion found a natural end, when someone said, 'Well, all this could have happened in Pithoragarh yesterday.'

Hearing of government schoolteachers spending their evening watching a serious Persian film in a small town in India would surprise many. The depth of the discussion following the movie and its broad range would be heartening to anyone. They were not critiquing the film as art, but as a human document directly relevant to their lives and to education. It's unlikely that there will be any deeper insights from the film in the seats of intellectual power anywhere. It's not as though there was an announcement made about the film show that evening and the teachers just showed up.

It's a group that meets and works regularly on matters of education. They meet on some evenings during weekdays, on some weekends and for longer durations during the vacations. The focus of their sessions ranges from matters directly in the curriculum to other practical matters facing them in schools and to things (like this film) that have a broader relevance to education. For example, in the past three months, many of them have participated in a five-day residential workshop on maths, in weekend sessions on gender issues and on the Constitution of India and their evening sessions have ranged from colonialism to gravity.

This is a vibrant peer-learning network focused on the professional development of its members—the teachers. Like any such effective network, it has its own norms and commitments, but is informal and not closed. The members participate and join of their own volition. They want to become better teachers. This group has not come together on its own. A few people have worked hard to develop it and stay committed to keeping it vibrant. They also make sure that there is a steady flow of dialogue with people outside the group so that it doesn't become insular or stop growing intellectually. You will encounter teacher groups of this kind and such individual teachers across the country.

The need for such professional development is naturally felt by most teachers, driven by the complexity of their role which demands deep expertise, street smarts, moral commitment, a humane approach and a Buddha-like disposition. And all this requires a lifetime of work. Providing active support and an enabling culture for such professional development of our 8 million teachers is perhaps the most urgent intervention required to improve the quality of education in India.

PS: Sadly, Abbas Kiarostami passed away on 4 July 2016, and the world is poorer for it.

7 July 2016

Schools and Sand Dunes

It was the first time I walked on sand dunes. The winter evening sun converted the sand to gold. He was wearing a craggy closed-neck coat which had thick black and white vertical stripes in the weave. We had walked half a kilometre into the dunes. He pointed in one direction,

'Two kilometres that way there is a school,' then another direction for another school 3 km away.

'The four of us are responsible for 600 schools,' he said. Some schools are in places where they can take their bikes; for others they leave the bike on the road and walk, such as the two he pointed out across the dunes. There is no winter evening sun through the year. There is the heat and the sand storms. Through this they reach the schools, it is their job. This is the Education Block Resource team of Chautan in Barmer district of Rajasthan. They are there to support the schools of the block.

His face shows the effect of trying to connect 600 schools through the sand and heat. It also shows how alone each of these schools is, and how isolated the teachers may feel. A teacher from one school said, 'There is God, and then there is me, that's it.' He was not being dramatic; his reality is that he has to fend for himself completely. Clean and maintain the school, handle thirty to forty students in every way, deal with the community, manage the mid-day meals, fill up reports, manage vaccination camps, respond to the officers and the list is much longer. Two other teachers were not fatalistic. They said, 'We can live here crying, or we can live here laughing.' They are all on their own. Many of them live in the schools, since there is no place to rent in the village and it is not possible to walk a few kilometres every day in that terrain from elsewhere. In Jaipur, they call this region kalapaani, for Barmer is a pretty hard place to be in. Every aspect of the district emphasises the isolation of teachers, although their reality is not different elsewhere.

Fifty kilometres outside Bengaluru, just off National Highway 4, I walked into a school. No one had visited them in a year. The teacher had been to the block office for supplies; he had virtually no real connection with the system.

There are demands on the teachers and the block education authorities to file administrative reports very often. However, interactions between different parts of the system are rare, let alone a genuine connection on their real work—education. This is the story across India. The task of organising good education for even a single child is perhaps one of the most challenging things that a person can face. The reality of being a teacher and doing this for thirty to forty students makes this exponentially harder. This role becomes even more complex in India, given our diversity and socio-economic characteristics. The design of our schooling system with schools within a kilometre of each habitation has solved the problem of access, but has added further complexity. It forces teachers to handle children across age groups together. It has also contributed to the isolation of teachers and other education functionaries. The Barmer example makes this stark: teachers in remote sand dunes, on their own. But, let this not suggest that the issue of isolation exists only in the so-called hard places. This is the reality everywhere for our teachers, even in the heart of our cities too.

This is because physical disconnectedness is only a part of the problem. The core issue is that our large, bureaucratised education system does not recognise the importance of intellectual and social connectedness of a teacher for her ability to perform her role. This arises partly from the mechanising, de-individualising tendencies that are common to most large organisational systems. Unlike industries, which thrive on scale, schools need to be smaller networks, connected to communities with substantial autonomy for teachers and school leaders. Problem arises when there are doubtful assumptions about a teacher's role, ignoring its complex and creative nature. Complex, creative professions such as filmmaking or being a scientist thrive on intellectual and social connectedness; we think of this as natural. Such connectedness is equally crucial for teachers. It is just that we don't think of the teachers' role as being similarly demanding and challenging, when in reality this is very much so.

I have seen repeatedly that it doesn't take much to enable this connectedness. It is often about someone playing a facilitating role to bring together a group of teachers. It does require persistence and thoughtfulness. The block- (and cluster-) level resources are ideally placed to do this, but they are thinly spread, and themselves in need of some help to build their capacity to play this kind of a role.

20 February 2013

The Education Battle Cry

Let me present two proposals for your endorsement, advocacy and, in case you are in a seat of power, for immediate implementation. Both are about improvement. The first is about how to make India a serious contender for the football World Cup. We must implement a rigorous system of assessment for our footballers. We should do this at all levels: from the schools up to the national team. This will help separate the good from the bad, who can then be given a few chances to improve. If they don't, they can be asked to play something else. A few other things will also need to be done, but the pivot will be this rigorous performance-based accountability system, which will quickly put India in contention for the World Cup.

The second proposal is about improving the fortunes of the multi-business, multi-geography, multinational company which has continued to perform poorly. Since business is all about selling, we must focus on where it really happens. A transparent system of performance-based incentives and accountability should be set up, rewarding sales people who do well and getting rid of those who don't. This will surely help regain market share and improve margins.

I can hear your protests on the short-sightedness of the preceding arguments, if you have taken them seriously. It's obvious that if we have to become a football superpower, we will have to improve infrastructure, coaching, facilities, community engagement, marketing and more. The last thing you would do is to discourage already engaged footballers, because as is obvious, bad footballers are not stopping us from winning the World Cup. In the case of the corporation, with its uniformly poor performance across businesses and regions, the one thing that you can be sure of is that its precarious state is not because of the sales people in the trenches, it has a much deeper set of strategic problems.

These are both examples of scapegoating accountability on the least empowered people in a system. The root causes of such systemic dysfunction are complex and interrelated, and such scapegoating improves nothing. If anything, it creates disengagement and fear in the 'trenches'. So why do we not see the short-sightedness of such approaches in education? Why do we think scapegoating teachers is a solution for the state of our education?

One popular battle cry is: let's fix teacher accountability. This is imagined to be done by having a standardised assessment of learning of students. This is identical to the football and troubled-corporation examples. For sure, there are good teachers and bad teachers, most of them are the average ones, but sifting them on the basis of their performance as reflected in student-learning will not lead to a positive change in a system which is overall performing poorly. An aside: managing truant and misbehaving teachers is not an educational issue (requiring student assessment); it's a socio-political issue.

For the past ten years, the US has driven an assessment-based teacher (and school) accountability system through the No Child Left Behind programme (and its cousin: Race to the Top). It has failed to make any differential positive impact on US education. If anything, it has fostered a culture of teaching-to-the-test, narrowing of curriculum, fear in teachers and schools, the disadvantaged getting further left behind and widespread cheating.

What has happened in the case of the No Child Left Behind programme is a result of the essential nature of education. Such external (not done by the teacher herself) assessment of students, its usage and implications end up corrupting and vitiating the process of education. In the field of education, scapegoating teachers is doubly dysfunctional, like in any other field, because of its vitiating effect on the very core of the educational process. There is no doubt that the role of the teacher makes her responsible for her students and their education, and she must discharge this responsibility to the best of her ability, within the constraints that face her. A sensible, empowering approach to managing teachers, including a fair multi-dimensional performance management system, will help substantially.

The current system, however, does not empower her, nor support her adequately. The inadequacy of our teachers is a symptom of the deeper problems of our education system: the alienating management systems, pathetic pre-service teacher education, dysfunctional and misaligned institutional structures, inadequate investment, archaic examination and textbook system and ineffective community engagement. This is without even considering the daunting and special challenges of India: socio-cultural-economic diversity, large majority of first-generation schoolgoers, linguistic complexity, etc. We need to work on all this and refrain from finding scapegoats.

Much of our popular imagination (from that of the politician to the average parent) continues to crave for performance-based accountability of teachers. This is just another expression of the desire for quick, simple fixes, which never work, and often cause harm. The same popular imagination is unmindful that the teachers themselves have another set of ready scapegoats: 'What can we do if the students are so bad?' This creates a full circle of dysfunction.

23 January 2013

Groundwater and Equality

As a schoolboy I spent many of my summer vacations in the searing heat of Sarangarh. In this small town ('kasba' describes it best) in Chhattisgarh, bordering Odisha, I saw multiple instances of the practice of 'untouchability'. Not perhaps in its most heinous form, but visible and clear to a child's eyes; for example, someone merely touching the water pot made the water immediately undrinkable, impure. This was the late 1970s and early 1980s.

In hindsight, what intrigues me most is how this practice was conducted. It was open, yet it was hidden. People seemed to know clearly that this was ethically unacceptable, besides being legally unacceptable, but they just had to do it. It was a bit like the newly corrupt taking bribes.

My own revulsion with this practice was not shaped by the law, but by my reading in school of Munshi Premchand's *Sadgati*—one of the many telling blows on social injustice by the great writer. There were other things that shaped my feelings, but *Sadgati* stood out.

Sadgati was not the only piece in my school education that was about untouchability. In fact, it was just one instance of how the whole curriculum, from Class I to XII, was infused with the notion of 'human equality' as an axiomatic good. The point to note is that this notion of axiomatic goodness of human equality was not just a chapter in one subject, but was infused in the entire curriculum. Not just mine, but in the entire country.

A question worth asking is: can we afford the same slow shift on ecology as has been happening with human equality? I would conjecture that this also had some role to play in the consciousness of the ethical unacceptability of untouchability in Sarangarh despite the low levels of efficacy of our education system. 'Human equality' is a work in progress in our society, but infusing education with this notion has certainly helped in the task of changing.

Upper Wainganga, which few of us may have heard of, is apparently the largest surface water reservoir in India. In the period between 2002 and 2008, in Haryana, Punjab and Rajasthan, the groundwater depletion was equivalent to a net loss of 109 cu. km of water, which is double the capacity of Upper Wainganga. This water is gone, vanished in six years, pumped out by millions of borewells. Groundwater vanishing continues at an accelerating pace. What would happen in ten, twenty, thirty years is merely a matter of simple numbers—unless we do something directly about the vanishing.

Whichever part of the ideological spectrum we reside in, our rational mind should not let some of these numbers escape us. Other such numbers are about the human population. Around seven billion humans are consuming at a growing pace the ecological capital of the earth. At the beginning of the twentieth century, the world's population was around 1.6 billion, not to talk of the dramatically different consumption footprint of humans then. In thirty to forty years, there will be 9–10 billion of us.

One doesn't have to be the proverbial Malthus to know that in some ways, probably in very significant ways, these numbers matter. Whether we are believers or non-believers of anthropogenic climate change and its effects, of increasing severity of water scarcity, of the impact of biodiversity loss and a host of other such things, these numbers should matter. This is simply about—staggeringly—more of us being dependent on the same capital stock of nature, and it tells us that action must lie in the direction of changing our relationship with this capital stock.

How can we use groundwater such that it doesn't vanish? Or,

the larger question, how does society move towards redefining its relationship with nature, with ecology? Obviously, this will be a complex, non-linear, systemic process. One element that could help is infusing education with the notion of 'ecological sensitivity' as an axiomatic good, much like 'human equality'.

This is not merely about teaching children 'EVS' (environmental sciences) as a subject. It's about infusing education with this axiomatic good in a deep, fundamental manner—across the curriculum and through practices. It would find expression in stories in languages, conceptually in economics, integrated in history, explored in engineering and so on. Education needs many kinds of reforms and changes; this is perhaps one kind.

Ecology infused into education cannot, in itself, guarantee a shift towards redefining our relationship with ecology, with the natural capital stock, but it will indeed be a significant force. The shift will happen slowly, as it has with human equality. The question worth dwelling on is: can we afford the same slow shift on this issue as has been happening with human equality? The issue of ecology is not just an ethical one, it is also about humanity's survival.

A few centuries of slow progress towards equality has been too slow, but a few centuries of slow progress on ecology may be too late.

17 June 2010

Every Child Can Learn,
Our Beliefs Matter

Construction has been slow. That is usual on these steep mountainsides around Almora. And this is a big campus. A medical college is coming up with large buildings. In the mountains, labour is local, but large projects often use labour from outside the state. The labour force at this site is mostly from Bihar and Odisha. Many of the labourers live in shanties near the site with their families, including young children. All children aged six and above attend the public (government) primary school in the nearby village of Lama Singh.

Children of migrant labourers grow up in the most difficult of circumstances. The economic hardships they face are compounded by the frequent uprooting of their lives. Most of these children don't get to attend school. Those who do usually find the school an alienating place. Age-appropriate curricular learning is impossibly distant. For teachers and schools, teaching and handling these children is one of the biggest challenges.

Radha Ballabh is one of two teachers at the school in Lama Singh. He and some of his students were at the *Baal Shodh Mela* in Syalidhar, which I wrote about in my column ('India's Capable Teachers Can Solve All Education Woes'; goo.gl/G8LQKu). In the past few months, the number of students in his school has gone up from fifty to seventy. All the new students are from the construction site. Ballabh and his colleague visit the shanties regularly to ensure that all children are enrolled and attend the school. They have also arranged for two people from the village to accompany the children every day from their homes to the school.

In the melee of playful children around us, he lists the achievements of his students. His greatest pride is in the students from the shanties. He says they are wonderful. They learn with interest, behave responsibly and live with good cheer. That is his experience with scores of these children in three years. He calls out to two of his students, who are passing by. We talk, and they are all that he claims.

Why is his experience with migrant children different? Why are they doing well in his school while other teachers find it difficult to handle them? His response to these questions is precise: 'Working with these children does require more effort from us in the school, because of the hardships they face in their lives. But then there is nothing else that is different. I believe that all children are good and can learn, while many other teachers believe that these children are not "normal". And that is the only reason.'

Those few sentences capture the gist of both the accumulated wisdom and decades of research in school education. There are multiple influences and determinants of the learning of children in schools. Teacher characteristics, learning resources, school culture, peer groups and home environment are some of the factors that deeply influence learning. While a precise model of the interaction of these factors and their influence on learning is impossible, their contributions and interrelationships are reasonably well understood.

One of the most important of these factors is the belief of teachers in their students. If a teacher believes that every child can learn well with appropriate interventions, despite being different in many ways from one another, it has a significant direct positive impact on learning. On the other hand, if a teacher believes that some categories of children, or an individual child, are less capable of learning, it has a direct negative influence on actual learning. This phenomenon would be unsurprising to any observer of human behaviour and relationships.

This is not just a pernicious Pygmalion effect. After placing the onus of failure to learn on the students' inability, the teacher absolves himself of his responsibilities. This often directly affects his efforts, triggering a negative spiral. Unsurprising as this is, not much is done about it. Educational theory discusses this a great deal. However, the reality in schools is that efforts to work with teachers, for them to examine their beliefs and thus change them, are very rare. And since the vast majority of our teacher education programmes (Bachelor of Education) are in shambles, nothing can be expected at the stage of teacher preparation until a quality revolution happens.

Many kinds of teacher beliefs impact student learning. Gender, caste and class prejudices are some of them. But the belief that some children cannot learn or cannot learn as well as others has an effect on every dimension of learning. There are two kinds of such false beliefs: one is the idea that children are either 'smart' or 'dumb' and that the latter can't learn. The second is a specific manifestation of group-specific prejudices—that children of the economically poor, of Dalits and tribal communities, and of minorities, are incapable of, or very bad at, learning.

These beliefs about children, which have not the flimsiest empirical or theoretical basis, are among the most intractable issues that we confront when we work with teachers across the country. Relentless, patient dialogue is what helps. Demonstration by us that children learn equally is better. But the best is a teacher like Ballabh, demolishing these myths through his actual work. There are thousands of teachers like him. They need to be celebrated and emulated to make a real difference to this ignored but critical matter, while we await the revolution in teacher education.

19 July 2018

A Dark Day in April

On that dark day, the mountains loomed high, merging into the black clouds. The steady rain did not belong to April, it was from mid-monsoon. The Bhagirathi was a sheer drop of 400 m from the right edge of the loose gravel road. On the left, the road hugged a cliff, a grey wall of flaky mud.

The rain was washing the mud down the cliff, on to the road and into the river. We didn't seem to be in danger, but it appeared that the road would get blocked by the sliding mud by the time of our return journey. That would force us to take another route, three hours downriver, to cross the next bridge, and then four hours back to return to Uttarkashi. We decided not to take that risk and turned back instead. We had to skip the visit to the school at Chhoti Mani.

The road wound down to the bridge nearby. We crossed it, and turned downriver toward Chinayalisaur. We were now just across the river from where we had turned back. That spot was a speck on the over 1,000 m-tall cliff of slipping mud. The ribbon of the road itself was not visible against the grey background and the low light. The foolhardiness of having tried to drive on that stretch, in those conditions, was apparent from this side of the river. It made everything even darker. We now had time on our hands, so we stopped by the government primary school in Badethi.

Sanjay Kuksaal, the head teacher, was an old acquaintance of my colleagues Sanjay and Jagmohan. He was preoccupied with uploading some data on the DISE (District Information System for Education) website. He welcomed us warmly while continuing his work. We did not want to interrupt him, so we asked him if we could talk to some of his students. He suggested that we visit Class VI, since the teacher was out for training and the students were studying on their own.

Jagmohan went into the class with me. There were fourteen children—an equal number of boys and girls. Predictably, the second question they asked us was where our homes were. This led to our asking where their homes were. That question can be one of the most difficult for some, as it seemed to be for one boy. That this was an unusual class was apparent from the early banter, but the way the class rallied around the boy, in answering that question, pulled at me even across the depth of darkness I was in.

The boy was from a distant state. That this was the reason for part of his discomfort, we understood. But there was more, which we did not want to get into. After his first hesitant statement, his friends did not let him speak, at least five of them saying, in their own words, 'He is one of us, his home is here.' He smiled, and all was well. When girls and boys sit together, mixed up and not separately, it is usually a sign of a better school.

The banter continued. I told them I was ninety-eight years old, and they rolled over with laughter. Then they guessed my age to be anywhere between forty and fifty-five. They asked Jagmohan his age. He said his age was five years less than half of my stated age. In an instant, they figured out his age. That is remarkable for Class IV in any school. To be able to solve a maths problem posed in that abstract a manner, in an educational culture that only teaches procedural skills, speaks of the quality of the school. When we were leaving, I told them that they were very smart. They responded, 'You are very smart, sir,' and then they turned to Jagmohan and said, 'You are also very smart, sir'—they did not want to make him feel excluded.

An hour that could have only brightened life, deepened my

darkness. I could only see the little girl from Kathua everywhere. Going by her photograph, she would have fitted well into that class.

I knew the resolution of the tumult in my heart and mind. I knew what to do with the rage that was fuelling the darkness. But knowing what to do is light years away from doing it, and that interaction made it much worse; every moment an excruciating reminder of what she would have been.

We went to see the airport under construction near Chinyalisaur, on a high plateau over the town.

Standing on the middle of the runway, I got a call from a friend, 'I want to drop all this that I am doing and go to Kathua.' 'What will you do,' I asked him. 'Maybe hang them,' he said. '*Jinhe naaz hai Hind pe wo kahan hain?*' he asked.

Sometimes, giving counsel can be therapeutic. Every day a new depravity haunts us. In just these weeks, we have had Kathua, Unnao, Surat, Bareilly and Muzzafarnagar (places where children were abused). Education cannot change and solve all this, but we should fight the fight that we can fight best. Especially when it can make a real difference, even if not all the difference. Our challenge is to harness our rage into our work.

We must do a better job with education, and faster. If education can help grow children like the fourteen I met, we must go for it. And if children like that are the future of this country, then every little girl may be safer, and perhaps even happy.

I reminded myself and my friend that even the timeless lament of Sahir from *Pyasaa*, which he quoted, ends with a challenge, not with despair: '*Jinhe naaz hai Hind par, unko lao!*' It's a challenge to us, '*Kyonki naaz humme hai Hind par*'.

26 April 2018

Countering the False Narrative

Landing at the Jolly Grant airport, we drove through the mountains for five hours to Chinyalisaur. At 6 p.m. when we reached, a group of fifty teachers was discussing the challenges that children encounter when trying to understand place value in maths. Teachers shared what had worked well in their classrooms. Each experience was critically appraised by the group, and a few fell apart in the examination. As the facilitator of the session was wrapping up the session, the teachers asked me to speak. We were familiar with each other, since I had been visiting them at least once a year for the past five years.

It was 7.30 p.m. We had to drive on to Uttarkashi and they had to go home. Some had come for this evening meeting of the Voluntary Forum of Teachers from as far as 20 km, on their two-wheelers. That meant a forty-five-minute ride back in the dark in the mountains. I said it was too late, but they insisted. They wanted me to speak about the *Teacher Absenteeism Study* that we had published in April 2017. I have written about the study in these columns (see 'The False Narrative of Teacher Absenteeism'). The gist of the study is that the absenteeism numbers for teachers from schools is about 2.5 per cent. This is sharply different from the popular imagination of absenteeism, with numbers between 25 per cent and 50 per cent routinely brandished, with no basis. The study also delves into other research reports, including one from the World Bank titled, 'The Fiscal Cost of Weak Governance: Evidence from Teacher Absence in India', which when studied carefully point to absenteeism numbers between 2.5 per cent and 5 per cent. I described the study. They listened carefully and applauded at every key point.

It's unusual for a research study to receive applause anywhere, let alone in a small town in the mountains. But if you have talked to teachers this would be unsurprising, because the conclusions of the study demolish the core myth behind the false vilification of teachers that is rife in our country. Rarely does any non-teacher attempt to understand their reality, and even rarer is any public counter to the false narrative.

One of them started narrating, as many joined in, an incident from the previous week. A local newspaper had a story with the headline: 'Sub-divisional-magistrate Conducts Raids in Schools, Finds 54 Teachers Missing'. The sensationalist headline was supported by the misleading story, which made no attempt to explain that fifty-three of the fifty-four teachers were not in schools because they had been sent for training on government orders. They were not missing. Over the next few days, the protestations of the teachers were ignored by the newspaper. After all, in today's media world, truth is not sufficient to stop catchy headlines and stories shaped by ideological commitments.

That newspaper in Garhwal is not very different in its quality on this matter from *The Economist*. The British weekly ran an editorial and an associated story last week on Indian schools. The two pieces are full of pedestrian analysis and sanctimonious prescriptions. It dishes out the weekly's all-purpose medicine for education, increased private schooling through vouchers. It has not even paused to consider that through the Right of Children to Free and Compulsory Education Act, 2009 or Right to Education Act, 2009 (RTE) norms, India already runs the world's largest virtual voucher programme. And that as private school enrolments have risen in the past ten years, learning levels have declined. The cavalier vilification of teachers by the two pieces is exemplified by their blasé assertion that a quarter of teachers play truant. Of course, there is no basis to this. But who is going to listen to Indian government schoolteachers in the face of an editorial from the venerable newspaper, *The Economist*?

In that week, I must have met over 300 teachers in Uttarkashi, Maneri, Barkot, Naugaon and Purola. These meetings were of groups of teachers, who meet regularly to learn from each other, to improve as teachers. All the meetings were in the evening, the teachers investing their own time and money. In every meeting, we went through the same conversation as in Chinyalisaur. The conversations acted as balm, however temporary.

The next week, I was in central Rajasthan. I met 200 teachers in similar meetings in Newai, Tonk, Malpura and Aligarh. The conversations were similar. The refrain echoes across the country.

Teachers live singed by the injustice of their vilification. Especially when in reality they give everything to perform a complex role, often in very trying circumstances. The weak are always the easiest to convert to folk devils and witches, and burnt at the stake. And that is what we are doing with our teachers.

That is not only unjust, but ineffective. Education can improve only as much as classroom pedagogic practice and school culture improve. This improvement is dependent entirely on teachers. And that cannot happen by shaming them or with fear and threats, especially because teaching is a complex and creative endeavour.

We need teachers to be enthusiastic leaders of change, on their own. We need to invest in teachers and support them. Most of the 8.8 million teachers across the country are at it already, and will respond even more if this is done. But too many of us have cobwebs in our minds, and treat the 97.5 per cent teachers in the image like the truant 2.5 per cent, egged on by the likes of *The Economist*, that have no stake in our future.

22 June 2017

The False Narrative of Teacher Absenteeism

Almost all my columns are based on experiences involved with the work that the Azim Premji Foundation does in school education. But I have rarely written about what we do. Our work ranges from working directly with government (public) schools and teachers on the ground, to working on matters of curriculum and policy with various government bodies.

The most complex work is what we do on the ground, at the grassroots. Our team of about 1,000 people is spread across forty-four districts in five states. Most of these districts are disadvantaged on multiple socio-economic parameters. While our engagement in these districts is very intense, we are also active in another fifty to sixty districts in the same states. So, in all, we work in over 100 districts.

We are focused on the professional development of teachers, principals and other functionaries of the education system. We also collaborate with the state governments to help improve academic and institutional processes. All of this requires direct, continuous and sustained engagement with teachers and others. With this kind of deep engagement over many years, not much is hidden between us and the teachers. We get to work in this manner with hundreds of thousands of teachers and thousands of schools.

The past sixteen years of these engagements have taught us a lot. Perhaps the most important learning has been that most government schoolteachers are committed to their work. In my assessment, their commitment is markedly more than that of the average employee of a business organisation to their work. This reality of teachers is in sharp contrast to the popular narrative, which paints the average government schoolteacher as irresponsible and disengaged.

At the core of this popular narrative is the notion of very high teacher absenteeism—meaning that a large number of teachers just don't show up at work. People easily talk of absenteeism ranging from 25–50 per cent. This matter has such grip over the popular imagination that it is often talked of as the single biggest problem in Indian school education. Many of our policymakers tend to believe in and feed this narrative, and use it to inform policy action.

With all our experience, across years, with hundreds of thousands of teachers, we have never seen absenteeism rates even close to the numbers that are often talked of. So, a few months ago we decided to conduct a field study to systematically assess the rate of teacher absenteeism.

While there are nuances to the method, it basically involved going to schools unannounced on an average working day and noting down how many teachers were not in school and for what reason. The study involved 619 schools across six states, and is available on our website under the title *Teacher Absenteeism Study*.

The study observed a teacher absenteeism rate of 2.5 per cent. This is similar to the conclusion of other research studies when looked at closely, with their observed absenteeism numbers not more than 5 per cent. These numbers are clearly not even remotely close to the numbers in the popular narrative.

Some of the other studies are: *The Fiscal Cost of Weak Governance* (World Bank, July 2016), *How Much and What Kind of Teaching Is There in Elementary Education in India?* (World Bank, February 2014) and *Para-Teachers in India* (*The Economic & Political Weekly*, March 2010).

In our study, the overall percentage of teachers not in school was 18.5 per cent. As mentioned before, 2.5 per cent were playing truant, 7 per cent were out of school on other official work, including attending training, and 9 per cent were on bonafide leave.

These numbers are not very different from what you will find in any workplace. Most employees of any organisation are eligible for twenty-five to thirty days of leave of various kinds, which means 10–12 per cent of the total working days. This implies that it should be expected that in any such large workforce, on any given day up to 10–12 per cent people can be on leave. In fact, factories plan headcount and workflow on the basis of such an estimate. And is it so surprising to find 7 per cent of the people of your office out of the office on some legitimate and useful work?

The kernel that has been used to feed the frenzy of teacher absenteeism is the overall number of teachers out of school. Absence from schools for legitimate reasons has been conflated with absenteeism meaning rank truancy. This is done inadvertently and also deliberately. Fortunately in these post-truth days, filled with alternative facts, I don't need to attempt to explain how such a false notion can grip the popular imagination.

This false narrative is deeply damaging to Indian education. It vilifies and demotivates teachers, who are the most important actors in education. It often leads to ineffectual policy actions, all about controlling and monitoring teachers, rather than enabling and supporting them. It also feeds a culture of mistrust and suspicion, which is profoundly dysfunctional. Even 2.5 per cent absenteeism is unacceptable, but clearly it is not the biggest problem in Indian education. Would you demotivate 97.5 per cent of your employees for the sake of disciplining 2.5 per cent?

The average Indian teacher, committed to her work, dealing with some of the most challenging working conditions, performing the most complex of roles in our society, needs our support and not vilification. We can start by getting rid of one alternative fact, that of high teacher absenteeism.

2 April 2017

Superstitions and Science

For the past twenty-five years, I have been running in the morning, six days a week. Even when I travel, which I do often for work, I run. My estimate is that I have run in over 300 places in India. Finding a nice route is easy in small towns, but cities are a different matter. In cities, public spaces are virtually absent. We haven't bothered to build and nurture them. The roads are a mess in most places. But when I am home in Bengaluru, it is a pleasure to run. This is because the University of Agricultural Sciences, better known as Gandhi Krishi Vignan Kendra (GKVK), keeps the gates to its beautiful 1,600 acre campus open to the public. I wish more institutions would do the same across the country, creating more public spaces.

On any weekday morning, there are more than 200 people out walking or running in GKVK, most of them people like me, from outside GKVK. On weekends, these numbers swell to over 400. There are days on which the numbers drop to about half, say, the morning of Diwali. But on the morning of 22 July 2009, the drop was unprecedented. I ran for an hour at my usual time of 6 a.m. and saw only two people walking. After the first few minutes of running, seeing no one, where I was used to seeing scores, it occurred to me that I must have missed some crucial news—there must be a curfew.

But then it dawned on me that it was the day of the full solar eclipse. Only a partial eclipse was visible from Bengaluru, but it was a big event. Soon, I was able to test my hypothesis; there was another solar eclipse on 15 January 2010. Sure enough, there was the same sharp drop in the number of runners and walkers.

Life in India is suffused in superstition of various kinds, from the most bizarre to the innocuous. Everyone has their own stories and many their own superstitions. But I find the GKVK solar eclipse incident emblematic of a particularly curious aspect of superstitions in India. The surrender to the superstition of malign influence of solar eclipses is remarkable when it happens in the precincts of a science university. To see the grip of superstition so dramatically displayed in this modern tech city, in a science university, is astonishing. Does this have to do with our failure to separate religion and faith from belief in the supernatural? Or is this the result of shallow education, especially science education? Perhaps both. Scientific understanding can dispel superstitious and magical thinking without us losing our sense of wonder. Those who are deeply religious need not fear this. Religious life does not need magic and miracles to sustain itself. Instead, the very people who should know better, those who study, teach or research science, seem to be equally in the grip of superstitions. The proportion of such people doesn't seem to be different from the general population.

Some of this behaviour is probably a version of Pascal's Wager—that is, respecting a superstition may be a minor inconvenience, but probably a worthwhile one just in case there is some truth to it. Even this line of thinking, however, betrays a kind of muddled thought, which ought not to be there in a life of science scholarship and teaching.

All this is unsurprising given the nature of our education. Our curricular objectives may be very worthy, but the reality of education in the vast majority of our institutions is that it is merely memorisation of facts and procedures. This is true for humanities, social sciences and the physical sciences. It is also true of applied fields like engineering, medicine and law. For example, physics is reduced to facts, formulas and procedures, with no attempt at building conceptual understanding, let alone developing the capacities for application of the methods of science. And most important of all, the development and fostering of a scientific temper is neglected entirely.

Our classrooms are embroiled in conflict, animated by the beliefs of the educator being vastly different from our educational goals. How effective can a science teacher, who is in the grip of unscientific thinking, be? If a teacher's superstitions are visible on their gem-laden fingers or in the black mark to avert the evil eye, what scientific temper can they foster? While I am emphasising the matter of science in this piece, similar conflicts arise from the prejudices and beliefs of teachers about gender, caste, religion and more.

This is our messy socio-cultural reality. It is not going to change overnight. And it won't change by heaping derision on such people. As with most matters, even in this, there is no substitute for reasoned public and private dialogue. But, in addition, there must be explicit recognition of the responsibility of the educator to which they must be held accountable. Within the school or the college, their manifest behaviour must be in complete consonance with our educational goals—on the matter of scientific temper, and all our constitutional values—even if their personal values are conflicted. But sustainable resolution and real progress will happen when our teachers are transformed by their own education and their private and public lives are consistent with these intellectual and social values.

The same goes for our public figures, those in authority. If they live double lives full of belief in magic and the supernatural, then their actions will signal the same ambivalence. The full benefit of science and technology will never accrue to society till we reconcile this contradiction.

15 February 2018

Gender Equity in Education

The inner quadrangle of the school in Gulbarga was huge, and full of shiny triangular frames, wheels and other assembly parts of bicycles. In one of the corridors along the quadrangle, ten men were skilfully and rapidly assembling cycles. They were all from eastern Uttar Pradesh, and said that in another five days they would move on to a school in Sindagi. Through the summer these people, and many others like them, move from school to school across states, assembling cycles while schools are on vacation. When the schools reopen, the cycles are ready to be distributed.

Year after year this massive operation is run across the country, to help the education of girls. In Karnataka, the cycle scheme was launched in 2006. All girls from disadvantaged families in rural areas in Class VIII, in government and government-aided schools, are given free cycles. Unlike primary schools which are within a kilometre of all villages, schools with higher classes are at a distance away from most villages. These distances have a role to play in the higher dropout rate of girls. Commute across these distances present problems of the cost involved, the very real troubles girls face in commuting on foot and discriminating social norms. The cycles help with the commute, which also helps the family to make up its mind to let the girl continue studying in higher grades. Many states have a similar scheme, which is one amongst many that help girls get into and stay in schools.

From the early 1990s there have been sustained and massive efforts to drive gender equity in education in India, with a special focus on the education of girls. The Union government has played a central role, and the state governments have played their role. While the matter of gender equity was much talked about earlier, the real push came after the education policy of 1986. The District Primary Education Programme launched in 1994 and the Sarva Shiksha Abhiyan from 2001 had specific mandates of achieving gender equity. These nationwide programmes had multiple schemes and mechanisms to help enable this mandate. One crucial goal of gender equity has been achieved in India. The gender parity index which was 0.76 in 1991 is now 1 for primary schooling.

What this means is that in 1991, for every 100 boys in primary schools there were seventy-six girls, and now there are 100, that is, complete parity. In fact, this complete parity was achieved in 2008. To realise the full import of what has happened, this development has to be seen in the context of the dramatic growth in overall student enrolment numbers in the same period. Enrolment has gone up from about 65–70 per cent to 99 per cent. That is, earlier 65–70 per cent children of school-going age were enrolled in schools, now almost all children are in schools. Put another way, just about twenty-five years ago, 45–50 per cent of girls in India were in school, today almost all girls in India are in schools. This is a commendable achievement. As much as we ruminate over all that is wrong with our school education, we must pat ourselves on the back for this achievement.

In the same period, the gender parity index has gone from 0.6 to 0.9 for secondary schools and from 0.54 to 0.8 for higher education. That has also been significant progress. It's not as though all this progress is the result of only government programmes; there has been significant civil society mobilisation around this issue. Overall, the improvement has been driven by improvement in access (like more schools, cycle schemes), by changes in core educational factors (like teacher awareness and sensibility, inclusive texts) and by the evolving, changing social norms and expectations, which are partly influenced by the spread of education itself. Every month I meet parents of students in rural government schools; often, many times a month. I always ask them, why they send their children to schools. The responses are always complex.

In the case of boys, the response is a mix of economic, developmental and social aspirations—he will get a good job, he will gain confidence, there is no respect without being educated, education is the only path to higher status. In the case of girls, the responses rarely have direct economic aspiration, and have some different developmental and social aspirations—she will gain confidence, she will be able to take care of herself better, she will go (get married in) to a better family, it's necessary for respect. These differences in the reasons for sending girls and boys to school merely reflect the reality which we know well. Patriarchal attitudes and gender discrimination are very much within us, in the family and even in classrooms. That still must not diminish the achievement of gender parity in primary schools. For it tells us that we can make progress, with sustained and focused effort. Which is was what we need to do, on all the fronts in education that are in need of improvement.

30 April 2015

Politics and Education

He is a District Education Officer (DEO) of a district where even political parties hesitate to claim that India is shining. He spent two days with me, visiting schools. That is unusual. Many DEOs don't see any need to visit schools. He questioned the teachers empathetically but relentlessly. Officials treating teachers as fellow human beings is also unusual. The questioning was focused on two things: how to get the out-of-school children back and how to help the ones from most disadvantaged homes to learn. He was driven and socially sensitive, but also had a sound educational understanding. He regaled us with stories of skirmishes with the mightier powers in the system, of which he seemed to have more than his share.

One was about the local MLA (Member of Legislative Assembly) insulting him in a public meeting. He responded by announcing in the same public meeting that he would see to it that the man lost the next election. That man did lose the election. The DEO did have a role to play. He mobilised the teachers to campaign village by village. His political leanings were clear, so I commented that he ensured his own party candidate's defeat. He agreed and said there were greater things than party affiliations—nation-building is one of them—and added as an afterthought that you can't insult people in public and get away with it, whoever you are. This man is just about as good an educational administrator as one gets. He is also a political animal. It's his intense social purpose that fires both his educational work and engagement in politics.

This shouldn't surprise us; education is political in both a narrow sense and also in a broad sense. In the narrow sense, it is often directly part of party and electoral politics, with teachers and administrators directly participating and influencing the power equations of their communities and constituencies. But education influences politics deeply and fundamentally in the long run by altering the very way in which politics is structured and citizenship is exercised. We will get to the deep politics of education; let's first consider some things on the surface.

Teachers constitute 20–40 per cent of the state government workforces. As much as 99 per cent of the villages in India now have schools within 1 km. This provides direct reach to the most basic geographical communities in India. This structurally deep and comprehensive coverage of India by the school system enables teachers and teacher unions to play a role in politics on a continuing basis, and often significantly in elections. This political engagement is not merely for the sectional interest of teachers, but is an integral part of the on-the-ground organisational jostling of political parties. This shouldn't convey the impression that all or even most teachers are flag-waving members of some party or the other. But certainly, enough are to be an important element in the local political equations. No wonder, a big national-level politician recently threatened teachers in a particular state with dire consequences, unless they supported his party.

Education is widely recognised, understood and used as one of the most important social processes for the development of individuals and the society. Most choices and practices in education, at their core, will also have political roots and implications. This is true for aims of education, curriculum, institutional arrangements, inclusions and exclusions, school practices—almost everything. For our school education, the basic political roots are expressly drawn from the Constitution. Let's take a few examples.

The National Curricular Framework, 2005 emphasises,

within the aims of education, its role as an enabler of democracy and in developing individual autonomy. The Right to Education Act, 2009 is aimed at an inclusive, egalitarian society. The various mechanisms of support for disadvantaged or discriminated groups directly draw from constitutional frameworks. But these constitutional roots only set the limits and inform education at a very fundamental and broad level. Often choices within this constitutional framework are the real issues of politics. It's much like the rest of the polity: people and parties operate (or profess to) within the Constitution, but have sharply differing agendas and policies.

The real political battleground in education has been in textbooks, in school culture and policies related to language. For example, glorification of the Soviet Union, vilification of Tipu Sultan and sprinkling a dose of ancient texts in science are all political choices. Textbooks have become weapons of insidious politics, given their significant influence over actual education.

Political battles in school culture have been fought through rituals—choices on celebration of events, of festivals and assembly prayers. Choice of languages taught in school, the variants of language that get primacy, for instance, sanskritised Hindi over Hindustani, and treatment of English have been political instruments and statements.

This deep politics of education can't win immediate elections, but when done systematically and then sustained, can shape the political character of society significantly. When we vote in polling booths, most of which are in schools, it's in a way symbolic of the influence of schools on politics at multiple levels.

30 April 2014

Education: Who Is Accountable?

There is a lot of talk of accountability in education. This is directly related to the increasing anxiety about performance of schools, across the world, as well as in India. Most often, the talk is of accountability of teachers. The explicit subtext is that the key reason why our school education is in poor shape is that schools and teachers are not accountable. Why is this issue so vexed?

Shouldn't it be quite simple, that is, teachers and schools should be accountable for the learning of children? Let's consider some aspects of this issue; let's start with the word 'accountability' and its usage. Much of the usage of that word today has roots in the notions arising from the world of business. Those notions are modelled on mechanistic systems, where people are given tasks, made responsible for something and then they are accountable for delivering the results. This task would have dependencies, resource constraints and environmental challenges. The world of business recognises all this, and factors it to some extent, but on the whole approximates to the mechanistic model. Sales people are accountable for their targets, factories for their output and quality and chief executive officers (CEOs) for earnings growth. The mechanistic model struggles with accountability of human resource people and R&D engineers, but businesses gloss over that as aberrations which need to be accommodated as best as possible within the model. The use of this mechanistic notion of accountability for social institutions and processes is a basic problem.

If we think of the Parliament being accountable for developing a better India, we will get a sense of what I am talking about. Indeed, the Parliament is responsible for developing a better

India, but not alone and not in a mechanistic manner, unlike achieving sales targets for soaps for the year.

Schools too can be easily misread as mere service delivery mechanisms. It doesn't help matters that many schools do behave as commercial outlets. This makes them seem fit for the mechanistic model of accountability.

This is fundamentally flawed. Schools are anything but mechanistic systems; they are some of the most fundamental social institutions. And education is a complex process based on human relationships, with broad humanistic, social and democratic aims. This certainly includes what are generally talked of as the basic goals of learning (like in language, maths), but goes well beyond and deeper than that. So, in systems like this, is it not possible to talk of accountability?

Indeed it is, once we dump the notion of mechanistic accountability. Teachers and others in the school system have significant space for creative and good work, which gives them definite responsibility, but not mechanistic accountability. One way to think of it is that school systems have a web of accountability—including for learning. Participants in this system have various accountabilities, all linked and related to each other. For the system to function well, these accountabilities must be aligned with each other, and with the aims of education.

Schools as organisations have an accountability to the regulations that govern them. Teachers have accountability for certain hygiene factors, like showing up at work, banishing corporal punishment, etc. Teachers also have a deep accountability to a code of professional conduct and behaviour, which arises from the idea of education, of which they are the most important custodians. The community around the school is accountable for nurturing the school. Parents are accountable for getting their children in school and (many of them) for the complex interplay of the home environment with the school. Some sets of experts are accountable for developing a curricular framework and structure, which is educationally sound and responsive to the ideals of the society. The teacher-education system is accountable for the preparation of our teachers. Those who conduct school-leaving examinations are accountable for the examinations to assess real education. 'Higher-up administrators' are accountable for the culture, effectiveness of mechanisms and providing support where required. The government is accountable for the level of public financing and regulatory structure of the school system. We—you and me—are accountable for the societal expectations that we set for education and the relative priority that we give to it in reality.

This web of accountability is not a snapshot of a moment, but has built cumulatively, historically over time. For example, there is no one group of experts accountable for the curricular framework, but many groups collectively over the past few decades. This whole account would be enormously frustrating for those looking for who to hold accountable for the learning levels in schools. Can we think of a war in the past 6,000 years, where the soldiers can be held accountable for defeat? That's not because soldiers are not important; they are in fact the most important. But we know that the complexity of war is such that soldiers in themselves are not accountable for the war and its outcome. Education is far more complex than war, and not just because it's a continuing social enterprise.

There is no simple way of thinking about accountability in education.

19 March 2014

A Day on the Road

Till about four years ago, I lived with severe acrophobia. Garhwal cured me. I don't understand how, but driving for hours on narrow, crumbling roads, with 400–600 m drops on one side did this.

The cure was tested to its limits two months ago by Jagmohan. He took Anant and me to villages in the mountains that had been completely cut-off by the deluge in June 2013. The roads to these villages were being repaired, but it was taking time. The purpose of the visit was to see how the schools in these villages had coped with months of tenuous connection to the rest of the Uttarkashi district. We would drive for a few hundred metres and then there would be no road. And Jagmohan would say, '*Ye thoda risky hai.*' (This one is a bit risky.) He is an understated person; this phrase was in keeping with his character.

Anant is a man of the mountains. Even he sat tense through each leg of the journey. It didn't affect me any more than him. That night we met Col. Ajay Kothiyal, principal of the Nehru Mountaineering Institute, who has climbed Everest twice. He has played a key role in the relief and rehabilitation operations in that area since the deluge. He raised his eyebrows in surprise when he heard of our day's journey: 'Well, that's something.' That's the top medal for me.

The schools haven't got any medals. They opened up three–four weeks after the deluge. To operate, they have to manage a range of activities; in addition to teaching, for example, they have to get the salt and rice for the mid-day meal, have to report back on what's going on in the school, have to get paper and chalk. All of it is simple elsewhere, but not here, where every narrow mountain road fades into a narrower crumbling dirt track.

The teachers have to be there to run the schools. How do they get there? Usually, most teachers commute from wherever they live to the villages they are posted in. With the bad state of the roads, the daily commute has become much longer and riskier. They have figured out solutions; some have taken up rooms in the school. The district education administration has also got volunteers from each of these severely affected villages to help out at their local schools. So, somehow the schools go on. Three of the schools that we went to brought to life an example of alternative roads in life.

The first one had two teachers and about fifty children. The head teacher had been transferred from some other school a few months ago. He was not very happy. The children seemed disinterested. He seemed like a reasonable man, but couldn't get his mind away from how unreasonable his transfer was. During the time that we were there, he had no interaction with any of the students. He has been a teacher for over twenty years.

The second school had one young teacher. She was living in that village, which was perched somewhere high in the mountains. Her family lives 50 km away; she visits them on the weekends. The children were playing enthusiastically in the sun. The teacher was energetic, and had incisive comments about her pre-service teacher education programme. The kids seemed to like her.

Even in the brief conversation, she seemed to flit between enthusiasm and uncertainty about her profession. She liked teaching and the kids, but she felt alone in the school. The community was supportive, but living away from her family was not practical. Every sentiment had its opposite in her.

We walked down a steep slope for thirty minutes to get to a third school. It was a two-room building with a verandah facing west. As we walked in, we saw two teachers sitting there, surrounded by about sixty children, engaged in intense activity. They were completely engrossed and did not notice us. When one of the teachers saw us, she was embarrassed. They continued to sit there with the children, and work with them, while they talked with us. They had been teachers for over twenty years and loved their work. It felt like a good school, and Jagmohan said it was.

The young woman in the second school may end up like the teachers in the third school, or like the one in the first school. Which road she will take depends on many things, but certainly also on the kind of support the education system provides her.

Our system design has the required support mechanisms in the form of cluster- and block-level resources, but we have to make them function. My thoughts about the road ahead for the young teacher faded away as we took the non-existent roads back to Uttarkashi, leaving just the wonder of schools that work every day where even a day is an adventure for most of us.

8 January 2014

Seeking Philosophers

Whichever university I go to speak at, I make it a point to say that we are recruiting philosophers, especially those interested in school education. Once, a professor came up to me and said that his philosophy department had thirteen people pursuing PhDs. In other places, even the memories of a philosophy department aren't there, let alone thirteen active PhD students. The head of the philosophy department arrived later and began with an apology. Recruiting from his PhD student group was not possible. All of them were middle-level officials in the state government's animal husbandry and fisheries department. He told me that they had no interest in philosophy or animals or fish, their only interest was to add to their list of degrees.

We have not had much success in recruiting philosophers. Good philosophy departments in India are few and far between. The en masse desertion of the social sciences and humanities by middle-class students has hurt philosophy more than other disciplines. 'Philosophy *karoge kya?*' (You'll study philosophy?) is a form of derision, covering not just the discipline but also any other tendency to think versus do. It is often compared to something more 'real' like pursuing a course in enterprise resource-planning implementation or English for BPOs. But why are we so desperately seeking philosophers?

Actually, we are not seeking philosophers as much as those who can think about issues that are within the broad area of philosophy of education. This thinking includes relating it to education practice, and working with others on these issues. It needs rigorous, critical and systematic inquiry into basic questions. This is what (loosely) constitutes the method of philosophy. A good student of philosophy is better placed to do this, so long as she is interested in the questions relevant to our work. Others interested in the same questions, with willingness and ability to employ the philosophical method, do equally well. So, what are these questions and issues?

I can give only a partial, illustrative list: what are the aims and functions of education? Is education about the transmission of knowledge and conformity, or is it about the development of autonomy? Is education for personal liberation or social change? What should form the content of education and why? What is to know, to have learnt something? Should all children have the same education or different groups have different kinds of education? Should the content accommodate views and perspectives of all social groups, and if so how, and why at all? What is the difference between educating versus teaching versus training versus indoctrination? What notion of good and good society must education foster, if at all? All the preceding questions need not be discussed in the bipolar manner that they have been posed, it could be a bit of this and that, and then the questions that arise are about which bit where, and how that is to be decided. But why are we interested in these questions and their implications for the practice of education? Aren't these so basic that they have been sort of settled or aren't they at such broad a level that they have no direct relevance for most people in education?

Let me go back to where I started. We need people who can deal with these issues, because we need them in our work, not because we have some particular fascination for philosophical enquiry. Our work in education ranges from the capacity development of teachers and administrators, to curriculum development, to running an education-focused university. We have worked in education for years and others have worked far longer. All of us have learnt that these questions and issues are immediately and directly relevant to all kinds of work in education. Those who are most effective have learnt to deal with these in relevant ways, whether they call it philosophy or not.

Let's take an example of how this comes to life every day. Should a student accept something as true because the teacher says so? Or should the teacher develop a reasoned argument? Why should the teacher do this—because it's important to develop autonomy of thought or because of respect for a fellow human being who just happens to be their student? What should the teacher do if that reasoned argument confronts the child's cultural beliefs? Exposure to issues of philosophy of education will help the teacher recognise and resolve these questions. Given the process of learning, the nature of education and its purposes, philosophy and practice are inseparable, even though the practitioner may not recognise it. All practice often involves unexamined assumptions that are ripe for philosophical scrutiny. Since education has a deep impact, for better or for worse, on the next generation, it is important that teachers, principals and administrators become reflective practitioners. While philosophy alone will not do the job, it is an essential ingredient. That is why India needs people able to philosophise rigorously about education, even if they are not academic philosophers.

21 August 2013

Expectations and Understanding
of Education

There is a 600 sq. km area with twenty-four villages, called Bhakhar, in Sirohi district. It's all low hillocks, with scores of streams criss-crossing at the foot. Living conditions are tougher than in adjoining areas. Getting around is more difficult, and there is hardly any cultivable land.

There was a community meeting in a panchayat hall in Bhakhar. It was a dialogue on how to improve their schools. After a lively discussion, a lady asked a question and then many lent their voice to it. They all wanted to know why examinations were being stopped in schools. How would they know whether the children were learning, if they didn't get examination scores?

There are very sound educational and pedagogical reasons for using methods like continuous and comprehensive evaluation (CCE), despite its implementation being complex and difficult. The country is discovering these challenges, now that the Right to Education Act, 2009 has mandated CCE up to Class VIII. In CCE, every child's learning is assessed on an ongoing basis, and that is used in an integrated manner to teach the child better. For example, if a child is having problem with fractions, he or she is assessed in the class, the issues carefully noted and then relevant strategies used in the next classes to help the child. This method is in sharp contrast to the child taking a test at the end of the term and getting poor scores on fractions, which is of little use, aside from telling the child 'you didn't do well'. The CCE system develops a rich document of a child's progress on multiple dimensions, through the term, which is pedagogically useful. But it doesn't give any scores or 'marks'.

It was this issue that was being referred to in the panchayat hall in Bhakhar. We had a long discussion on that question. We tried to converse about CCE in common language, not education-speak. The simplicity of scores, the clarity of pass or fail, and the social importance of 'marks', all this and more were battling with CCE in their minds. The conversation didn't leave them satisfied, but there was some progress.

Elsewhere, in a big city there was another meeting. It was a plush conference room, uncomfortable despite its size and the air conditioner. The minister of education of a large state was sitting opposite me. It's because of this that he kept looking at me, as he asked the question, though it was addressed to others as well. The question was the same as in Bhakhar, though his interest in it was for different reasons. He said that since 'you educationists' had decided to drop exams, it must be the right thing to do. But he didn't understand why it was so, and when the people in his constituency questioned him, he felt at a loss. There were more than twenty of us whom he had classified as educationists. We didn't give him a satisfactory answer. The educationists didn't speak a language to which he could relate. Some dismissed the question silently as if it had a self-evident answer. He didn't leave any better informed.

CCE is an example of the wide gap between the average person's expectations and understanding of education, and our policies and curricula. Our curricula and policies increasingly reflect what I have said elsewhere called the 'progressive consensus'. This consensus includes attempts to move away from rote learning, building analytical ability, learning-to-learn, etc. It is informed by developments in fields as varied as psychology, neurosciences, sociology and philosophy. It is based on the nature of knowledge, the principles of how children learn and develop, the integral role of social context and the humanistic, liberal democratic aims of education. In their design, our curricula bring together what is educationally effective and is socially important.

While there is a large gap between the curricula and policies, and their implementation, there is clarity on which way our education is supposed to go. It is important to preserve this broad consensus. Can we take this for granted? I sense a significant risk.

Many stakeholders, including parents, political and community leaders and a large number of teachers, are more comfortable with the older methods which seem to be more easily understood, as in the case of assessment. Their expectations are also influenced by current social factors and the history of education practice.

This gap between the progressive consensus and expectations of people, in the backdrop of broader social-economic dynamics like commercialisation of education and political polarisation, makes the consensus very, very fragile. Not from within, but from outside. I fear that the primacy of the consensus in determining policy may wither away, and it will be left only in name in a few documents. We need to recognise this risk, and work on it as much as on the policy implementation gap. We must avoid the temptation to ignore those who disagree or (we think) do not understand. This requires a genuine dialogue, in a language that people relate to, and not from some intellectual high ground. It is important that the minister and the people of Bhakhar remain part of the debate.

7 August 2013

Redemption of Faith

Sardar 'Pinder' Singh Bhangra was an adventurer. Even he had a tingling sensation when he saw the spectacular sight of the 6,316 m high Bandarpunch Peak. This was somewhere on the long, winding and climbing road to Uttarkashi. In an exercise of local myth-making, that spot is now called Tingling Point. I also felt the tingling, but not because of the view of the peak, which I couldn't see at all as it was covered by clouds right from the bottom of the Assi Ganga Valley, but because of my chat with Dhiraj. He was selling vegetables at Tingling Point. It was cold, but the twelve-year-old didn't seem to feel it at all. We negotiated with him the price of thorny bitter gourd, and admired his strength that allows him to carry 20–30 kg of vegetables up that steep hill and down the deep valley. He takes two days off every week from school to sell the vegetables. The days are set— Monday and Wednesday. From the way he spoke, he seems to be taking school seriously. He said, *'Aaj ke liye sabji, aage ke liye school* (Vegetables for today and education for the future); wisdom indeed, for a twelve-year-old; enough to leave me tingling.

It was another day, another stop, on another winding road in the Garhwal; this time for lunch, at Lakshmi's hut. I hesitate to call it a 'dhaba', because the word has acquired pop grandeur, and this really was a hut. My shepherd and friends, Anant, Jagmohan and Prakash, know Lakshmi well because of the countless trips on those treacherous roads. We had carried spinach, potato and tomato, knowing that at the precarious height of Lakshmi's hut, vegetable supply is unreliable. She was quite upset with that. She said: 'Don't you know in this season, our patch gives enough vegetables?' Anant, Prakash and Lakshmi then cooked the best meal I have had outside of home in a long time. She kept chatting with us, like an old friend.

I learnt that her husband is a daily wage earner. He is skilled as a mason, but he does whatever work he gets. He leaves early, and is back after nightfall. Her old father-in-law helps her in running the kitchen, and growing vegetables in season (which they also sell). On a good day she may feed twenty travellers like us; on a bad day she has to be happy with none. I asked her how much money they made. Enough to survive and to send her two children to school and her brother to college, she said. That, according to her, was the central, long-term issue: education. She kept the vegetables which we had brought only after much cajoling, and we left on the winding road.

The plains of Raichur in north-east Karnataka do not have the aesthetic or spiritual succour of the Himalayas. They can grind a visitor down, especially in the summers. On such a hot summer afternoon, Raghavendra showed me videos which he had made on an inexpensive camera. It was a patient investigation of why schools have low attendance during the cotton-picking season.

Children don't show up at school because they are especially 'capable' of cotton picking: they don't have to bend to pick the low-growing cotton balls, since they are short, and their hands are gentler than that of an adult. This is in addition to the simpler fact that when cotton has to be picked, it has to be picked, so it's sort of all-hands-on-deck. Anyone familiar with those areas won't find this surprising. What is actually (pleasantly) surprising is that these children are enrolled in schools, and at most other times they do go to school. This is the first generation in these communities going to school. They do it because they have started believing that school education is important.

The massive increase in enrolment numbers in schools over

the past two decades or so, across India, isn't an adequate picture. It hides actual attendance numbers of children and there is also a bit of fudging of data on the ground. But the massive increase is real, and does accurately reflect a very critical change across our country: across class, caste and creed, there is a dramatic increase in the importance of school education.

Battling every conceivable physical, economic and social shackle, 200 million children are showing up in Indian schools. They show up with the faith that education is their future. Lakshmi works for that, Dhiraj pauses work for that. They put their faith in the education system and entrust it with their future. We know the state of our school education. The schools do not deserve this faith of millions yet. The only redemption is in giving it our best shot; we have generated the faith, now we have to at least try our hardest to fulfil it.

The state of school education, as I have argued in these columns, needs fundamental change at all levels: teaching, curriculum, assessment and school administration.

14 November 2012

Good People, Hard Places

Hoshangabad is 60 km south of Bhopal. Many paths in Indian education lead there, because that is where they started. You may know of the city only as a train station on the Delhi–Chennai line. The city now has a population of 1,50,000 and it's a district headquarters. Glimpses of the present are unmistakable in the city, even though it seems to be still in the 1980s. It's not hard to imagine what it might have been really like in the 1970s. In the '70s, the city's sole claim to fame rested on the superhit *Naya Daur* having been shot 10 km away in Budni. That is when the quiet revolution in education started there. The fires were lit with the Friends Rural Centre and Kishore Bharati, which evolved into the Hoshangabad Science Teaching Programme (HSTP).

Good thinking and good work in education had happened before HSTP in India, of that there is no doubt, and it continues to happen. But there had been nothing like HSTP. There never had been an attempt in India to improve education in government schools, where improvement meant scientific temper and learning to think, with good education as a path to social justice, at the scale and in the reality of real India. HSTP attempted to do this across the district of Hoshangabad. It was inspiring and inspired. HSTP itself changed and evolved, spawning efforts on a larger scale, and then eventually shut down. Over the past three decades, HSTP has continued to inspire and influence education in India: through its ideas, its people and its methods.

You can see the spirit of HSTP in the National Curricular Framework, 2005, in the excellent NCERT textbooks, in the various kinds of activity-based learning methods in many states, in the hundreds of people and organisations that carry its fire.

But most of all you can see it in the now-legitimate mainstream idea that education is about learning to think and about social justice.

This column is not about HSTP, which will need a few reams. It's about the starting point of HSTP. The starting point of HSTP was the decision of people like Anil Sadgopal to go and live in Hoshangabad. Actually, he lived in Bankhedi, a village 90 km from Hoshangabad.

He was a Caltech (California Institute of Technology)-educated scientist at the Tata Institute of Fundamental Research, when he decided to make the move. The revolution of HSTP was also fired by similar decisions by Kamal, Sadhna, Hardy, Vinod, Anjali, Anwar, Syag and many more.

They were (and are) all good people. Most of them were from large cities. While for all of them the choice to serve a social cause was the fundamental point, HSTP would not have happened had they not willingly moved to Hoshangabad. No amount of their commitment and capability would have fired the revolution that happened, if they had chosen to live in Delhi.

Over time, I have come around to the view that to make change happen where it is needed most, the central question is: how will good people move to those places? I sense that this is true for all social issues, while I have experienced it in education. 'Those places' is most of India. The country's 680-odd districts have over 6,000 blocks. Your guess is as good as mine as to how many of those places people want to move to, or to continue to stay in, if they have ambition and capability. In fact, the greater the need in a district, the more 'difficult' it will be. The reality that we can't escape is: to make change happen in education, we need strong teams in each of the districts, with presence in each of the blocks. Without that proximity, the deep, sustained and continuous academic support that schools and teachers require is impossible. So that we don't go on a tangent: technology can help, but can't replace this on-the-ground effort and you can't 'send people for training'—no amount of short-term training away from their context can help.

Each of our districts has between 800 to 4,000 schools; put together any two–three districts and they are like Finland. One can imagine the depth of expertise required locally to make any real change happen. The government has created structures with this reality in mind. There are block-level academic support people and each district has a District Institute of Education and Training.

However, either these positions are staffed with people who do not have the required expertise or the positions are vacant. Do 'good people' need to only move from outside? In a sense—no; over the long term, the capacity of people who live in all places can be developed. But to make that happen, we still need people there—sort of pioneering groups. My experience suggests it's possible, it's happening. Often it only needs one man or woman to say, 'I will move'. Then people follow.

Sounds romantic? But it does happen. Anil has shown that, so have many others, including people that I work with every day in Yadgir, Barmer, Uttarkashi, Dhmatari and so on.

5 September 2012

Profits and Schools

The 6 ft 3 inch frame, and a boxer's build, suggests that Prabhu can handle whatever may be required to be handled in Bellary. Although, what Prabhu handles is altogether more innocuous and a lot more meaningful than what is usually handled in Bellary. He runs a well-regarded school.

When I met him last, he had come back from a short course at the Harvard Graduate School of Education. He narrated in a matter-of-fact manner, how he started more than ten years ago with the belief that he would run a high-quality, financially self-sustaining school, and how hard that has been. His experience has taught him that the attempt to run a good-quality school is very hard to make financially self-sustaining. His ideas of quality have taught him to respect a set of basics, and he doesn't compromise on these basics. These include: the number of teachers in school, their compensation, their professional development and that of other staff, improvements in curriculum, curriculum support material and infrastructure. In his experience, the cost structure built up by the basics demands that he charges a price in the market (school fees), which is unavailable. The size of that segment of the market that can pay that fee is so small that the costs are unsustainable. And this is Bellary, not exactly the most impoverished of places in India.

Prabhu has an MBA, with many years of history in business; he is not a dreamy-eyed idealist. It's just that he wants to run a good school, without compromises. He bravely trudges along on the edge of financial abyss, often supporting the school through income from other business and contributions made by like-minded philanthropists.

His story is, in no way, unique. There are hundreds of such people, across the country, striving to provide good education, within their means and context. There are also many more running schools for profit. They will never state it as their goal, but that is the truth. You can see that in the compromise that they make on the basics, often shockingly so. While in a country as large as India, there are always exceptions, there are few other ways to profit in schools.

Profits and money are not just important, but essential, in any society. But money, finance and economics may be very limiting and invalid perspectives, in certain contexts. Actions driven by them may just not work, in these domains.

It doesn't work in schools. A closer look, even through the limited view of education as a 'service', in the framework of markets, is enough to highlight some of these reasons. One set of issues arises from the ever-present information and knowledge asymmetry between the provider of education, that is, the school, and its users, that is, children and parents. In a situation like this, the provider must do their best—an honest attempt to deliver good service—irrespective of whether the user discriminates between what is good and not-so-good.

This is a professional obligation. You do expect that a doctor would do her honest best for her patient, although the patient may have no idea what is good (or best). The school situation is akin, but the professional obligation on the school is even greater. This is because of two reasons: one, at a real, practical level the ability of the user to 'shop around' for alternative providers is very limited, because the rhythm of schooling makes location an almost insurmountable constraint. Two, the school is responsible, in very deep ways, for the present and future life of the child, and by the collective future of its students, it also influences society.

In this situation of asymmetry, to do an honest job of its

professional obligation, the school's cost structures become such that the fee required to make it sustainable (forget profitable) is not available; primarily because it's simply unaffordable by a very large majority in the country.

The unfortunate fact is that there are hundreds of seemingly respectable schools giving short shrift to the basics of good education. This pursuit of profits through short shrift is scandalous. In the doctor analogy, this is like, 'I will keep charging you a relatively low fee, because that is what you can pay, but not cure you, though I know what it takes to cure you; because this is my business.'

I have just scratched the surface of the issue of profits and education. Let me leave for other occasions attempts to talk about even more fundamental issues in this regard—what the value of education is, which, in turn, is linked to the issue of the purpose of education, the long term and often immeasurable impact of school education and so on.

At the heart of all this is an acceptance that money and economics are not necessarily the most relevant frames of reference for all human endeavours. And that profit is not a legitimate pursuit in a social relationship of trusteeship such as education.

2 July 2011

Land and Livelihood

Through the flawless, unbroken white of February snow, driving for hours at a stretch, I would cross silent villages of a dozen or so houses every 20-odd miles. I was blessed to have a job that let me drive around the stunningly beautiful landscapes of Sweden. That beauty never hid the extreme challenge of living in such places, where 20 degrees below zero counts as normal. And I would wonder: why do people live here?

I asked the same question late on a May night, thirty years ago, driving with my father across the dry, cracked plains of interior Chhattisgarh in an official white Ambassador, unrelenting heat radiating from the land. That question—why people live in extreme physical circumstances—has a complex answer. One critical strand of it is that people are deeply connected to the land that they live on. This connectedness is difficult for most of us city-dwellers to feel. It comes from living off the land.

Outside the city, whether in Sweden or Chhattisgarh, land is livelihood. So, people live (often in migrant modes) where the land is, braving all that comes along. Sitting in an office in Bengaluru or Delhi, this deep and complex dependency is hard to empathise with. Which is why we don't easily understand that it is not possible to make 'rural India' self-employable simply by 'skilling' people to be plumbers or electricians. Rural India needs sustainable 'livelihood' improvement.

Because 72 per cent of India is still rural, most of this livelihood is related to land. The National Sample Survey says that 89 per cent of rural India depends on self-generated livelihood (agricultural and others) and related labour. This will no doubt change, but only over decades.

Hence, having skills and developing them are necessary, but woefully insufficient. Livelihood requires more—knowledge and networks, both social and cultural. It requires access to natural physical resources—forests, grazing lands, water sources (what I have collectively called 'land'). Beyond all this, it depends on rights—legal and social. The micro reality of this complex mesh that constitutes livelihood is determined by our macro socio-political choices. It depends on our model of development, followed consciously and unconsciously. The inevitability of urbanisation, the importance of industrialisation, expansion of services, sustainable development, steady state economy or Hind Swaraj—it doesn't matter where our hearts and heads lie. What matters is that over 800 million Indians live off the land that they live on—a fact that won't change much for decades to come.

This land is under pressure. Population growth in the past few decades has doubled the human burden on land. At the same time, land productivity has declined, and there are now legitimate competing uses for a declining quantum of land. The methods of agriculture and subsidies, which delivered the Green Revolution, are no longer effective, and are actually significantly degrading sustainability.

To address livelihood issues, the ten-year-old Swarnajayanti Gram Swarozgar Yojana was transformed into the National Rural Livelihoods Mission (NRLM) in 2009-10. A reading of its plan shows the scale and complexity that it tries to deal with. It doesn't skirt the basic connection of livelihood to land, and to social, cultural and political dimensions.

Yet, the average Indian realism will say that some of that complexity will never be addressed with any degree of efficacy. NRLM was allocated Rs 2,914 crore in the recent budget. That in no way seems to be an adequate resource. Perhaps it's not just the money, but also the approach. NRLM still makes me hopeful, because it attempts to deal with what is necessary, but is usually an afterthought—a footnote in all the discussions on our grand pursuit of 8–9 per cent growth rates.

Working with education in rural India, we have a ringside view of this extremely complex issue. Livelihood affects education, and vice versa. The simplistic notions of 'vocational training/ education' have little use: when livelihood is so inextricably linked to land and the local milieu, apprenticeship within the family and village is the only practical vocational training. And this is usually how villages operate, though we (and they) may not call it apprenticeship. But this is the subject of another column.

The connectedness of education to livelihood, as of livelihood to land, is deep. But we either seem to miss it, because we have lost it; or ignore it, because it's too complex to deal with. This may be a spiritual issue, but in the here and now, it is at the core of the economic well-being of well over 800 million people.

10 March 2011

PART FIVE

THOSE WHO GROW TREES

Those Who Grow Trees

The three trees towered over everything. There was nothing else of their great height in that rocky plain, making them visible from a few kilometres away as we approached the school. They stood in a straight line at the edge of the school grounds, about 20 m tall.

We sat in a room on the first floor, under the trees. In the two rooms of the ground floor, Classes I–VIII were in progress. The only teacher for the eight classes, with fifty-three students, was sitting quietly in the room with us, in a corner. He had given them an assignment, which allowed him to participate briefly in our discussion. Alumni of the school filled that small room as well. There were seventeen of them. Three had taken a ten-hour overnight bus to reach the school. The others had travelled from an hour or two away on their bikes or public buses. Only two of them now lived in the village. As the introductions progressed, so did my bafflement. Why had all these young people turned up, travelling for hours? It was just a usual school visit for me, one of many every month. It was supposed to be just a chat with the teacher and students and, if possible, with local community members. This was not a ceremony of any sort.

Their answer was simple. It had been years since someone interested in education from outside that area had visited their school. They wanted to ensure that the story of their school was told properly. They did not believe that the teacher, who had been their teacher too, would do that. So, they came to tell it themselves.

A long time ago, when they were little children, the school had had another teacher. He was kind and caring. Their days in the school were full of joy and excitement. He would teach them well and bother about each child. Not just their learning, but also their health and families. One day, the teacher and the kids decided to plant three trees. They chose badam. They couldn't recollect why, perhaps just because no one imagines badam trees in such hot, rocky and arid terrain. Life in the school went on, busy and fun. They tended to the trees, which turned from green to purplish to grey, as badam trees do. But, the next year, they encountered a storm.

Their teacher was transferred to another public (government) school and two others were brought in to replace him. One teacher was indifferent, the other was cruel. They have banished their memories of the details after that. In just a year, all but two of the thirty children left the school. Some enrolled in the public school in the nearby village. Many dropped out altogether. They left the school, but they did not leave the trees. They tended to them, watering them, pruning them, protecting them and they grew.

The year passed and, in the summer, the two new teachers were transferred out. They were replaced by the quiet man sitting in the corner. He took charge of his two students and of the three trees. The two children talked about him every day in the village. The children who tended to the trees saw that they were being cared for. Then he went out and spoke to those who would roam the fields all day, grazing the goats, or just drifting. The ones who had dropped out. He persuaded them to return to school.

One after another, all of them did. They were followed by those who had enrolled in other schools. Within a year, they were followed by children from nearby villages, having heard of the quiet man who could 'teach everything to any child' and was so kind, as only a child could be. When the cohort of the eldest children reached Class V, the government expanded the school to a middle school so that the children could stay in the same school with the same teacher. There was no additional teacher appointed. The teacher started running the school all seven days of the week—having to teach all eight classes. In time, the eldest cohort graduated from Class VIII and left to join the nearest high school. However, they did not really leave. They would all be back on Sundays and evenings and holidays, so that their teacher could teach them.

More than a decade has passed. The quiet man goes about his work every day, as he has done all these years. Life is much the same in that school. However, life is not what it was for his students who had gathered there and not for the scores of others who were not there. Life for them now is what they could not have dared to imagine in their small, poverty-stricken village. Two of those who took the ten-hour bus ride work for a leading global IT firm. Another is a doctor. The rest of the seventeen are police inspectors, teachers, public servants, successful businesspeople and one is a rising politician.

'We have come here to tell you this story. He is the God we believe in. Only we can tell you that. So here we are.' He was squirming in his chair and at the first pause in the conversation excused himself to go to the classes.

When we finished, he came to see us off at the car with a gentle radiant smile as though he was with his pups. 'Don't believe them, Sir,' he said, 'they exaggerate everything. They are just very good children.'

Our car sped away, everything receded as we looked back, but the three trees did not.

Anything can grow to a great height, in any terrain, if you care, care enough.

12 March 2020

Kisko Fursat Hai Jo Thaame
Deewanon Ka Haath

The pride of the crimson tilak on his forehead did not determine his demeanour. His posture, voice, words, all were courteous to a fault. But the tilak and the name revealed his identity. We will let him remain nameless; he would want it so. He was waiting at the gate of the school to welcome us, having seen us walk down the mountain path from the road where we had parked the car. We had no plans to visit his school; we had chanced upon it.

Even the scorching summer of an Indian May fails to reach the mountains beyond a certain altitude. And the winter at those heights freezes everything, including schools. So, schools at that height and beyond have a short summer break but no vacation; the winter vacation is long. We had been driving around, looking for such a school. We made one wrong call, reaching a school amid a thicket of pine trees, that was shut for the summer. We drove further up through the forest, hunting for one that was open.

He was the principal of that government upper-primary school, which had 125 students, across Classes I–VIII. For the sparse population of the mountains, that is a big school. After the brief welcome, he led me to the classes. We entered Class VI and without preamble, he asked a girl to get up and start reciting the periodic table. She went halfway through it before stumbling. He asked a boy to take over, who completed the task without pause. We moved to Class VII, with a repetition of the performance by a couple of students.

As we walked from Class VII to Class VIII, I noticed the periodic table painted on the wall; a marker of a curious obsession,

I thought. But I also noticed something else. On the right, down the steep slope, on another level, there was a half basketball court. I had never seen a basketball court in such a terrain.

I asked him about it. He said 'Well, it's a good game, and we can't have a football field here, so I put in my money and got some from the villagers and got the court made.' And then he shared his view on the importance of sports in schools and the ease with which activities can be organised, if the teachers take initiative. By the time we finished with Class VIII, a game was on at the court. With over twenty kids in that half court, it was more rugby than basketball. It was a wonder that the ball remained in play, with the steep slope on two sides of the court.

We went to a room full of things that the students had made. None of it was the 'projects' that every second school in the country displays—these were unusual. There was a shear to cut branches from a 3-ft distance. Another contraption to pluck wild berries. A beautiful 12-inch-high tree made from wound copper wire, and more. He then asked me to speak to all the students of Classes VI–VIII. I did not want to disturb the classes, but he argued that classes happen every day, while a visitor to this distant school is very rare.

Over fifty students were collected in one room. We needed no time to thaw; the conversation got going from the start. Soon I asked what I always do with this age group—was there inequity and discrimination based on gender, caste, religion or class, in their villages? The first set of responses were denials, as it always is. But unusually, unprompted by me, this first set was cut off quickly. A little girl narrated in a firm voice discriminatory treatment at the local shop based on caste. A boy talked about the designated and separated places for eating in village functions. Then, child after child had a story.

He did not say a word during this conversation. He sat at

the back of the class, looking content. It was clear that he had fostered the consciousness and candour on these most sensitive of issues, which most schools would never talk about, let alone confront. So, I asked the kids, what should be done?

The kids talked about persuading their parents and relatives. They talked about changing the world. And then another little girl got up and said, 'First, we have to change ourselves. All this is within us too, right here. If we change, then we can change the world.'

He still sat quiet. There was no reason to speak. The fire he had lit, blazed in the children. He insisted that he would climb up to the road to see us off. At the car, I reached out to shake his hand in farewell. He clasped my hand in both of his, and eyes tearing up, he said, '*Kuch to kariye is desh ke liye.*' (Please do something about this country). Holding on to my hand, he said it three times.

What broke in a man who had the spirit to fire that blaze? And why with me? Perhaps in my questions he saw a kindred spirit. On that lonely mountain top, the battle that he wages is even lonelier. He has not left me with the burden of his hopes, but with the privilege of his solidarity. I will not leave the hands that have clasped mine, whatever happens.

PS: Some of you may not be familiar with Hindi and/or this allusion: '*Kisko fursat hai jo thaame, deewanon ka haath?*' It is the exquisite lament from Sahir's pen, in Guru Dutt's immortal *Pyasaa*, to the tune of S.D. Burman; it (roughly) means, 'Who has the time in this world to support those who are possessed (unsaid: by some higher calling)?'

26 September 2019

Coalitions on the Ground

The school was invited to lunch in the village. The lunch had been arranged with the elders in attendance, and the whole community was present. The public (government) primary school was doing good work, led by its lone teacher, Sachin. It's his fire that had changed the school. At the door of the house where the lunch was arranged, some of the students were told not to enter, but sit outside and eat. These children were from Dalit families. Sachin spoke to the organisers.

He wanted that there be no discrimination; in the school there was none. The organisers would not let the Dalit children eat with those from 'upper-caste' families inside the house. The teacher did not relent. As the argument escalated, he decided to stop the lunch. Either all of them ate together or they would go back to the school. Frantic negotiations started among the organisers. In the end, the kids sat together.

This teacher is an exception. Even those who never discriminate between their students on any ground inside the school find it hard to take the battle out of the school. They and their students face such conflicts daily, on every dimension of prejudice and discrimination—caste, gender, religion, poverty and more. This is not a trivial issue. We expect school education to play a crucial role in developing an equal society. But the school is fully embedded in this very world of discrimination. Teachers have to have the understanding and the courage to battle this inside the school and outside. What can support and enable the teacher to develop this understanding and have the tenacity to fight these battles day on day?

On a hot September evening, fifty-three teachers were watching the television screen showing Shyam Benegal's *Samvidhan*. The room in the government upper-primary school was about 600 sq. ft, and sweltering. My colleague Ravi was running the third episode of the ten-part series on the screen. The full series was scheduled to be screened on ten consecutive days. This was in a small town called Dhorimana. The word means 'mountain-like sand dunes'. This is 55 km from Barmer, in the Thar.

Ravi would pause the show at crucial moments, throwing a question at the gathering. There is a particularly poignant moment in the show when Rajkumari Amrit Kaur and Hansa Mehta discuss the depth of patriarchy that even they have to face. Ravi paused the show and asked, 'How are things today, almost seventy years after the Constitution?' It sparked a furore.

There were ten women in the room. But the debate was not divided along the lines of gender. A few men admitted that despite progress in these seventy years, patriarchy and gender discrimination were alive, even within themselves. The discussion moved to caste and then to religion. A minority confessed to the seams of discrimination and prejudice running on all these dimensions. Ravi brought the debate to a close; the intention was to light a few sparks, not to conclude.

The next time he stopped was after an intense segment where B.R. Ambedkar, Alladi Krishnaswamy Iyer, Syama Prasad Mukherjee and others debate the right to freedom of expression. Till one man spoke, seemingly there was agreement that we had secured freedom of expression for all in the past seventy years. He said, 'What about that woman Gauri Lankesh? She was killed for expressing her views, wasn't she?' I was surprised to hear that in Dhorimana. But it did spark a fiery fifteen-minute discussion. Ravi managed to end the session, without the intensity going down, but with no animosity remaining.

Thirty-five teachers attended the show across the ten days on an average, with a low of twenty and a high of fifty-eight. They came because they were interested, there was no order or incentive. It was an intense ten days of exploring the Constitution. All in the context of the reality that they live in. Much after the ten days had ended, we asked the teachers the value of the 'Festival of the Constitution'.

Understanding the Constitution was only a part of it. The real matter was the discovery of like-minded colleagues. A peer network, which could provide sorely needed support on conflict-ridden matters. This sense that there was someone close to you was a spur for action in the school and outside. Policies and curriculum mostly enable the teacher. But that is inconsequential, when confronting all this within her community and social relationships. There are those few like Sachin who may have the inherent courage. Many of them, too, wilt over time. Most who would like to battle discrimination find it hard to act, even within the school.

These biases are deeply ingrained in our society. The question to ask of ourselves is: what supports the teacher (or anyone else) in her daily life in the quest for our Constitution's ideals? There doesn't seem to be much. Most of those who battle to bring our Constitution to life, in the Dhorimanas of this country, feel alone. They need not, because they are not alone in Dhorimana. Once they get talking, they build a coalition for the Constitution. But while this has to be done, it doesn't happen on its own. We cannot await Godot, we have to do this ourselves.

20 December 2018

Folk Tales from the Mountains

The elderly man was pleasantly drunk at 10 a.m. He was minding the shops, two of seven, on the main road. Most people who were not out of the village earning their livelihoods, including some of the shopkeepers, seemed to have gone to the government primary school where we were headed.

The path to the school wound down the mountainside. The valley had a sharp drop, common in that part of the Kumaon region. Around a bend, the school became visible in the distance. It looked like a movie-set piece, perched on a distended platform overhanging the valley, framed by the high mountains behind. Even from a distance, it seemed abuzz with movement and colour.

Over 100 children were at the playground, which was most of the rectangular platform that was a natural outcrop of the mountainside. Some were painting on old newspapers stuck to the wall of the building, while others ran about helter-skelter, playing some game. The three rooms of the school, on one edge of the playground, were filled with people from the village. They were visiting the Bal Shodh Mela (Children's Research Fair). The mela was a joint effort of the school at Syalidhar, which is where we were, and the government primary schools at Lama Singh and Raialkot, both about 2 km from there.

The walls of the rooms were covered by posters with stories of two kinds—original ones written by the children, and local folk tales. The rooms were packed with visitors. The children were being called in repeatedly to explain their work. A few of them would squeeze in, but would soon sneak out, pulled by the activities outside, with no desire to talk about what they were done with. Many of the visitors' reading abilities were limited, but they were as awestruck as those who could read well. It seemed impossible that those long interesting stories were written by their six-, seven- or eight-year-olds. Teachers from other schools also visited the mela through the day.

When the crowd of visitors thinned, Sudha Pande and Geeta Khatri, the two teachers, narrated the story of the mela. Teaching children reading and writing with expression and comprehension, and not as mechanical reproduction of letters, is one of their biggest challenges. A large proportion of their students live in homes with a deep economic disadvantage. Far from having any books, many of the parents can't read and write. Everyone is out long hours, struggling to earn a living in the steep step-fields or as daily wage earners in the towns. The children often take care of their siblings.

These challenges are faced by almost all our public (government) schoolteachers. The complexity and difficulty of these challenges are usually underestimated, which is part of the reason why teachers don't get adequate systemic support. Instead, they are often saddled with simplistic techniques, including packaged early-language curriculum, all woefully inadequate in developing reading and writing as integral to expressive language.

The exercises leading up to the mela had started six weeks earlier, sparked by a workshop that the teachers had attended. The children were asked to get local folk tales from their families. On the first day, only one child had a story, from his grandmother, which he narrated to the whole school. The fun snowballed and, within some days, each child had a story. Soon, each had many, and they had to be divided into groups.

Each of the groups had children from Classes I–V, with a few who could write. In the next stage, those who could write wrote down the stories as they were narrated by each child. Then the stories were read aloud. There was a scramble for stories to be written and read before anyone else's. Next, each child used the written text of their own story to write it themselves with the help of those who could write well. The two teachers were deeply engaged with each group, supporting each child. This exercise went on for five weeks with variations, such as days being reserved for creating original stories. Over this period, the children became more and more independent with written language. The last week was spent preparing the exhibits.

The two teachers were as awestruck with their own experience as the visitors were with the exhibits. They had never seen such progress. Those who were beginners had made progress that used to take a year or more. Students already familiar with writing had gained fluency and become substantially more expressive. But their greatest sense of achievement was that all children had become keenly interested in reading and writing.

The two teachers attempted this pedagogical experiment with enormous effort. The mela in itself played a crucial role, energising the teachers and students, engaging the community and teachers from other schools. But the real value was in the overall experiment, especially for the two teachers, who developed an effective approach for language teaching.

No official had asked them to do this. No official stopped them either. Their desire to get their students to learn better had fired this effort. This fire, or its early sparks, are there in a large proportion of our teachers. We need to fuel this fire. India's educational challenges can only be addressed by such efforts of engaged and capable teachers in school. All efforts, at all levels, must be informed by this reality. Not by grandiose ideas cooked up sitting on perches of power of policy or academia.

5 July 2018

Hope Remains Alive in Education

Let me tell you five stories from my encounters in different parts of India in 2015.

In the hot and green plains, every day, the teacher goes to his student's house. He picks him up because the child has no legs, seats him on the bike, and together they go to school. The child is a part of the school, he is not different. Everyone makes it happen, but the teacher is at the centre. When school ends, they go back together on the bike.

Up in the mountains, she considers the whole valley her beat. She goes to each small habitation once a week to see if any child is not in school. That's how she found Asha and Khushi, two little girls distant from hope and happiness. Their families were perpetual migrants, searching for daily wage labour. She cajoled, charmed and bullied the parents, and got the two girls enrolled in her school. She would go to their hut every week, knowing that she could never let go. Then one day, they were gone. She didn't know where, but surely in search of more stable daily wage labour. They stayed for a year, they learnt to read and write. Whatever comes their way in life, this year will matter. She continues relentlessly, on her beat every week, and teaching in her school every day.

He was the most senior official in the state in school education. Two months after he had been transferred to the role, rumour was rife that he would be transferred out in a month. In those two months, he had soaked in as much as anyone can in education. He read and listened, late into every night. He had a tentative list of priorities to work on. He was methodically going about rustling up resources: money from the department of finance, good people from his own department and help from outside. On being confronted with the possibility of imminent departure and the futility of what he was doing, he just put his head down and kept on going. Fortunately for that state, he has still not been transferred out.

The lady has big, shining, laughing eyes. With the broom, she whips the place into shape every morning. No wonder the school is clean, so clean that you can eat from the floor. This is not her job; she is the cook for the mid-day meal. Why does she do all this? Well, if the government is organising free education for all kids, and the teachers work so hard, shouldn't they do something for their own school, she asks. She forces the awfully sweet tea on me before charging about to whip up the quorum for the school management committee.

The quiet man in the group was the first to come and last to speak. All the complaints in the room died after he spoke. He reaches the school—of which he is the head teacher—at 8.30 a.m., and opens the place. He then teaches and does everything else that is required to run a school, along with two more teachers. An hour before the school closes, he takes his cycle, rides 10 km to another school. He opens that, and runs that till late in the evening, and he is the only teacher there. He will do this till the other school gets a teacher. He is not sure, but he thinks it's just a matter of a few months. He has taken it up himself, else the kids in that school may lose the whole year. He smiles and looks like the Buddha.

All these stories are from our government schooling system. Among the many privileges of my role, one is that I meet such people every week. One day, a colleague who had joined us recently asked me whether I did not understand that every time that I travelled in the field, I would be deliberately taken to meet such people, skipping all the truants and the rogues. Having seen it for years, I could respond to him immediately. If week after week, year after year, I could keep meeting such people, imagine how many good people there are. Isn't that much more important than all the negativism that we feed ourselves anyhow?

This is not only my experience. Everyone who is willing to leave their high perches, in Delhi or Bengaluru, or wherever they are, discover the same. There are good people doing good work across the country. As we enter another new year, I am not merely giving some new hope. I am just suggesting that any strategy for change in education will work only if we make sure that all these good people are equal, enthusiastic owners of change.

Demonising the millions in public education, trying to beat them up to improve, is just poor strategy. There is a force within us—we don't even need to awaken it—and if that's new hope for the new year, then so be it.

23 December 2015

Being Superwoman

The inspector of schools knew that only one student in that cluster of villages had passed Class X in the first division. When the schools opened after the summer vacation, he went looking for her. He couldn't find the girl in any school. She had not taken admission in Class XI. She was up in the high mountain terrace farms, working in rice transplantation. Word reached her family; she went and met the inspector, who insisted that she join school. That was over thirty years ago.

Last Thursday, she was walking uphill steadily in front of me, leading me to the school in Baun. The visible strength of her forearms, within her small frame, tells of a lifetime of hard work. Harsha, the same girl who couldn't join Class XI, was now the deputy block education officer of Dunda in Uttarkashi district in Uttarakhand.

The maze of narrow paths took us through a steady climb in Garhwal to the far edge of the village. At one place a bent figure carrying a big bushel of millets crossed us. The person was not visible. Harsha bent down to look under the straw. It was a young girl. Harsha chatted with her, enquiring why she had not gone to school. She made up her mind quickly that the girl had to go on, so she told her to study tomorrow what she had missed today. Her tone and decision came from having lived that life herself. Through the climb up, she kept chatting with whoever we came across—the owner of a small shop, the ex-Pradhan of the village and an old lady drying wheat. She seemed to know most of them. Her responsibility includes 192 schools across 140 villages. Each village is a steep climb up and down, across mountains spread over 1,200 sq. km. How does she know most people in any village?

The school in Baun is a good one, and needs its own telling. The kids at the school also knew her. We were there for two hours, the last forty-five minutes spent with all the teachers together. She let them do the talking, but for briefly praising the principal and the teachers. A couple of times she intervened with precision on an academic matter that came up. She was recording what support the school needed in a well-used diary. She had last visited them in May and had a summary of what had happened on their issues since then. For many of the matters that came up, she suggested a solution immediately. For example, how to get school uniforms for some children who had joined late.

We left, as energised as the teachers. When we were coming out of the village, she walked into a tea shop at the other edge of the village. Five men were sitting there; they cribbed that the teachers had not got any award from the district administration despite their school being the best in the whole area. Her response closed the conversation: 'What can be a bigger award for a school, than five men sitting in a tea shop, demanding an award for the school?'

As the day passed, we were in another school in a valley. It became clear quickly that the school was wanting in many ways. We couldn't have figured out the cause of the problems in the brief visit. She had a clear understanding. There was chronic squabbling amongst the five teachers. She just tore into them in an even voice. It was awkward, sitting there as she took them methodically through their problems. The intensity of the admonishment was carefully calibrated, having set it up in the previous visits.

We left the group shaken. She sat in our car and cleaned the film of dust on the audio system with her dupatta. At 3.30 p.m., we got only a stew of instant noodles with onions and tomato for lunch in a small shack at the bend in the river. She had taken charge of the recipe, talking affectionately with the cook. That is what she is like, aware and active, every moment.

After finishing her schooling, she had to move out of the village to Uttarkashi. Then she became a teacher. Her elder sister and a friend, who was an accomplished mountaineer, encouraged her to join a course at the Nehru Institute of Mountaineering. It led to her trying to make the Everest team. She climbed a 7,000 m peak, then a 7,300 m peak and then a 7,600 m peak, which was enough to get her into the government-sponsored team in 1993. She had to abandon her Everest climb at 8,300 m because of bad weather, just 620 m short of the summit. When she is tired of covering her 192 schools or disheartened by something, she invokes that memory and says, 'If you want to work, nothing can stop you, and anyone can do a lot.'

Why do you climb a mountain? Because it's there. Why are you a superwoman? Because that's the job. Does education really require this kind of effort? It does. As long as we don't understand that, we won't climb Everest.

15 October 2014

School in the Desert

He is an imposing presence, the kind that would immediately put the lid on anyone's road rage, even in Delhi. The white crown of hair on his head reinforces the intensity of his eyes. It's almost as though he is continually glaring. Our exchange of pleasantries in his office was much shorter than the usual. He wanted to move to the classes. The March sun was also glaring down on the sand dunes. Out of the sun, the shade was still pleasant.

He took us to Class II which was sitting on the floor in the verandah. There were about fifteen kids. There was no preamble; he stooped just a bit, and threw the words at the kids. '*Ye Bangalore se aaye hain.*' His presence, his voice and his eyes, all told me that the kids would wilt now. The smallest girl in the group pounced up, eyes dancing from him to me.

She screamed, 'He has come from Bangalore.'

He said, '*Wo aadmi sadak pe khadaa hai.*'

A boy responded, 'That man is standing on the road.'

He said, '*Wo ek gaay hai.*'

Another kid said, 'That is a cow.'

This rapid fire continued. There was not the slightest change in his demeanour. The kids loved it; they were competing to respond. After witnessing this game of translation for ten minutes, it was quite clear that the kids understood English; it was not some parrot-speak of rote-memorised phrases.

This is the government upper-primary school in Hardoni-Meghwalon-Ki-Dhani, on thorny sand dunes, 50 km from Barmer in Rajasthan. His name is Shyam Lal Sharma. He is the head teacher of the school. There are 139 children in the school, which has five teachers. It's a nice, neat building, with a walled, naturally sand-filled, 1 acre playground. This seems to be quite the norm for government schools in Rajasthan, especially in western Rajasthan—pleasant and spacious.

The location of the school is such that over 80 per cent children are from the most disadvantaged communities, the other 20 per cent only relatively less so. If you venture beyond the tourist settings of the desert, it's hard to figure out how (and why) people live in those conditions. But they do, with an equanimity which perhaps only living with an eternal natural foe can bring, a foe whom you then befriend.

We moved on to where a maths class for Class IV was in progress. Chotu Lal Meghwal was the teacher; he was very young. They were working on fractions. Sharma observed silently for a minute, and then he wrote on the black board: 23 23/27 + 63 17/8 + 97 15/33

Even before he had finished writing, a boy volunteered to go to the board and simplify the number. I sat with the kids on the floor. The boy went about it slowly and methodically, writing every step on the black board. There were three girls around me; two of them were engrossed in the problem. The third kept looking up at the pace of the boy, trying to beat him.

All of them were clear about the steps, and reached the solution. The girl, who was competing, made an error in one addition in the end. I pointed that to her, she instantly realised her error and corrected it. They continued with other fractions as we walked out.

The next room had Class I. Even before Sharma said anything, the kids started making a racket. It was obvious that they liked him. He asked whether anyone wanted to say the pahadaa, that is, the multiplication tables. The din only increased. Finally, he had to point at a kid to start; he said he would do twenty-three. I thought I had misheard him. But he started and finished the table of twenty-three up to ten, in one breath. The class was uncontrollable after that; they were all reciting tables, and each of their own choice. It ranged from two to thirty, and it seemed like they were playing a super-exciting game.

The level of learning in the school (with genuine comprehension and understanding) in maths and in English, which is a third language for the students, is quite something. The easy confidence, engagement and energy of the kids, makes it a fun and exciting place. It deals with every conceivable disadvantage that the children have, and overcomes them. It's a good school.

The key is, of course, Sharma. We chatted as we were leaving. He said he did not want to take any promotions. That's because as you grow in the system, you become distanced from children, he said.

That was the third good government school I visited in the dunes that day. I am sure there are some in your vicinity. Go and visit them, and you will realise just how false is the popular narrative of most government schools being shoddy and teachers being absent. India's school education is not in good shape, but if we continue to hold on to superficial narratives, we will not be able to find real solutions.

2 April 2014

The School on the River Tons

If I could do it, the only temple I'd build would be for Karna (one of the central characters in the epic Mahabharata). I think there is no one more worthy than him for a country that is in short supply of heroes. When my friend Jagmohan heard this from me, he was convinced that it was Karna who pulled us to Mori.

We drove to Mori from Purola in Uttarakhand in an hour, through a pine forest which had no break. We had decided to make this trip the previous day on a whim, to meet Prem Singh Rawat. I had heard about his transformation from a disinterested block resource officer in the education department, thinking of Mori as a 'punishment posting', to a man driven, almost possessed, to improve education in the block.

Mori is just about as far as you can go on a road in this country. It is a very small town in the Uttarkashi district, on the River Tons. Even in this mountain land of divine rivers, Tons is a category of its own. Its furious flow and blue water dominate even the majestic mountains. No one drinks its water. That is because the origins of Tons define a tragedy: the loss of the righteous Kauravas to the Pandavas. The people of the valley, all followers of the Kauravas, cried and cried on this cosmic injustice and thus, from their unstoppable tears, the River Tons was born. When I saw the Tons, the myth sounded almost believable. Jagmohan then told me about the wooden temple of Karna, 7 km further from Mori, which is when he suggested that it was my hero who pulled me there.

Rawat was in a training session, so we had some time. We decided to visit the government primary school in Dei, a village on the other bank of Tons. It has forty-six students in Classes

I–V; a neat building with two rooms and a verandah, which is used more than the rooms. With the blue Tons flowing below and steep wooded mountains all around, few places can be more beautiful, and fewer places more distant. In this last mile of India, it is a wonder that there is a functioning government school, a wonder that we take for granted.

It is functioning because of Aruna and Mirchu Lal. Aruna commutes two hours one way from Purola to reach Dei; Lal treks three hours a day to and from his village. Aruna lives in Purola because her husband runs his own (private) school there. She has been at the school in Dei for nine years.

She told me the tale of Dei. It was originally located about a three-hour climb from where it is today. The people of Dei saw patches of cultivable land on the banks of the Tons, so they set up a few huts there. Over time, there were two Deis, one on the Tons and one up in the mountains.

Over time, all families shifted to the village on the river. They would go up to the original village only for some rituals; one such was a festival for which they would go up for a month. So, nine years ago, Aruna encountered this puzzling problem: all the children would disappear, mid-session, for more than a month. She climbed up three hours to see firsthand the cause of this puzzle. She then started a dialogue with the village community, trying to convince them that Dei-on-Tons was as much their home as the Dei-on-the-mountain and so they could celebrate the month-long festival on the Tons as well.

In time, she succeeded. Now the village doesn't migrate for a month, and so her students don't miss a month of classes, which is what she wanted. I asked her why she took the trouble of trying to change the village. If I was looking for any grand answers or deep motivation, there were none. She was very matter of fact. 'If as a teacher, you have no students in your school for a month, what do you do?' You try to bring them back, that's all.

Every child in that school can read and write, with good comprehension; we tested it. They talked with us confidently and thoughtfully. We saw a remarkable project that they had done together as a school, an insightful analysis of the problems that development had solved and created in Dei. Aruna chatted with me in the same matter-of-fact tone. She saw nothing out of the ordinary in her school. She said she was not doing anything special. She was just the ordinary teacher, merely doing her job.

This ordinary teacher is one of thousands. As we fulminate over policy, crib about financing and don't really do anything to support them, these thousands go on doing their jobs. That's a reason for hope. I will be back in Mori. I missed meeting Rawat (his session had not finished by the time I left) and I couldn't go to the Karna temple; so, two heroes beckon me. Although I did get to meet another one—the one who just does her job diligently.

31 October 2012

From the Ruins

The rock stands erect amid the rubble around. I can't read the Brahmi on it, but I have read a translation. A part of the edict says, 'Devanampriya does not value either gifts or honours so highly as this, that a promotion of the essentials of all sects should take place. This promotion of the essentials (is possible) in many ways. But its root is this, guarding one's speech, neither praising one's own sect nor blaming other sects should take place on improper occasions, and that it should be moderate in every case. But other sects ought to be honoured in every way.' He speaks to us directly in his own voice, across 2,300 years. The voice is not that of the all-conquering emperor he was, but of meditative wisdom. Which is why we listen.

After this communion with Ashoka, I went to a village not far away, to visit its government elementary school. The smooth metalled road ended at the village, whose narrow lanes were broken mud tracks. On both sides were open shallow drains, overflowing in all directions. Refuse from a temple was mixed with that from toilets in front of rows of shanties. Mounds of degraded plastic blocked the drains at regular intervals, forcing the slush into the lane.

Seven murders have marked six years in the village. The two dominant and warring clans of the village have been relentless in their pursuit of vengeance. Each killing has escalated the brutality of retribution. The rest of the village lives with this terror and with chronic poverty. Most residents are landless agricultural labourers.

Now, along with some henchmen, the lone surviving chieftain is in jail. That has paused the killings. But he still runs the village from within his penal abode. Even the School Management Committee cannot take any decision without his blessings; important bodies like the panchayat are tightly controlled. The school fits in this wilderness of decay. The walls are crumbling, half-loose rough tiles make for floors, and its small quadrangle has mounds of garbage.

Class IV has ninety students. On an average day, attendance is about seventy; others are out working in the fields. The kids cram into one classroom. The teacher teaches them all the four subjects—maths, environmental studies (EVS) and two languages. Given the precarity of life in the village, I will neither name the teacher nor the village.

The ambience of the class has no semblance to the village. The kids talk confidently, smile and laugh easily and remain focused on their work. With seventy kids to handle, the teacher has divided them into many groups. And then further into groups of threes. Each group has children with varying abilities, to help each other. He moves from group to group. He forms and reforms these groups through the year. At the beginning of the year, he focuses on those who have not learnt to read and write in the earlier three classes. He ensures that in a month or so, they learn the basics so that they can subsequently reach roughly the same curricular level as the other students. The syllabus does not force his pace. He could spend ten days on a lesson, which has two days scheduled, so that the children truly learn. And at the end of the year, he is ahead of the syllabus.

Stories are the foundation of his teaching. The children tell each other stories, create their own stories, hunt for stories in their homes and narrate them in the class, complete each other's stories, read stories aloud and in silence and convert pictures to stories and stories to pictures. The small classroom has six taut strings tied at a height of about 6 feet, and clipped to these are books, which the kids borrow. This is their hanging library. He ensures that the writing keeps pace with reading. Stories remain the cornerstone of his teaching of EVS and maths, and he connects these subjects to the world around the child, instead of being bound by dry abstractions. He has meticulously collected portfolios of the work of each child, which reflect their remarkable progress, not only on the subjects taught, but also in their thinking, imagination and perspectives.

His completely white, trimmed hair, and unbroken serenity, make him appear older than he is. He was appointed a block resource person, a position of some power in the local education system, but he preferred to teach in this school. That role would have also eliminated his daily 40 km commute to this village from his home. When asked why he did that, his precise response is, 'There is nothing more fulfilling than these children learning and being happy.' And then he adds, 'especially here'. He refuses praise, denies that he is doing anything special and asserts with the same precise simplicity that this is his duty.

The village is the debris of the ideals of Ashoka and the wreckage of our Constitution. Is there redemption? Can the rubble that we see ever be the edifice for equity, justice and peace? We have no choice but to believe. If this frail, tranquil man can embrace these ruins, and build bit by bit from there, we have no choice but to keep the faith. He stands upholding the possibility of a better world, as have the rocks for two and a half millennia, bearing the voice of Devanampriya Ashoka.

7 November 2019

The Heart of the Forest

The thick sal forest had only one large clearing in miles, which housed the school. The school had closed for the day, but some children had lingered, playing in the yard in the winter afternoon's fading sunlight. Through the iron grill of the window, I could see right up to the edge of the misty playground where the wall of trees began. Kiran Deo Singh was narrating his life as a teacher. As he went from his college days, to his first year in a school and then to how he found an anchor in an elderly retired teacher, all the lingering children left, disappearing into the wall of trees.

A boy and a girl, probably eight and six, respectively, visibly siblings, returned to the playground from the forest. They came running into the room. Singh gave them the glucose biscuit packet that he had opened for me, and asked them why they had come back. The girl was eating three biscuits at once. The boy replied: *'Abba door desh mein hain, aaj raat ko nahi aayenge.'* (Father has gone to some distant place, he won't return tonight.) They went out and started singing loudly just outside the room. Singh continued the story of his life.

In a few minutes, we finished the conversation and were ready to leave. The children were still playing outside. I asked him about them. The story of Afzal and Anjum is unremarkably common, but for them it is their life. Their mother passed away, and their father is a daily wage labourer. He is a caring father, but has to go where work takes him. Once in a while it is so far that he can't reach home the same night. Their extended family lives in another village. The neighbours are fine people and help within their meagre means. However, the children prefer going with Singh to his house on such days.

'So, will you take them home with you?' I asked. He replied in the affirmative, while locking the doors. 'How many times does this happen?' One lock was giving trouble, so with some delay he replied, 'Once in a while.' I got into my car, while Anjum and Afzal were squabbling about who will sit right behind Singh on the bike. They came to some agreement and left, as we, too, left.

The cold was biting even at noon, held to the ground by the thick forest. It was another school, in another clearing, two days later. The dull sunlight outside was better than the inside of the dark, freezing rooms. It was a large gathering of about fifty people sitting in a circle, on durries, on the ground. There were teachers, principals and other education officials from across that area. I had reached a bit late and a place was kept for me next to the officer, who was clearly the boss. I noticed Singh, with his heavyweight boxer's height and build, at the far end of the circle.

Without looking at anyone else, the officer started speaking to me. He rattled off his heroic efforts in this remote district. After ten minutes, he turned to the group and gave them a five-minute rapid-fire speech on their duties and told them how those who wouldn't improve their schools would be taken to task. Then he left. After his departure the meeting came to life.

The discussion was without artifice. Quickly dividing the group was one matter, with opposing beliefs—all children can learn versus not all children can learn. The second group, which was in the majority, explained their belief by saying the children of the poor just don't have the capacity to learn. The other side said that it was all about trust; if you believed that all children can learn, then they will. They had a punchy back-up argument. They took the example of the officer who had departed. If he were to trust that they would do a good job, most of them would do much better than they were doing today. That was a statement that none of them would refute.

These are all oft-used arguments in groups of teachers. Like the others, this discussion too tapered to a stalemate. Some found validation, a few may have even moved a bit, but it hadn't really changed anything. Till Singh spoke up. '*Pyaar to karke dekho,*' (Try loving them) he said. If you love them you will know that there is no difference between children. If you love them, all challenges will be trivial. If you love them, it will change you, and that is why they will blossom.

This was a different battlefield. Not even the most hardened cynic was able to argue that children should not be loved. They may not do it, but they knew not to oppose this. Some had a glow of insight on their faces: a few from gaining that insight, some others from hearing Singh articulate so clearly what they knew.

I was saying farewell to Singh when I asked him about Afzal and Anjum. They were still at his home. Singh spoke to their father the day we had met. He was getting five more days of work at twice the standard wage rate, but the place was so far that he couldn't commute daily. So, Singh told him to stay there, work and earn, while the children would stay with him. How many times does this happen, I asked. 'Once in a while,' he said. '*Mere hee bachche hain.*' (They are like my own children.)

My father is eighty today. He has dedicated his life to education, about which he once said, 'The heart of the matter in education is that it is a matter of the heart'. He could have said that about life. I wish more people would listen to him or Singh: '*Pyaar to karke dekho.*'

31 January 2019

What Does the Desert Have?

The crimson sun set on the sand dunes of Chohthan. All its hues yesterday were the same as five years ago. I had never seen the sun set in the sand dunes before. The temperature dropped by 10 degrees in thirty minutes. The colour of the sand changed every minute with the sinking sun. But the reds of neither the sand nor sky matched the palette of red in the pagadi (turban) Satyapal Singh had given me.

That day five years ago, I had gone to the public (government) school 7 km from Chohthan, where Singh was the teacher. We had just begun working in the district of Barmer. Chohthan with a population of 12,000 is the headquarters of a block in the district. I listed the warnings that we had received about Barmer in Jaipur.

It was called 'kala paani'. The terrain was so hard, the heat so scorching, the poverty so wrenching and the water so absent, that no one but the desert-natives could live there. Singh laughed and said all that was true, but the last. Then he added '*Yahan log rote hue aate hain, aur rote hue jaate hain.*' (People move to Barmer unwillingly, but leave equally unwillingly.) Because Barmer may have nothing, but its people have big hearts.

When we were leaving Singh's school, they wanted to put a pagadi on my head. They had one each for my colleagues Shobhan and Gautam too. Ramphal, while a member of our team, seemed to be equally theirs, so there was none for him. We refused to take the pagadi. He stamped out our arguments by saying 'The pagadi will be the responsibility on your head, for working with us to help improve the schools here.'

Singh was there yesterday too. It was a workshop on

developing teaching-learning material (TLM) in maths from whatever resources were available to the schools. Through the two-day workshop, the twenty-five teachers developed a bagful of such TLM to take back. During the closing debrief in the evening, Singh pointed out that even after two days of hard work, the teachers didn't want to leave. Another teacher mentioned that the most important thing that they had learnt was that they had innumerable resources around them to make learning effective and exciting for their students. Meagre budgets did not have to be a limitation.

Battling the physical conditions of the desert, while taking care of all aspects of their schools—many of the teachers alone with thirty to forty students—is hard work. The twenty-five teachers' faces and physiques reflect their toil. But their spirit is resplendent like the crimson sun. As it is in each school that I had visited in the previous four days. The tenacity of these teachers in the face of every conceivable challenge is epic. A few lines can be no more than a blurb for these epics. Let me share three such instances.

Moolaram and I met for the third time in three years. Each time, he was the head teacher of a different school. The frequent transfers have not left a mark on him. But he has left each school much improved. Teachers from all around seek him out for advice. There had been a school which I had been to before Moolaram. The 1 acre campus in the sand was sparkling earlier as now, but the learning of the students had transformed. After the tiger ate seven of the twenty-three goats in the village and I bought thirteen more goats, how many goats were there? Children in Class II find that question very hard, even with pen and paper. These kids answered this and many more orally. He worked with each teacher to make this happen; Moolaram is a master-teacher.

Ganesharam and Mahesh run a good school but they didn't think this was enough. They decided to learn English so that they could teach English. I hadn't heard English for three days in Barmer, till I heard the Class IV children speak in that school. They are far from fluent, but for students of two teachers who themselves started learning English that year, it was a marvel. They have built an oasis in the school, a grove of neem trees with fifty happy, fearless children. As we were leaving, Ganesharam pointed to his own house across the blazing dunes; he must live in his karmabhumi—a word with no accurate English equivalent.

A different Moolaram has been a teacher for four years. He is the lone teacher in the school, teaching fifty-six students three subjects across five classes. Like the other schools, his students battle life in poverty every day. Along with education, the school is a succour to the children and their families. Every month, part of his salary is spent on the school. All alone that he is, he craves to learn from others. He has bought a bike recently. Earlier, he would walk miles, to meet other teachers. He says, '*Mushkilen ginaane se kam nahi hoti.*' (Counting difficulties doesn't reduce them.) His wisdom rests easily on his slight frame and youth, with roots in experiences of his tough and driven life.

When the terrain is so hard, the heat so scorching, the poverty so wrenching and the water so absent, all that's left is the human spirit. And that fills every breach, tends every heart and keeps bodies together. These are not just schools, but crucibles from which faith in humanity comes out forged every day. The crimson sun is just one part of the intimate beauty of Barmer. If you go there, you will not leave willingly. When you do, it will be with a bit of faith in humanity restored.

22 November 2018

The Ordinary People

I signed off 2017 with the column 'The Continuing Importance of Being Stubborn'. I am 'ziddi' in my heart—the Hindi word's depth and nuance is not conveyed by the English 'stubborn'.

On a cold night in Jamshedpur recently, at the twenty-five-year reunion of my MBA (Master of Business Administration) class at XLRI, a sozzled and close friend drew out a kind of gist of the piece, riffing off Antonio Gramsci. It is about the unrelenting optimism of the will in the miasmic pessimism of the intellect today. The words are sort of heavy for me, but it certainly is one way of saying it. His question was, 'What fuels your optimism, aside from weird genetic wiring?' That question is a great start to 2018.

In 2017, I spent 105 days in the field. That was much like 2016, and will be so again in 2018. That is where the action is. For me, it means the districts across seven states that we work in directly with public schools and their teachers. These are some of the remotest districts in India: from the mountains of Uttarakhand, to the deserts of Rajasthan and dense jungles of Chhattisgarh, and more.

On each of these 105 days, I met ordinary people going about their work without any fuss, doing what they think they should be doing. Let me sketch the typical example of such an ordinary person.

At 7 a.m., a woman gets into a jeep cab with ten other people. She gets off after an hour-long drive on the non-existent roads winding up and down. Then, she climbs on foot for thirty minutes, one of those gorgeous, treacherous slopes in the Garhwal region. She opens the school and checks the provisions for the mid-day meal. With the help of the students who are in early, she cleans the two classrooms, the small playground and the toilets. By then, thirty of her thirty-three students have come in. Two babies have tagged along with their siblings to the school, since there is no one at their homes during the day to take care of them. She starts the morning assembly.

The thirty students vary in age from six to eleven. She takes five classes simultaneously, teaching Hindi, maths and environmental studies (EVS) through the day. She is not comfortable with maths. Her subject in college was Hindi, and she has studied maths only up to Class X. Her B. Ed. (Bachelor of Education) degree, with its archaic curriculum in a dysfunctional college, was of little help in preparing her to become a teacher. She has learnt to be a good teacher by paying careful attention to each child and participating in every professional development opportunity she can find.

The six-and-a-half-hour school day is a roller coaster, as it would be with any thirty children. A scuffle breaks out among three of them, she sorts it out. The mother of a student shows up and wants to discuss whether she can take her child away for an extra ten days during the Diwali break. Two eager children are pulling at her sari because they have finished solving the problems she gave them. She wants every child to learn with understanding; she shuns rote memorisation in her school. Meanwhile, she has had to arrange for the two babies to be fed. Then she discusses the EVS project that the Classes IV and V students have finished. And so on. At 3.30 p.m., she closes the school.

She is not done yet. She climbs the slope to go to the house of the child who hasn't come to school for three days. She knows that the child is not well. She spends some time with the mother. And then searches out one of the panchayat members of the village, asking him to go and talk to the block education officer, because funds for repairing the toilets are not being released. By the time she reaches the road, the 4.30 p.m.-shared cab has left. She reaches home by 6.30 p.m., to another part of the full life awaiting her.

She has done this for fifteen years and will do it for another twenty. An ordinary woman doing what she thinks she should be doing. Some days are quieter, some crazier. All spent with children, who learn a bit more every day, the foundation of their life being laid by this ordinary person.

A life of such ordinariness in its full arc is the kind of heroism that upholds the world and animates the progress of humanity. If called heroic, such people shrug and move on, to the next ordinary thing. To be done to the best of their ability. Often in the face of the sclerotic and disempowering culture of the system, with little or no resources, while being the target of blame for the entire country's failings. In 2018, let's listen to these ordinary people on how to improve education in India. Next fortnight, I plan to write the sequel to this piece, called 'Every Ordinary Public Schoolteacher's Wish List for 2018'.

Encountering such people, hundreds of them every year, is fuel enough for my optimism. The 105 days in the field with such encounters is a privilege that my role brings to me. Your life and work may or may not give you the same opportunity. If it doesn't, then go out in 2018 and meet some ordinary people like her. You may not have to go far, the country is full of ordinary people doing extraordinary work.

But go with empathy and compassion. And the fires of optimism will be stoked in plenty. Then we can ask ourselves the question: how can our own ordinary lives fuel optimism rather than pessimism?

4 January 2018

One Woman Alone

The thorny, overgrown shrubs scraped our car as we entered the village. On the road stood a girl; she was probably fourteen years old. She remained on the road and so our car had to stop. She was stooping and turning around slowly on the same spot; there was a wound on her left cheek.

She paid no attention to us, with eyes focused past us, on some distant nowhere. Then in a flash she was gone. The car started and we reached the school.

The thorny shrub is the plant of the hot semi-arid climate of Yadgir district. The surprise is when the landscape breaks into acres of lush paddy fields. Wherever the waters of the Upper Krishna Project reach, landowners have shifted to paddy cultivation. They used to grow coarse cereals suited to the region's naturally arid climate and land. The effects of this change in cropping, incongruous with natural conditions, are not understood well and many are apprehensive. If the irrigated tracts have led to livelihood improvement, it is not visible in the villages.

The houses and the people, even along the lush paddy fields, look scorched by generations of poverty. Most locals are farm labourers, excluded from the economic benefits of the irrigation projects; the landowners live in Hyderabad. Halbhavi—the village that we were visiting—seemed to be on the same precarious edge of economic survival.

The school has one large classroom on one side and a kitchen on the other. It is an old building, but one that wears its age well. Thirty-seven students of Classes I–III were together in the room with Chandrakala, their teacher. The room was crowded. Charts hung from the ceiling. One wall had open cupboards neatly stacked with files and books. The opposite wall was lined with teaching-learning material.

Everyone was sitting on the floor, in five groups, each in a circle. We sat along the wall in the front as the teacher and her students went about their work. The movements and the voices echoed the confidence of being in a space that is their own, of enjoyment, and of trust. Two seven-year-olds came to us asking us to look through their notebooks. Their arithmetic seemed sound for their age. They read Kannada fluently. They had also written words in English. There were simple words and more complex ones; for example, 'cow', 'evening', 'agriculture', 'girl', 'canal'. Many of the complex words were misspelt, but phonetically all were faithful to the spoken word.

Then the two children started a conversation with us in halting English. They found their own effort amusing and giggled. My colleague Rudresh commented on their proficiency in English. Chandrakala said that her own English is very limited, so it is the children who teach each other. By now many children had gathered around us.

A nine-year-old girl and an eight-year-old boy both held their baby siblings on their laps throughout the ninety minutes that we were there. Both were cheerfully engaged in the proceedings. There were three other babies in the room playing on their own—siblings of other students. These babies are not students, but unless the children and Chandrakala take care of them, their siblings will have to stay at home and drop out of school.

On a whim, Rudresh asked the children around us if they knew the great social reformer and poet Basava's vachanas. It was impossible to stop them after that. Everyone wanted to recite a vachana, and most of them did. Rudresh played along, and asked them if they knew the districts of Karnataka. An eight-year-old girl made a song out of the names of all the thirty districts, almost without taking a breath, knocking out our breath.

The children then launched into a rapid-fire round of questions. They knew the capitals of every Indian state, and those of many other faraway countries. With each correct response they would laugh and clap. Chandrakala laughingly dismissed all this as entertainment, saying real learning was in their language, in their conceptual clarity and in their confidence. That classroom seemed like a magical mystery ship of happiness to us. With generations of social discrimination and unrelenting, debilitating poverty, most of the children are living in extreme circumstances. These conditions have a severe, adverse effect on them. To overcome much of that in the educational context, and to bring these children to where they are, is magical.

I asked Chandrakala how she does this. She said that it's her job and she tries to do it responsibly. There is nothing more to it, she added. I persisted with my question. She said, 'Well, it is 1 per cent because someone like you comes in a very long while and says I am doing something good, but it is 99 per cent because I am responsible for the future of these kids. What else do they have?'

Hundreds of thousands of teachers in our country face similar circumstances and identical battles. This is the real front line of the war for justice and equity, for social change and for economic development. The teachers need all our support in this long war. By then the girl with the stoop and distant eyes was sitting outside the door of the classroom. She had a pen in hand and was making undecipherable patterns on a notebook.

Chandrakala tries to care for her; she wishes she could do more. There are no limits to her sense of responsibility. There is no limit to empathy and compassion.

30 March 2017

The Quiet River, Narmada

It was a still, cool evening. The clear sky was awash with the orange of dusk deepening into hues of red. From the top of the ghat, the Narmada held perfectly still. A lone boatman stood erect on an unmoving canoe much like a statue in the middle of the river. The azaan wafting from a distance melded into the quiet. A minute after the azaan stopped, a gentle kirtan started in the temple a short distance away. In the school at the top of the ghat, a large classroom was dimly lit by a single lamp. A group of teachers sat discussing the hippocampus and its role in learning.

Narmada, the giver of pleasure, the eternal river of sustenance, holds multitudes. There was nothing incongruous about the still evening beauty, the religious range and the quest for knowledge flowing into one another on the ghat in Mandleshwar.

But in the multitude that the river holds, not all is quiet and serene. It also holds the turmoil of the dammed development, the epicentre of which has been Barwani, not far from here. It holds more. One could hardly do better than to read Hartosh Singh Bal's remarkable book, *Waters Close Over Us: A Journey Along the Narmada*, to understand how this river permeates everything in that land.

Next morning, the teachers at the government elementary school in Bediyaw wrapped up the morning assembly quickly. It was already hot out in the sun at 10.30 a.m. The assembly finished with all the students chanting in unison, '*Narmada hare hare.*' Everyone there owes everything to the river so it is fitting to end the assembly by thanking the river every day, the teachers explained to us.

This school and the village are an amusing study in how to find practical workarounds for our outdated and often impractical governance systems. While Bediyaw is one village, the historical local revenue records show three villages. This implies that over time, three schools were sanctioned and built. But the residents built each 'new school' around the same playground. So, in effect, they built and expanded one school. On record, there are three villages, but in reality, there is one. On record, there are three schools when actually there is one.

This works because the teachers who are posted to the three different schools laugh away the formal separation and run the school as one. The primary classes (I–V), where we spent time, had an unusually confident group of students. They did not hesitate in the slightest in engaging in a sweeping conversation with us and their teacher. They played a game trying to guess my name and where I came from. Then we talked about eating habits in Kerala, which is where Anish (my colleague) is from. They were fascinated by the importance of fish in Kerala cuisine. It soon became a discussion about who among them ate fish and if not, why not. That led to a discussion about gender equity. A few stating clearly why they thought girls and boys were not equal, and then listening intently to a description of how women were flying fighter jets.

Having heard about it before, I asked whose parents had studied in the same school. One of them cleverly riffed on my question. The Hindi word for 'studied' is 'padhe', which can be made to sound like 'pade', meaning lying around. He said, 'None of our parents are lying around, they are all working hard,' and that got many of the children rolling and laughing uncontrollably.

It's a happy school.

The partnership between the two primary-class teachers, the twenty-six-year-old Piyush Trivedi and Santosh Patidar, who has been teaching at the school for twenty-six years, appeared to be the source of this energy in the school. Like many good teachers that I meet, they exercise the creative freedom that is inherent in a teacher's role, while remaining committed to some core educational principles.

They have designed the school timetable such that every day ends with a common activity for all students, not feeling constrained by any externally determined schedule. They gave a fascinating description of how they conduct activity-based learning (a pedagogical approach), using the local language. Patidar narrated an incident of how one official was taken aback by this approach of theirs, and then kept quoting them as an example of how to be responsive to local reality, and not become rigid.

Twenty-six years is a long time to be teaching in the same school. Yet rather than burden or fatigue, Patidar's demeanour reflects satisfaction and commitment. The satisfaction is about how the village has changed for the better in many ways, including a dramatic reduction in alcoholism, and the fact that most of the school's alumni have stable, adequate livelihoods. That evening, teachers gathered to discuss some exceptionally good books on education. I had to leave early, but the discussion went on well past 8 p.m. These groups of teachers meet regularly to learn, so that they can teach better. No one has asked them to do this. They do it of their own will. It takes time and dedication to make a difference. But life on the banks of the Narmada has a sense of perspective.

Twenty-six years is a long time to be doing anything. But when lived with purpose, the years are enough to change the world, at least a small bit. Teachers changing the world bit by bit need all the help and support they can get. Many go on, on their own, fired from within—much like a quiet, eternal river that flows on, holding multitudes.

16 March 2017

Making the Choice to Fight
for Dharma

The Alaknanda river is blue in November. It seems still from a distance, but is raging. From a place where the river was out of sight, we started climbing after getting out of the car. Despite the clear skies and direct sunlight at 1,800 m, it was cold. We climbed for about thirty minutes on a 45-degree-incline mountainside on a winding path. On the way, we passed a few houses—all with grains drying in the sun. When we reached the school, my shirt was soaked with sweat. It was the familiar extreme discomfort, which would go away if I sat still for five minutes in that dry, cold air.

She asked me whether I would have tea and I said yes. She was sitting with Classes I–III, and a group of younger children, in the sun. The small courtyard hung out on the slope, like a stage in the sky. The mountains across the valley seemed dwarfed by the glinting 7,000 m peaks of Chaukhamba, though it was almost 70 km away.

I chatted with the students of Class I while she worked on maths with Classes II and III. Their ability to read and write, with comprehension, was unusual. Without hesitation, they wrote the following sentence in Hindi, 'Uma was sitting under the tree, when the cow came near her.' And then they went on to develop the sentence by adding, 'Uma got up and took the cow home.' And so the exercise continued.

The Class II students were doing multiplication of three-digit numbers. The younger children were not students, but she was taking care of them, since their elder siblings were in the school and parents were out working.

Inside the neat two-room school, all the children from Classes IV–VI were together. They had no teacher; the head teacher who is the only other teacher in the school, was on leave. The students from these classes were busy sorting out leaves and fruit, categorising them and then writing down details of the plants, including their use in daily life. They stopped and started a conversation with me. They were familiar with my city— Bengaluru. Most of their interest was focused on what it was like living in a big city.

I went back to the courtyard and sat down with her. She asked me whether I was visiting because I knew that the head teacher was on leave. I told her that was not the case. We talked about why all fifty-six of her students seemed to be doing well on everything I could observe. She responded that there was no great mystery to it. All children are good, the real question is whether the teachers try or not. And whether they have empathy in their hearts. I asked about her challenges and problems, and she said that her only problem was the head teacher, but she had almost solved it.

The head teacher was transferred to her school two years ago. He was ten years older than her. He arrived with the bluster of a bully legitimised by official authority. The happy school was stricken with terror. The children went into a state of shock.

Violence, both physical and verbal, was never far away. She would often be the target of his verbal assaults, as would the lady who cooked the mid-day meal. He treated the parents of the children no better, especially the mothers. He was a misogynist—perhaps even to the core. With twenty-five years of experience working in schools, he had figured out how to cross all lines without leaving a trail. He was also known to be politically connected. Even as she described her nightmare, she did it in an even tone. For six months, she remained terrified and conflicted;

all her friends and family wanted her to take a transfer out of the school. But she chose to stay and fight. Like most bullies, he stopped mistreating her when she confronted him. Thereafter, it was a hard, grinding struggle to get him to change. She rallied the parents, talked to sympathetic officials and kept pushing back against him. His behaviour became worse before things improved. As her relentless mobilisation gathered momentum, he couldn't take it anymore, and he disengaged from the school.

And that is how it is now, he is often absent. When he does show up, he sits sullenly, all alone. Why fight and take its misery? Her response was a lot more poetic in Hindi than it sounds in English. She said, 'My retreat would have been the end of education for these children.'

That November night in my hotel room, sleepless like millions, I was exchanging emails with my colleague Indu on the state of the world. She wrote back to me: 'Went back to the Mahabharat today—to a conversation before the war. Draupadi realises she is going to lose all her children, and is furious. And Krishna says: "Did I ever tell you that you would get happiness and prosperity after this war? This war is to re-establish dharma—that's all. Fighting for dharma is not your duty—it is a choice you make. And you take all the consequences that come with it."'

That brave teacher in the hills, she has chosen her battle and taken the consequences on her stage in the sky. We must make our choices, on our own stages. The world is unmade and made by that.

PS: I have masked her identity, since her battle continues.

24 November 2016

A New Battle in Talikota

The ruins of Hampi are haunting. Among impossibly balanced giant boulders, with intermittent lush paddy fields, and the quietly flowing Tungabhadra, they soak you with a sense of the impossible having happened there. Hampi was the seat of the Vijayanagara Empire. The definitive date for the end of this empire is 26 January 1565. That day, the empire's armies were defeated by an army of the coalition of its neighbouring sultanates in the Battle of Talikota, about 180 km from Hampi. Like every such battle marking a watershed in history, there are claims and counterclaims about what happened on that fateful day. What is not disputed is that the Battle of Talikota marked the end of something remarkable.

Today, Talikota has no marker for this important role it played in Indian history. No memorial, no ruin, just vast rolling plains around a town that's completely like any other small town in India. But memories can't be erased, even after 500 years. All conversations with outsiders invoke the battle. And so it was with Ameensab Mehboobsab Nazkatti, the head teacher of the government elementary school in Talikota town. He started with the battle, but moved quickly to responding to our question. He told us his story.

In early 2015, he requested a transfer to this school. He wanted the transfer, not because it reduced his commute or some such convenience, but because he had studied in that school himself. The school was established in 1876, and had a rich history of having been a key educational institution of that area. But over the past decade, it had decayed. Teaching-learning had declined to virtually zero, and worse, it had become a den for the local heavies. Fisticuffs inside the school were a usual sight, so were bottles of liquor and heaps of stinking trash. He could not bear to watch the school that made him what he was, and many more like him, descend into this abyss. He had four years of service left before retirement, and so he asked for a transfer to try and improve the situation as his last assignment. After moving in, he realised that the underlying dynamics were far more complex than he had anticipated. The school was a free-for-all, both as a physical and social space, with no concern for education. Its decrepit physical infrastructure reflected its culture. It had really and metaphorically become a pigsty.

After observing the situation for a while, he gathered the local community leaders, cutting across political and caste affiliations. This is much easier said than done; it required enormous tenacity. Once he had got them, the question he asked them was whether they wanted the image of their community to be what the school portrayed. The ways of the school were well known in that area. His point was simple—a community is known by the school it runs. No one was unmoved. The reasons varied from genuine feeling to hurt pride, but they did want to do something. After a few discussions, this group concluded that to change matters, they had to involve some of the younger leaders who moved in the same circles as those who were involved in the problems in the school. Once this was done, the action on the ground started. The School Development and Management Committee played a key role. One track was about protecting and isolating the school from outsiders, and the other was about building greater community ownership.

The early moves were enough for the teachers to go to school regularly and teach. Some got the message, and some got the courage they needed. The community helped in cleaning up the place, then they contributed money to build a 6-ft-high boundary wall. Many other things were done and it culminated in a grand cultural programme that the students put up for the community.

Everyone swelled with pride at the work of their children. As we walked about the school, the lady in her mid-fifties who cooks the mid-day meal stopped us. She said that she prayed morning and evening for Nazkatti, so that he would stay in the school for many more years. Tears streaming down her face, she narrated how the goons would beat her up and how happy she was now.

After bringing order to the school, the head teacher is now moving on to the next steps. He is committed to improving learning in the three years that he has left. He is working with the teachers for this, and with the community, which has contributed to better equip the school and to start an informal preschool in one of the empty rooms. After many years, student enrolment has gone up from 170 to 230.

It would have been better if India did not need heroes, but it does. Fortunately, we have many—one of them has a slight build, wispy grey hair and faded white apparel, all belying the battle that he is waging in Talikota today. Unlike 1565, this time, it is the beginning of something remarkable.

1 September 2016

Inequity among Teachers

We were in a small central hall in the school, sometimes used as a classroom. Two kids ran in announcing that there was a snake on the steps outside. In the seconds that it would have taken us to reach the steps, two men had appeared from outside and caught the snake, with one of them gleefully holding it in his hands. They were snake catchers by trade. How odd that a snake appears in a school while you are visiting it, and it has two snake catchers in tow. In that village, almost anyone could have caught the snake, including many of the children, since it's a community of nath-jogi—experts in catching snakes. The head teacher of the school, who has been there since 1997, has also learnt to catch snakes. This school is in one of the most disadvantaged districts of Madhya Pradesh.

In 1997, the current head teacher was in his early twenties. He received an appointment letter from the government's department of education, as a teacher in that village. When he reached the village, he learnt there was no school there. Its dwellings were at best temporary shelters, made of plastic sheets, thatch and logs. When he asked the department officials what he was to do, he was told that he was supposed to start the school. He occupied the shelter of the largest tree as the school. It was a lot more difficult to get the children to school.

The community had no notion of schools or education for their children. They thought that this man from a nearby village had showed up to show off. After some negotiation, a few children were sent to the tree, along with a few curious onlookers. A few days later, all the children vanished, along with everyone else from the village. The community would regularly go to nearby towns and cities, and beg by showering the blessings of the snakes they had caught. They would be gone for two to three weeks at a time. He had to shut down the tree school as soon as it started.

He has been there for eighteen years now, with an unchanging focus on the school. He has got most other things to change. The community changed its practices; it stopped taking children on the begging trips so that they could go to school. The Sarva Shiksha Abhiyan funds were used to build a nice school building. It's a pretty, 2 acre campus now, very well-maintained. The school has grown; it now has ninety-nine students and three teachers. Scores of students have passed out of the school, many have done very well, and some have become part of the urban middle class as engineers and technicians. The village has pride in its school, and the whole area recognises it.

The journey from under the tree to the 2 acre campus has been an everyday struggle for him for eighteen years, which he doesn't refer to. Thousands like him have similarly, painstakingly, with no recognition, built our public education system. In the places they have toiled, most of us won't even go for a day.

The day we were there, the head teacher was on strike. He was protesting. His compensation is about half of the majority of teachers with similar tenure. This is an outcome of the state government appointing teachers in different 'cadres'. While the original intent of this practice may have been different, most will freely admit that over time it has become only a tool to reduce the state's wage bill. The result is blatant inequity—teachers doing identical work, with identical background and capacity, differ in compensation by a factor of two. It was a state-wide strike by the discriminated cadre. While he was on strike, he was still in the school. The children were also there and classes were going on. He seemed to have sorted it out for himself, as to how he could be working like any other day, and still be on strike. His sense of responsibility for children far outweighed any sense of injustice for himself.

Many states find themselves in a similar bind, developed over many years. Significant proportions of their teachers have been appointed at lower compensation levels and with worse service conditions—short-term contracts which just keep getting rolled over. These obvious injustices are not resolved because of fiscal considerations and apathy to the reality in the schools.

The situation remains on the boil continually and is managed politically. Unsurprisingly, all this affects the engagement levels of teachers and the school culture, especially in schools that have teachers from two cadres. The states must move to equitable service conditions for all teachers. It's no more complicated than that. In the meanwhile, thousands like this head teacher, who have given years of their life to the service of communities truly beyond the margins, will soldier on. The very human responsibility of the children in the class will continue to outweigh anything else.

12 March 2016

Bridging the Divide in Classrooms

The Katarmal complex has forty-six temples, built around the tenth century. The biggest temple houses the Burhadita, the old sun god, and is about 7 m tall. Some of the temples are less than 2 m. Large stone blocks have been used for the construction. Many of the panels have intricate engravings. But there is nothing particularly noteworthy about the history or architecture of this temple complex; it's one amongst hundreds of such complexes in this country. That's till you stand there and look down, from its perch on a mountainside at 2,116 m. How were the stone blocks dragged up that steep slope? Why did the Katuriya kings build the temples there? There are no adequate explanations. When I asked the students of the Government Upper-Primary School of Katarmal village about the temples, they narrated the local myth, the most important element of which is that the temples were built in one night. When I asked them whether it was really possible, they said it wasn't possible, and then the conversation went to how that myth may have been formed. Katarmal is about 20 km from Almora.

The temple overlooks the school, which is perched on another slope. The school has an unusual layout: four rooms open into one large central common hall, which has a sliding grill door, which once shut, closes the school completely. I haven't seen many rural schools like this, which can be completely closed by one grill door. It's a very clean school. I have seen many, but this one stands out.

As we chatted with the two teachers, Snehlata Bisht and Nirmala Uppadhay, it became clear as to how the temple looms over the school, and not just physically. The two teachers have been in this school for a few years. Their early days in the school were very difficult. Each day would bring a new disaster like smashed pots, muddied walls or human excreta in the hall. It was methodical vandalism by youngsters from the village. It's perhaps because of this that the grill door was made. For reasons that they didn't understand fully, the school had a history of a fraught relationship with the local community, and the vandalism was only one expression of the inherited hostility.

Inside the school they faced even more complicated issues. The children came from two different parts of the village, which were virtually two different villages, divided by caste. Local legends hold that the village of Dalits was the traditional home of the temple devadasis. This worsened the discrimination with the village. The temple devadasi tradition, even if it had been there, must have stopped a century ago. In the school, the children from the two villages would not even sit together. The teachers grappled with this fragmented school. While the educational activities of the school had the usual challenges, they decided that letting prejudices determine the basic character of the school made any other educational progress hollow. They felt that helping the children come out of these prejudices must be a core educational objective. They engaged with the community around. They revived the mechanism of the School Management Committee, which had parents from both villages. More important than that was the informal personal dialogues that they established.

Their efforts in the classes were equally sincere. They gave personal attention to all students, and fostered a culture of open dialogue. All these efforts in the school and the better teaching-learning environment were visible to the village community. The vandalism stopped after a while. After a couple of years, the teachers were invited to a wedding in the upper-caste village. They agreed to attend only if all the students were invited. After much consternation in the community, all students, including the ones from the other village, were welcomed to the wedding.

When we visited the school last month, all this was long past. The school was a cheerful place, with confident students. There was not the slightest sign of a divide; in fact, there was also no sign of the gender divide that pervades most schools. While the teachers were conscious that the divide in the villages remained, they were satisfied by the progress within the school. They have good reason to feel satisfied; the experience in the school has and will continue to influence the students.

Our educational aims and curricular approach would require that any school facing such a situation must act as these teachers did; this is just one dimension of the complex role expected of a teacher. What we want of education, in the context of our society and the natural environment of any class full of children, makes the teacher's role highly demanding and extremely complex. There is scant societal recognition of this basic reality, and it is reflected in the lackadaisical support to teachers, the poor teacher preparation system that we have built as a nation and the irrational scapegoating of teachers for all ills in our education system.

24 June 2015

A Tale of a Teacher Forum

The hills of Mount Abu glowed from the setting sun. The single-floor school complex, with the buildings on the edges of a huge rectangular playground, looked straight out on to this lovely sight. This was in Abu Road, a town of about 40,000 people, the railhead for Mount Abu. There were twenty-five teachers all sitting on the floor in a bare room, engrossed in a problem: given a length of rope, make a two-dimensional closed figure that would have the biggest area. It was a Wednesday, but a holiday because of a local festival. Figures were made, measured and unmade.

There was discussion on how to prove that a circle would have the biggest area. This led to what it means to prove something. Soon, there was a heated debate on whether certain mathematical concepts in the syllabus were too early for children of that age. In the end, the next meeting was scheduled for a Sunday about two weeks later. Many went to the nearby vegetable market on the way home.

These twenty-five are a part of a larger group of about eighty teachers, who live in and around Abu Road, and work in government schools across villages and towns in that area. It's a network of teachers, and is an informal group. Some of them are more engaged in the group's activities and some less. Unsurprisingly, each individual's engagement also varies, periods of lull following intense engagement, depending on other priorities in her life.

The group is called the Teacher Forum. In addition to meeting on holidays or after school hours to discuss specific topics, the group has other activities—supporting each other on academic issues, week-long workshops during the vacations, developing teaching-learning material. They also help teachers outside the forum.

The teachers do all this voluntarily, without any order from the government or any financial incentive. There is indeed nothing official about it. They are all investing their own time and also spending their own money for the commute. There is no political or mobilisation agenda to the group; it's entirely focused on academic matters. While it's called the Teacher Forum, many head teachers and other education functionaries also participate. All of them are involved voluntarily for their own professional development. They want to do their jobs better.

The Teacher Forum in Abu Road has not developed miraculously on its own. A few people formed the core of it and worked hard to develop it over the past five years. They battled cynicism, suspicion and disinterest. However, as it became clear that there was no agenda other than learning, and that it was a safe space with no possibilities of 'official' intervention, more and more teachers joined hands. Over time, local officials have started valuing this informal network, and support it in many ways, taking care that it doesn't acquire any tinge of becoming official.

The Abu Road Teacher Forum is one among ten such in the district of Sirohi in Rajasthan.

There are more than 800 teachers involved in these forums. This is not a phenomenon unique to that area; we see this across the country, from Uttarakhand to Puducherry. Whenever I talk about these forums with my friends, especially those who are wilfully uninformed and hold deep prejudices against government schoolteachers, I love making a comparison. I ask them as to how many employees in their organisations will show up regularly on holidays, paying for their own commute, to learn things so that they can do their jobs better, without any external incentive or mandate. They get the picture.

So, why does this happen with teachers? It's not that teachers are some special group of highly motivated people. The population of teachers very much follows the distribution of the general Indian population on all such individual characteristics and dispositions. Not the complete explanation, but a significant part of it lies in the inherent nature of a teacher's role.

At the most basic level, a teacher faces thirty children every day; she gets immediate and visible feedback of her efficacy. It's unavoidable feedback. It's like going out to bat in front of a packed stadium every day; who would not want to improve? There is something deeper.

Irrespective of why someone became a teacher, once she has children in her charge, an innate sense of responsibility takes over. This is not like any other job. It's the sense of being responsible deeply for the future and lives of the children. This affects most, other than the completely incorrigible.

While the teacher population is not different from the general population on basic characteristics, the nature of their role plays a key part in propelling them to learn and improve. This is perhaps the strongest lever available for improvement in school education. Decentralised, empowered and flexible mechanisms such as the Teacher Forum engage, energise and develop teachers. It does require patient work on the ground. And it requires including teachers as partners in change, trusted as a part of the solution rather than treated as part of the problem.

16 April 2015

One Man, David

David Horsburgh's Neel Bagh answered an eternal question in Indian education: 'What can one man do?'

David Horsburgh came to India in 1943 as a part of the Royal Air Force (RAF). He spent some of his leave, in what must have been an unusual pastime for an RAF person, in a small island village near Chittagong. Amid the waterways and paddy fields, he could see the village school. And he thought that was what he would like to do in life: teach in a village school.

In 1950, armed with a college degree from England, David returned to India. He lived here till his death in 1984. In 1983, he gave an interview to Rosalind Wilson, editor of the children's magazine *Target*. Wilson asked him, 'The general scenario of the education system in India … if it's so grim, where do you have breakthrough?'

David replied, 'I do not know what the answer is to this. I can only say, I am going to sit in my little village and try and produce what I think is very good education. Some children, perhaps educated in freedom—no fear, you know, not being competitive, being much aware, etc.—perhaps they will find solutions, which I cannot find with my background and my conditioning.'

In 1972, along with his wife Doreen, David had started Neel Bagh. A 100 km from Bangalore, just off the road to Madanapalle, the school was not in the midst of waterways and paddy fields. But it was what he had set out to do. The school had about thirty students, aged three to twenty, all from the villages nearby. Some were mad about Shakespeare. They would learn philosophy, aesthetics, music appreciation, carpentry and pottery. This was in addition to the usual mathematics, geography, physics and so on. There was a lot of emphasis on learning languages: English, Telugu, Kannada, Hindi and Sanskrit.

This eclectic, seemingly eccentric curriculum was just one facet of the deliberate design of Neel Bagh. The methodology, the culture, the physical environment and the community were all integrated to build a place where education happened as it should. The students would learn together in groups, but at their individual pace. The teacher would only facilitate the setting up of suitable learning situations. The focus would be on problem-solving and concept formation.

The students would engage in real-world activities, in reading, in discussion and in critical thinking. Almost all students were first generation schoolgoers. In short, Neel Bagh was the kind of school that we can only imagine.

Three years after David's death, faced with numerous financial and regulatory hurdles, his son Nicholas (who also worked at the school) handed it over to the Krishnamurti Foundation. The premises have subsequently passed to another organisation that runs a school there with great care. But David's Neel Bagh ended in 1987.

My friend Rohit tells me that David's bar would open at 8.45 p.m. In the long history of the British Raj, surely there were other Englishmen who would have spent their Indian nights at their bars set in incongruous rural settings. So did David, but along with an intensely debating bunch of 'student teachers', who interned with him. The bar would have opened to only continue what had started in the morning 'seminar'. These would-be teachers went through an intense education at Neel Bagh. David would invite them from all over India, and later built a house for them with his own hands. Rohit, Amukta, Reena, Malathi and a handful of others (only some of whom I know) went through this truly remarkable teacher-education programme. When you talk to them, the intellectual rigour of the experience and its absolute immersion shines through, as it does in their work. It changed them forever, and they are helping change Indian education.

David's small school showed that what should be done in education can be done, both for teachers and students. He ran the wonder that was Neel Bagh, largely supported through the royalties from the hundred-odd books that he had written (some with his son Nicholas) and with debt. Along with Rohit, I visited the premises of Neel Bagh earlier this year. It looks lovely and well kept. The houses that David built are still in place. For Rohit, every nook was infused with memory and meaning.

On that afternoon in Neel Bagh, I felt David had proved himself wrong. He did have the answer to Wilson's question. He gave the answer by producing as good an education as he could in a small village. That has made him a pole star for us—a star that guides and inspires breakthroughs—in this 'grim scenario'.

His legacy is alive in his books, his 'student teachers' and the many more that he influenced. The legacy is really a call to arms for good education. He is also an answer to another eternal question that faces most of us one day or the other: 'What can one man do?' The least we can do is sit in our little village and produce as good an education as we can.

5 May 2011

Education in India:
There's Still Hope

As I waited to meet the principal, the teacher's voice drifted out from the open classroom window. It was a dark room with the children on the floor. I couldn't make out more from the outside. The voice was repeating, 'Kanha is a national park. It is open till 6 p.m. in the summers and 4 p.m. in the winters.' After three repetitions, he instructed the children to repeat after him, which they did.

In a small town in Karnataka, a thousand kilometres away, the complete irrelevance of Kanha's opening hours is obvious. The dark room and the disembodied voice unwittingly portrayed a caricature that is often real, of teaching in India. All our stated educational policies and curricular approaches are dead against this kind of meaningless activity that passes as education. However, in the classrooms of this country, far and near from where these policies are made, this routine goes on.

The principal (and owner) was in his early thirties. We sat in a small room, which opened onto a narrow street. This was the only way in to the school; it was his control cabin. He narrated with some relish his success in building the school, starting with his disinterest in the family trading business and the desire to start a new one. He had some hesitation in talking about the economics of his school, but eagerly shared his triumph in being able to attract children from nearby villages within a radius of 6 km. In the half an hour that we were with him, we saw the effectiveness of his control cabin in managing his teachers, helpers and suppliers. We left him perched at his cash-counter, chatting with no interest with someone who had strolled in with no purpose.

In another small town, in Rajasthan, we were leaving another school. The principal was walking with us across the neatly maintained school garden to see us off. The little girl was in all red, both her thumbs in her mouth, perched on a platform built around a grand peepal tree.

She just kept staring at us wide-eyed. She is four years old, too young for school. Her mother had passed away a year ago; her father is a labourer. Her two brothers study in the school. With no one else at home, only they can take care of her. So Kaniram, the principal, has asked her father to send her to school, so that the brothers don't miss school. She hangs around the whole day and eats the school's mid-day-meal. Kaniram also arranges clothes for her.

Kaniram told me the story of the peepal. When he was transferred to the school, the tree was full of red flags, rotting flowers and decaying offerings. It was a totem, like many a peepal tree. But it was inside the government upper-primary school. Not only was it dirtying the place, but it would attract crowds who had no reason to enter the school. He got the flags and everything else out of the school, and burnt the heap. He was told by the horrified people about all the plagues that would visit them as retribution. His response was, 'The plagues will visit me, not you, don't worry.'

He uses less extreme methods to keep his school the way it is. It's an acre of leafy oasis, with fresh-smelling rooms and toilets with running water; a clean well-lit place. Aside from using his budgets well, he cajoles local people in the town, and also those who have migrated out, to contribute to the school. That's how he built the platform around the peepal, and is also able to organise an honorarium for a retired official, who helps with Class I, since the school has only four teachers to handle 245 children across the eight classes. His approach is 'negotiate for more resources from the outside, but must manage with what is there; the children can't suffer'.

All teachers in his school need to be able to teach all subjects. He regrets that experienced colleagues who had become really good teachers were transferred out, but gets on with developing the new teachers who have joined. We saw the Class VIII students working in a group, learning from each other. He doesn't know in-vogue phrases like 'peer-learning' for this, but gets it done. He politely refused to accept my compliments saying, 'This is my job, and every one of us has enough space to do it, if we want to.'

The first anecdote is constructed from experiences in a few schools, and is not about a specific school. That's deliberate because I don't want to sit in judgement based on brief interactions. However, such experiences are all too common. Schools driven by profit don't bother much about education, or about their students. Not all private schools are like this, nor do all government schools have a Kaniram. But without doubt, too many schools are run like cash counters. Fortunately, there are also enough people like Kaniram, with whom lies the hope for education.

13 November 2013

Empower the Teacher

An earthquake in 1991 flattened Ganeshpur. Twenty years after the event, you can still see the devastation that was caused by it. The village is 7 km from Uttarkashi. Its population is nearly a thousand and it has a government primary school. The school is still run from the temporary 'relief' structure constructed after the earthquake. It has two teachers and fifty-four students.

On entering the small walled courtyard of the school, I saw that a part of the wall had been used as a blackboard, with lines written in chalk. It was the news of the day from the village. The only tractor in the village had still not been repaired, the sowing of onion and potato crops had started, someone's flower bed was looking beautiful—titbits from life in the village that the children had found interesting.

Kailash and I entered one of the two classrooms. It was small for the twenty-five kids, cramping them. Kailash turned to the teacher, and quietly observed that there were many more girls than boys in the class. Standing in one corner, she just nodded, and said that that was the way it was. I asked her why it was the way it was. Her eyes flashed lightning, and her tone had a reprimand. She asked, 'Don't you know why?' She meant the obvious gender discrimination, with boys being dispatched to private schools.

After that we didn't move from our places for twenty minutes, standing and talking in the corner of the class. The children continued to do some assignment. Our conversation started with gender discrimination. We talked about the quality of education and what made it. We talked about the differences between private and government schools. We talked about the implication of those differences for the most disadvantaged and impoverished. Her insightfulness was matched by her complete fearlessness in standing her ground and challenging me all the way in that intense conversation. That was my introduction to Rekha.

With the Garhwal mountains rising around steeply, and the Bhagirathi flowing below, she seemed as much a force of nature. Her combination of intensity, thoughtfulness and courage is rare, very rare, anywhere. And she is a government primary schoolteacher in a village.

My colleagues and I sat down with her and Rajani, the other teacher, in a small room. They kept cutting juicy apples for us, fresh from the orchard nearby. We chatted about their school. We saw a collection of projects on which the school had worked for weeks. It was about children discovering firsthand the event that had shaped the collective memory of Ganeshpur, and its physical shape. These were authentic documents of the earthquake, authenticity of a child's curiosity researching personal cataclysms. We saw books that the children had written together with Rekha. The language, lucidity of expression and the stories would surprise anyone. So, it was no surprise to hear that a number of students had works published in children's magazines. None of these things are prescribed by the curriculum. But they are not prohibited either. Rekha's ingenuity has not let the system limit her. She operates within the same school system as others, but has discovered and created spaces, which lets her do all this.

This story of Rekha is set to the same tune these columns have sung before. Teachers matter more than all else in education. We have a shoddy teacher education system, and unless we improve that dramatically, our education won't improve. Our system must motivate the teachers, not disempower them. Despite everything, good people have enough space in the system to make a genuine difference. And there are many good people. But today's column does not intend to merely emphasise those larger, valid points. It's about that one exceptional individual that I met, and the question that she left me with. That first intense twenty-minute conversation ended in a way she probably wanted to avoid. We agreed with each other that besides socio-psychological factors triggering people to move their children to private schools, one key factor was the perceived quality of government schools. She agreed that if government schoolteachers were to do a decent job, it could make a big difference.

I asked her what was happening at her school. It is this discussion of her competence and the school's success that I felt she wanted to avoid. But she had to admit that the number of children in her school had been going up. Parents were moving their children from private schools in the vicinity to the government school. I told her what I felt: that she was doing a great job, that it is teachers like her that could really change lives. She looked at me. There was no lightning, no reprimand. She merely said: *'Har koi jogi to nahi ho sakta, na?'* (Everyone can't be a jogi, no?)

It's impossible to translate 'jogi'. It's equally impossible to convey the tone: the balance between a confession, a statement of finality and a question with hope. The Bhagirathi continued to flow furiously. I had no answer. We do owe her an answer, if nothing else.

2 November 2011

The Validation Phenomenon

My friends often say that every fortnight I seem to refer to a trip or two, which they wish they had come along for. I travel two weeks out of four in a month; some months it's three out of four. They also ask me why I travel so much. What makes me think though is their wish to accompany me on these trips. What I narrate from these trips is merely what happened. In that narration they probably see a world different from their own, infused with a sense of romanticism that beckons them.

The evening light was very faint, as it is at the bottom of any tree-covered deep valley. It was one of the rare stretches where the road runs level, just about 100 ft above the surging Bhagirathi river. We stopped at a shack-like dhaba open at the front, on the roadside. It was among a cluster of about ten houses, actually huts. There was no one in sight. We called out. There was no response. The temperature seemed to be dropping by the minute. We wanted tea, and couldn't wait. Anant fired the stove; Prakash searched for and found milk, tea and sugar. They made tea, as we stood shivering, looking down at the glittering river.

When the tea was being poured into the glasses, a young woman in her early twenties walked down the steep mountainside and into the shack. She was smiling, and asked, 'So you have made the tea?' It seemed like the most natural behaviour, on both sides. Leave your shack open, unattended, unguarded, because those who want tea will come and make it. We paid her Rs 30, and she returned Rs 10. She said that since the milk was less, the tea was less, Rs 20 was a fair price. She asked when we would return. That's the last we saw of her. For most of us in Bangalore or Delhi or wherever we are, the mental image of the evening-lit mountainside, the river and the woman's behaviour is so removed from our experience and expectation that it would certainly beckon us.

Let me point out: that's exactly the way it happened. I have not taken any creative licence. Many things happened on that trip; I won't write about everything. I do write about things that affect me positively. And so, perhaps I do infuse romanticism into the narration. Is it then somehow unreal, the picture of India that emerges? I don't think so, because such beautiful things happen week after week, across the country.

Another day, I was sitting on a boulder eating lunch, looking up a sparse forest on a gentle hillside somewhere in Karnataka. It was during a workshop for schoolteachers. One of the facilitators, a man who had worked on the ground in many parts of the country with schools for over thirty years, sat down with me. He said, 'We love your columns. We translate them into Hindi.' I was curious as to why someone like him would find my columns interesting.

Whatever I write about, he has experienced, understood and done immeasurably more in his thirty years with education. His explanation was simple. He said, 'You write about good people and good things. These are rays of hope for us.' He finds validation and reaffirmation in what I write. It's important for him, because he thinks that most of the mainstream discourse of the country has abandoned efforts like theirs, has given up on the public education system and is disconnected with the reality on the ground. His explanation reminded me of a lecture I gave at a university that lives on its glorious past, in a mid-sized town in north India. I am reluctant to give lectures because I don't know what to say. It seems as though I just end up repeating what everyone anyhow knows. At the end of that particular lecture, a professor came to me. She was in tears, which would not stop.

Through her tears she said that she had done for twenty years, what I had talked about, and she felt validated.

Over time, I have begun to see the importance of this phenomenon of validation. Some need it more, some less, but all need it nevertheless. The chasm between those on the ground, who face reality every day, and those who wield power and control discourse (or seem to) is large. The people on the ground often feel alone, disempowered and unsure. So, anyone or anything that can bridge this chasm through a simple reaffirmation— 'what you are doing is right and good'—is valuable.

People like me also need validation, for hope. Week after week, in schools, in offices and on the roadside, people reaffirm through their actions, that there is enough truth, beauty and goodness in this nation. What it needs is an attempt on my part to remain connected with those real people.

20 March 2013

PART SIX

IS BAHAKATI HUI DUNIYA KO SAMBHALO YAARON

Let's Not Talk about Education Now …

Twelve-year-old Jamlo died walking home in the searing Indian summer sun. She was among the lakhs who walked and are walking still, forced to flee the cities to the only places they can trust. Homes that they had migrated from, hundreds or thousands of miles away. While millions more try to survive wherever they are, picking on the wreckage of their livelihoods. Hungry today, fearful of tomorrow, haunted by the spectre of a plague and completely uncertain about life. This is our India now.

Why grudge those few who still enjoy wine-and-cheese evenings with friends on Zoom? Those who lack even a modicum of empathy for Jamlo, or who won't lift a finger to help the lady who used to iron their clothes as she scavenges for food today, can be ignored. They may have their private miseries. I learnt about the perils of comparing pains and tragedies a while ago from a wise one. All this should be accepted or ignored, so long as people recognise what has become of our India.

But deniers, there are aplenty, of what we have made of ourselves. Drowning in wine, or choking on their cheese, is the fate I wish for them, figuratively. This is not rage but just cold calculation about what will make for a better world. Many are deserving of such a fate, but most are sensible even if somewhat uncomprehending of the severity of the devastation across the country. Some from the latter lot have asked me in the past few weeks, 'So what should be done about the education of children?' My response has surprised them—we should do nothing about education. If children are not taught for a few months, nothing dramatic will be lost. Nothing that cannot be regained in the ensuing period.

Let's first guarantee that people have food, get them home and ensure that there is no repetition of what has happened over the past few weeks. Unless we get a grip on these bare necessities, there is no point in bothering about the education of children. Roiled by uncertainty and deprivation, no child and family can focus on education.

Even more perilous are the thoughts of 'online education' that many espouse while schools are shut.

First, the basics. Online education is ineffective. The education of a child requires intense social interactions between the child and a teacher. The child's physical presence, attention, thoughts and emotions must be carefully guided through multiple steps, often back and forth, towards the immediate learning goals. And then the sequences of these goals are sewn together into the complex tapestry that makes for education. None of this is even faintly possible through online education. It is a social and human process; technology cannot mediate it effectively. All theory and empirical evidence tells us the same, though this is not the place to recount that.

Children learning to bake from the internet is wonderful, but it is not education. Heavily marketed apps may help a child learn something, often because of energetic parents, but that is also not education. Online resources are useful tools, but they, too, are not education. The word 'education' does not mean mere learning, which can be of many sorts, both desirable and undesirable. Education specifically means systematically achieving the age-wise curricular goals of our schools.

Second, any attention to online education diverts scarce resources and energy down a cul-de-sac. Worse, just the act of 'doing something' lulls those in roles of responsibility into a false sense of achievement.

Third, the pandemic and the lockdown have magnified every vulnerability, amplified the inequities and their effects and, in too many instances, also sharpened the chasms of prejudice and discrimination. Online education will be just one more vector for exacerbating the deep inequities in education. The disadvantaged, who are the large majority, will get left behind further. Access to such social and physical resources as are required for online education are a pipedream for them—they are struggling for food. Online education in these times must not even be contemplated.

What should then be done about school education? After the 'bare necessities' are taken care of, schools should be opened up immediately. Without doubt, experts in epidemiology should weigh in on this decision. But there are three reasons to act with speed.

First, most schools will not increase the risk of the infection spreading. This is because they serve very localised communities, where kids intermingle all the time. Schools that serve wider communities can be opened with significant physical distancing norms, including, for example, operating on alternate days for half the students. Second, schools could be the real front line for generating awareness and building ownership among communities for the country's campaign against COVID-19. Third, as my friend Prof. Ramachandran, a veteran of restarting schools in every conflict zone across the world in the past thirty years, says, 'There is no better anchor for peace and stability of a community, than functioning schools.' In the long campaign against the pandemic ahead, communities will need this strength.

But let me end with what I would have not said even in my worst nightmare ever—let us not worry about education. Let us focus everything on penance for Jamlo. Not one of our fellow citizens should be made to walk home, nor remain hungry. We have burnt down enough of India's soul this summer.

21 May 2020

Ta-hadd-e-nazar Ek Bayaabaan Sa Kyun Hai

Busboys and Poets is a lovely bookstore-cum-restaurant in Washington, DC. The name is a homage to the Black American poet and activist, Langston Hughes, who earned a living as a busboy, a waiter's assistant. On 22 February, I was having lunch there alone, reading a book. The people on the table next to me kept looking at the book. They stopped near me as they were leaving and said, 'We don't think it is very serious, why are you reading that book?' They seemed curiously aggressive.

The book was William McNeill's classic of epidemiological history, *Plagues and Peoples*, perhaps one of the first to explore the deep influence of diseases on the course of humanity, from the early humans and the Neolithic era to the rise of civilisations and the modern times. I was not inclined to break my reverie, so I said, 'I am sorry, I won't read it,' and shut it. They went away.

That evening at Dulles Airport, as I was leaving for Bengaluru, the book came out from the bag with the laptop at the security X-ray machine. The security agent at the collection point on the other side looked at the book and said, 'That's the right book to read, man; it's coming.'

On 3 March, I was in a school in the village of Malpura, near Sitarganj in Udham Singh Nagar district, Uttarakhand. Children from three schools had gathered there and set up a Bal Mela, a children's fair, with exhibits that they had made themselves. It was not a big ground; there were about 200 people. I heard something like a chant from the distant corner, where a bunch of kids had gathered. As I walked across and nearer to them, the words became clearer, 'Coronavirus! Coronavirus! Coronavirus!' They were having fun with the chant and prancing around.

'What's this chant?' I asked. 'Who is this Coronavirus?'.

'*Bhayankar bimari hai*,' (It is a very dangerous disease) they replied.

'So, what will you do?' I asked.

'We must wash our hands,' they replied and laughed.

Through that week I travelled from the east to the west of the district, as I have done every year for many years now. In school after school, I discovered that 'Coronavirus' was well known, but not feared.

On 8 March, I returned to Bengaluru. In two days, we were considering closing our university, which we did two days before the government advisory to shut all institutions in the city. Those extra two days gave us the opportunity for a relatively orderly closure. The next day onwards, we stopped all non-essential travel. Thereafter, our decisions on response measures had to accelerate exponentially. With over 1,500 members of our team spread across over 200 small towns and villages of India, in addition to our concentration in Bengaluru, we were grappling with significant operational complexity. We further have over 350 partner organisations spread across the country.

My daughter was in London. She was calm, as she always is. My parents were in Raipur, wanting to get back home to Bhopal. At their age, it was inadvisable to travel, especially by public transport. Then India announced a virtual shutdown of its borders for flights boarding after noon GMT on 18 March. And since then, things have just escalated every day.

All of us are facing similar situations. Stranded away from those whom we care most about, with no way to help or even know. Many of us are much worse off, with livelihoods vanishing or risks multiplying due to already-fragile health, or both. We have not dealt with anything like this before, individually or collectively as a modern global society. We are probably not in the middle of it but at the beginning.

Until now, to respond as an organisation, we have used some common-sense principles. First, safety is paramount. Not only our safety and that of our families, but that of our communities. We must not become vectors of the virus in those remote locations. Second, heed all government advisories and only credible experts, ignoring the immense amount of misinformation floating around. Third, we must communicate many times more than we usually do. Every day, we have two teleconferences with over a hundred of our colleagues, who, in turn, speak to their teams every day. We also make sure to communicate clearly with our partners. Fourth, work must continue. This is very complex, and we are grappling with this. Work is important, but equally, it is an anchor for coping with this difficult time. Fifth, we must figure out a way to help others and contribute in tackling this crisis. Given the privilege of our resources and size, we must be out there, where we can contribute most. Sixth and most importantly, we must act with empathy. Each one of us is facing the same fears and confusions. We must stand together with each other.

I bought *Plagues and Peoples* in December last year, before the first news from Wuhan had leaked out. It was one of those strange coincidences. Let me quote the last paragraph of the book, 'Ingenuity, knowledge, and organisation alter but cannot cancel humanity's vulnerability to invasion by parasitic forms of life. Infectious disease which antedated the emergence of humankind will last as long as humanity itself, and will surely remain, as it has been hitherto, one of the fundamental parameters and determinants of human history.'

How profoundly this pandemic will alter the course of human history, we don't know. But we ourselves will be altered by it. Our actions make us who we are and who we become, slowly over our lifetimes. But there are times when a brief period can shape us profoundly. This is probably such a time. We can choose who we become, with thought, courage and empathy.

PS: The title is a line from Shaharyar's haunting *ghazal* (poem) about loneliness, used in the film *Gaman*, to wrenching effect. The line roughly means: why is there wilderness till as far as the eyes can see?

26 March 2020

Crossing the Bridge, Every Day

The crashing monsoon rain beyond the shut windows and the hushed tones is as alive as this morning. Blurting out my defiance of insufferable oppression with all the might of a seven-year-old is also vivid. So is the cutting glare from my Mausi, my best friend, barely having entered college then, and her whispered threat, 'You will also be jailed and so will all of us.' All this in the dining room of my Nana's bungalow in Bhopal, back in 1975.

Then they went back to talking about, 'JP, George and Dharia' in low voices. At some point, I heard Nana mention a king, and that had he been alive, he would have come, to struggle in solidarity, for the freedom of the people who gave him Gandhi.

These days, about once a year, I run past that house—and the others I have lived in—and their memories in that city which is home. Remembrances of that distant a time, form as they did in a child's head, must be jumbled. But not in mine. I asked Nana who this king of ours was, who could not come to save us. That is how I first heard of him—when Nana said, 'Not the king, but Martin Luther King, Junior.' Since then, King and Gandhi have lived together in my head. Even when I have playfully jostled with who was the better of the two, they were inseparable.

By the time the Emergency was lifted, I was soaking up books, which, even to me now, seems totally incongruous with my age then. The number was also abnormal. Almost a book a day. So, I just cannot recollect where I read of the young man who stayed up one night in Nashville, writing a list of nonviolent 'do's and don'ts' to help his fellow students if they got arrested. The last point in that list was: 'Remember the teachings of Jesus, Gandhi, Thoreau, and Martin Luther King Jr.' That this line was not a figment of my childhood imagination got settled only recently, when I read one of my most treasured gifts, Taylor Branch's *Parting the Waters,* in which the incident is described as I remembered it.

I can't recollect whether I read first about Dharasana or Selma. Both places are fused in my head. And into Webb Miller's wrenching words that were first read by millions in mid-May 1930: 'Not one of the marchers even raised an arm to fend off the blows. They went down like tenpins. From where I stood, I heard the sickening whacks of the clubs on unprotected skulls.'

The first skull to be cracked open on 7 March 1965 in Selma was that of the young man who led the 600 protesters across that bridge. And he was the same young man who prayed to the flame that passed from Jesus to King, through Gandhi and Thoreau.

Thus, John Lewis became muddled in my head with Gandhi and King and Thoreau. When I saw the terrifying Dharasana scene in Attenborough's *Gandhi* in 1982, I saw Lewis fall. I read more about him. Never methodically, but just along the way in my chaotic but copious reading. His preaching to chickens as a child because he wanted to be a priest, one of the original 13 Freedom Riders, leading the March on Washington in August 1963, and more. Forever in good trouble—as King had advised him.

While my heroes are muddled in my head, my memories of events are clear all the way back to the age of three, when sirens would blare at night during the 1971 India–Pakistan war. Lying on the floor in my Mausi's room, in the usual scorching summer afternoon of Raipur, I remember picking up a book with a green cover. It was 1979, and by then my Nana had moved from Bhopal to Raipur. I didn't drop it till I finished it late that night. The backflap listed the author's other books. The next morning, I went with Nana, who dropped me at his university's library, which by then was used to the odd requests of a kid. They searched for the other books, and got me *Under the Sea Wind* and *The Edge of the Sea.*

Mausi and I fought the next two nights. She wanted me to switch off the lights, and I would not, lost as I was in Rachel Carson's lyrical conjuring of the wonder of nature, magical enough to vanquish the atrocities of the Raipur summer. Ever since, a copy of *Silent Spring* has been with me, like the Gita or the Bible. And Rachel (she can't be called Carson) is among my heroes.

Some years ago, I started going regularly to Washington, DC. On every visit, I would think of trying to meet Lewis. And then my courage would fail. I was afraid that I would start crying when I saw him. He was himself and that was enough. But he was also King and Gandhi, and Selma and Dharasana. Not only because he crossed that bridge in 1963, but because he had kept crossing the bridge to good trouble, every day, since.

On 16 July 2020, I read one of Rachel's countless resplendent lines again: 'Against this cosmic background the lifespan of a particular plant or animal appears, not as drama complete in itself, but only as a brief interlude in a panorama of endless change.' The next day, the eighty-year-old Lewis passed away. And it dawned on me how completely wrong my hero Rachel was.

The life of Lewis and her own life are no brief interludes, but eternal flames of moral clarity and courage. When I fail to carry that fire, you and others still will. Because they lived.

30 July 2020

Chirag Dil Ka Jalaao,
Bahut Andhera Hai

Rumi, the redeemer of our hearts and souls, said, 'The wound is the place where the light enters you.' What if that light is from the funeral pyre of a nineteen-year-old child? With her tongue cut, spine broken and strangled, after being raped. Why call her 'child'? What is your nineteen-year-old daughter, if not a child? What when that pyre has not stopped blazing, from before Kathua and after? Unnao was but one burst of flames in this unceasing conflagration of depravity amid the countless that burn the nameless and powerless. Her pyre was lit on 30 September, the day Rumi was born in 1207 CE. What would have Rumi said to redeem us from this inferno? To her mother and father and sisters?

In another age, with the country aflame, the Mahatma fell, slain with 'Hey Ram' on his lips. The light went out—the light of moral clarity and courage. The strongest and tallest of our many leaders then—even one of whom being with us today would have been a lifeline—felt orphaned. They all collected in Wardha for three days, beginning 29 February 1948. From Nehru and Azad, to Kriplani and JP, all of them. To meditate over, 'Gandhi is gone. Who will guide us? What would he have done?' We can ask the same question of ourselves in this bleakness of dark light.

We know what that man who was born 151 years ago, almost to the day of that pyre, would have done. He would have gone on a fast to heal us. He would have searched for the truth of this never-ending blaze. He would have marched to Hathras, and we would have marched with him. What about his great follower from across continents? What would he have done?

Martin Luther King, Jr. would have preached love to save us. He would have organised to raise us. He, too, would have marched to Hathras, and we would have marched with him too. But neither would have let this pass.

They differed in what they invoked as their organising principle for their work and goals. Love for King and truth for Gandhi. That difference was at the root of my juvenile question one winter day: who was better, Gandhi or King? That was after she had wounded me by calling Gandhi self-righteous, and I her, by pointing out how flawed King was. It is not for us to judge who is the better of the two. We stand here today because of both; it is for us to carry the flame and pass it on, she said. That was the truth. In the long arc of history, their differences do not matter, each doing everything they could, to bend it towards justice. In action they were one. Against every injustice and for the weakest.

They were also one in prayer. I am not one for prayers. So, it's from them that I understood a prayer is only that which excavates the deepest wells of your commitment and courage to power ethical action. Anything else is a retreat from reality and humanity. So, I pray at Kalsi, to the words of Ashoka that speak across 2,200 years, with a pledge to uphold a just and humane world, and more. And you have the Serenity Prayer, or your own Kalsi.

Each one who lives by the Serenity Prayer underestimates herself. Not because she could do more for the good and the just. But because with that commitment, she is doing enough. Enough for the arc of history to bend towards justice and stay bent. Heroes and leaders cannot achieve that. Even if they are Gandhi or King, or the Buddha, or Yugandhar himself. A moral universe needs to be built and upheld by each of us with our Serenity Prayer.

Reinhold Niebuhr wrote the prayer differently from its popular retelling. He wrote, 'Father, give us courage to change what must be altered, serenity to accept what cannot be helped, and the insight to know the one from the other', and not as he is often quoted, 'God, grant me the serenity to accept the things I cannot change, courage to change the things I can, and wisdom to know the difference.'

The original sequence of the words, including the call to courage at the beginning, has the radiant spirit of this prayer. Not fatalism, but a vow to do everything one can. The followers of this prayer live by this spirit, but underestimate their role in cumulative history because of the words of the retelling.

If there were enough of us with the Serenity Prayer in our hearts, there will be no more vile light of such funeral pyres. Because it will be washed away by the light that King prayed for: 'Darkness cannot drive out darkness: only light can do that. Hate cannot drive out hate: only love can do that.' And Gandhi too, while remaining true to his organising principle: 'I am praying for the light of truth that will dispel the darkness; let all those with a living faith in non-violence join me in the prayer.'

Rumi's prayer presages all these prayers. For he doesn't leave us just with that incandescent line of solace and illumination. The redeemer that he is, he gently points towards the path to such light, at the very beginning, 'I said: What about my eyes? He said: Keep them on the road. I said: What about my passion? He said: Keep it burning. I said: What about my heart? He said: Tell me what you hold inside it? I said: Pain and sorrow. He said: Stay with it. The wound is the place where the Light enters you.'

We need both—the light of truth and the light of love. To enter the wounds of this blighted age.

PS: The title is a line from Majrooh Sultanpuri's vastly underappreciated glowing gem from the film *Yaadein*, in the voice of Mohd Rafi, beseeching only as he can, to the tune of Madan Mohan.

8 October 2020

Iss Bahakati Hui Duniya Ko Sambhalo Yaaron

He wears a raincoat and comes at me bounding, criss-crossing right in front of my legs as I run, till I stop. Then he licks my legs, barking excitedly. After a minute or so, he is satisfied that he has demonstrated enough affection for me, and then allows me to resume running. He accosts me like this once every three–four days on a stretch of my running route around 6.30 a.m. Only once have we met without his raincoat. I have not figured out which house he lives in, nor have I ever seen anyone accompanying him. He is a big dog. Our bond is very recent. I started running that route this year in June and encountered him then. I haven't seen him perform this marvellous ritual with anyone else, while he seems generally friendly with everyone. Why does he choose to douse me with his love? I don't know. It's my luck, I suppose, for the simple act of standing still for a few moments. But then, dogs are like that.

I used to be petrified of dogs during my childhood and they seemed to reciprocate the sentiment. As an adult, I made a reluctant and uneasy peace with them. Only in the past few years has their wondrous world of unconditional love and complete loyalty opened up for me. Because I have unlocked doors in my heart that I had kept shut. For a latecomer like me, the telepathic communion of some people with dogs is awe-inspiring. Magic, I have witnessed. A terrified aggressive street dog turned to putty of affection with an uncontrollably wagging tail, just by a gaze and a few gentle words, in the shadows of a beautiful monument in the winter dusk. That requires confidence seeped into one's very being that dogs are designed for love. And the insight that the species has evolved as a reservoir of loyalty and care for humans in the past 30,000 years. Thomas Mann's *A Man and His Dog* is a poignant study of this nature of dogs, as of us.

In April, with each passing week of the lockdown, the number of dogs on my running route kept increasing. In the vicinity of the first garbage heap I would cross, I started recognising five new dogs. Two of them had shiny black coats, they also had collars. One day I stopped, they wagged their tails around me, generally acknowledged my presence, and went back to ferreting the heap. One of the black dogs stayed around, wanting more. I patted it and it rolled over in pleasure.

During the day, I stopped my car and asked a shopkeeper nearby about the dogs. He confirmed my suspicion. The two black dogs had been abandoned by their owner. Only after noticing them looking lost, but not leaving the garbage heap for two days, had he recollected seeing through the corner of his eye a car stop at a distance and let them out. The other street dogs had joined later. He then mentioned what I had only read of, that people are afraid dogs could carry the coronavirus infection and are therefore abandoning them.

My running routes around my house add up to about 25 km. As April turned to May, there were more and more dogs on these routes. And now, I had an eye for any that seemed abandoned; over these weeks, I saw six to eight such dogs. Their body build, behaviour and breed, none were like that of street dogs. By now some good people had taken care of these dogs, finding them homes or safe shelters.

I have not hit anyone ever in my life, from what I can remember, even in my thoughts. But the rage in me would have exploded in a muh-pe-mukka (a punch in the face), if I were to catch any of those whom these dogs must have considered their entire world but who still chose to throw them out.* To throw out your dog, helpless and loving like your baby, is a depravity for which there should be no redemption.

Last week, I stood outside a one-room house as a colleague

of mine asked the woman inside a few questions. She had lost her job as a garment factory worker in April, and she was very confident that COVID-19 could not reach her or her family. Because, 'We make sure we don't interact with Muslims and Dalits.' She used a pejorative word for both communities. I have heard this refrain over the past four months across the country.

Why should we be surprised that the pandemic is totally out of control in our country? Our abysmal healthcare system, exacerbated by poverty and inequity, is laced with our prejudices, delusions and preposterous notions. Such as, 'This is a disease of Dalits and Muslims.' Such as, 'All is well.' Such as, 'Throwing out your dog can save you.' The result is what we have a scourge tearing through the entire body of our nation.

But this pandemic is an unchecked inferno because it is merely a symptom of a deep malaise in the soul of our nation. Throwing out your dog and scapegoating Dalits and Muslims are as emblematic of our moment of epochal blight as the disrobing of Draupadi in another age.

Like my hero Karna, we face an epochal choice. We can choose inaction as humanity and morality are disrobed at their core and in all their manifestations. Or we can throw ourselves into the same fight that Yugandhar did, that Gautama did, that Gandhi did, that millions have done, to uphold the world that we cherish.

Else, like with my hero Karna, a lifetime of righteousness and of heroism will not be able to redeem us.

PS: *Iss bahakati hui duniya ko sambhalo yaaron* these smouldering lines from Dushyant Kumar's *Yeh jo shahtir hai*. Those of you who do not understand Hindi, please forgive me; it is not possible to translate this line and keep its spirit.

10 September 2020

Our Tattoos

After reading my tribute to John Lewis and Rachel Carson, my brother asked me, 'What triggered you to read so much at that age?' He is three years younger than me, so he knows my childhood even more closely than my mother, having shared all of it.

That we lived in a house full of books, our conversations with parents suffused by them, is an insufficient answer to that question—when he asks it. Because at the end of our childhoods, as we left Bhopal, his circle of friends seemed to include every human being in that beautiful city, and a few books. While mine seemed to comprise all the books in the city, and a few human beings. So, what he was asking was, 'Can you explain this inexplicable difference?'

I cannot. All I can say is that over the past thirty-five years, our circles of friends have become more alike. Even as my realisation has grown of how much those years of frantic reading have shaped me and my commitments. Not because of the little that I understood or absorbed from what I read. But because whatever I absorbed mediated my life experience. Lewis, Rachel, King and Gandhi were all living in my head. Dharasana and Selma were holy places. It was a long list of haphazard reels from much that I read. All alive for me. So, when a friend laughed after reading the same tribute, 'Come on, how silly, you didn't even try to meet Lewis because you thought you would start crying?' I knew I would have. Meeting such a one as that, in flesh and blood, would have been too much.

But a shrine to one of them is a different matter. Those are flames I get drawn to. Every time I am in Dun, I want to steal an evening to go to Kalsi. Devanampriya speaks directly across 2,500 years through the edict on that massive rock. So, it was wistfully that I left Mori a few years ago, not having been able to visit Karna's temple up the Tons valley. A pilgrimage remained unfulfilled. He had been in my pantheon since I read Shivaji Sawant's stirring *Mrityunjay*, probably in 1980.

Abandonment and injustice from his divine and royal family at birth. Growing up nurtured by the love of ordinary folk. Mastering on his own all that was to master. Valour that was unmatched. Generosity that made his name the touchstone for generosity across millennia. And yet the butt of innuendo, derision and insult, only because of the ordinariness of his foster family—the very family that saved him and made him. Finding a friend in the prince emperor who saw in him a complete counter to his own mortal enemy. Anointed a king by the prince, but unable to escape the silent contempt of the times for his bonds with ordinariness. How can Karna not be in anyone's pantheon? He was amongst the very top in mine. If I was the kind who sported a tattoo, I'd probably have one of Karna.

The torrent of injustices in his life swelled with the three curses. Cursed by the almighty Earth for feeding a hungry child milk. Cursed to die when he, the mighty warrior, would be most helpless—for the honesty of admitting to the accidental death of a cow at his hands. Cursed by his guru Parashurama, for his martial knowledge to slip away when he needed it most. Because of his unhesitating loyalty to ordinariness—a crime for which there was no redemption.

Sawant's literary technique of each chapter as a soliloquy by a key character, while remaining more or less true to the Critical Edition (of the Mahabharata), inserts you into the internal torments of Karna. Most of all in the feverish twenty pages of the disrobing of Draupadi. Every step of his life, despite every torment and conflict, swallowing all ridicule and insult, he is ever righteous. Why then, at that moment of epochal blight, does he choose what is wrong, the only time he does so?

Pain and incomprehension haunted me over that failure of Karna. Even after reading and rereading, inspired and aflame by his final choice. That which must surely be one of the most incandescent moral actions in human literature and mythology, perhaps history.

Krishna holds his hands and reveals to him the mystery of his life. In a moment elevating him from ordinariness to divinity. And in the next, offering him the empire of all lands. If only he would side with his bloodline in the war ahead.

To the master of the universe, Karna refuses all three—divinity, the empire and an end to the bane of his origin. Instead, he embraces ordinariness, and allegiance to those who stood by him against the age and its norms. He says, 'What matters most in life are bonds of love, and not power over the world.' Yugandhar himself is brought to tears, blessing and validating him, 'Victory to Karna, Radha's son.'

A few years later, glancing through a literal translation of the Critical Edition, I noticed the passage of the night before he takes over as commander of the Kaurava army. He confides in his friend Duryodhana, the perpetrator, that he is tortured by the wrong he did. Then I also discovered how that poignant encounter between Krishna and Karna ends. He confesses to being haunted by his actions and inaction on that fateful day. Apologises and says that only his death would be sufficient atonement. And with that, I found my peace.

Karna was a hero because of the commitments he tried to live up to, but he was a perfect hero because he knew that he was an imperfect man. We are all flawed and imperfect, what matters are not the tattoos of commitment on the skin, but the tattoos on the heart.

27 August 2020

Phir Bhi Dil Hai Hindustani

As the predawn glow lit the east, I started running towards the dark west. And the phone started ringing. I cut it off, it was not a number I knew. I slowed to exchange affections with the five dogs who have become my friends, on the stretch before the highway. It rang again. And again. It wouldn't stop. So finally, I did, and picked it up from my armband, dreading a dire emergency facing a loved one, and a bystander calling me. The voice was unfamiliar, but the tone wasn't. *'Hum Hindustani bol rahen hain.'* (This is Hindustani speaking.) It was 14 May.

Waman, William, Mohabbat, Harold and Hindustani were the five young men I had met in the similar predawn of Labour Day, walking on the same highway, to their homes a few thousand kilometres away from Bengaluru. They had reached. Hindustani narrated their odyssey.

On that first day, they walked till noon. Then, a tractor-trolley gave them a ride almost till the border of Andhra Pradesh. Lest they get quarantined, the driver advised them to get off the highway and cross the inter-state border through the fields. They did so at each state border subsequently. Their first meal, of rice and sambar, was at 6 p.m., bought at a hut. They walked till 10 p.m. and then slept at a shuttered dhaba, and started at dawn the next morning till they could not bear the blazing sun. Resting under a tree and walking by night, they found another small but open dhaba. The owner didn't charge them, saying that the food would have gone waste. A truck stopped for a break, and the driver offered them a lift till beyond Vijayawada.

The ten days that followed were much like those first two. Walking in the scorching summer day, till they couldn't. Eating what they got. Struggling for water. On the constant lookout for rides in trucks. They managed seven. Four of them free, with drivers stirred by their plight. Two at reasonable charges. One fleecing them ₹500 each in a truck laden with sacks of grain.

'Ab ghar pahunch gaye, sir. Yahaan bhi khaane ke liye nahin hai. Phir bhi sab theek hai.' (We have reached home, sir. There is no food here too. But still, all is well.) When I met them on Labour Day, they had one question for me: 'Why was this done to us?' I had no answer. And I had two questions for them.

One, what made you decide to walk 2,000 km in the summer sun? Their jobs had vanished. Food was dependent on NGOs or on scrounging. Used to paying for everything with sweat and blood, now dependant on alms, they were deeply troubled. Everyone around was caught in the same web of hunger and poverty. The powerful people in their life, their employers, had turned away. Room rent, phone expenses and other small things had depleted their meagre savings. No end was in sight of the pandemic or their joblessness.

Two, will you come back to work in this big city? They did not want to come back. But they could not visualise livelihoods in their village. So, they felt they would have to come back. But they wouldn't till the pandemic was gone. Because they may be forced out of work again. They were ready to brave hunger in solidarity in their village. But they were unsure of how long they could last.

Hindustani and his four friends changed a practice of thirty years in my life. Now, I paused my running every day to walk with those walking to distant homes. I ran 350 km in May, which I had never done before in a month. By 24 May, I had similar conversations with twenty-six groups. I also went to railway stations and talked to 'shramiks' being corralled like sheep into trains. I asked them all those two questions.

Akin to those five young men, everyone's expressions of desperation were inchoate. But it pounded their hearts and powered their feet. To the only sanctuary they could imagine. Home. Even if it was a 2,000 km walk in the summer sun. Equally inchoate but certain was their acceptance, of being mere straws at the mercy of massive economic tides. All they wanted was some certainty for their heads and a bit of dignity for their souls.

The pandemic has sharpened discrimination, intensified exclusion and amplified the bad in us. It has also magnified selflessness and generated heroism, insufficient though it is in the face of our systemic ineptitude and structural moral failings. But if we care to look, it has clarified that the morally worthy choices vis-à-vis the organising principles of our society are also the most economically wise. Sound social security, strong labour laws and universal access to good-quality public healthcare and education will create an economy that could absorb almost any shock, because it will build resilience at the level of the individual and the collective around her. People won't have to flee to imagined sanctuaries. Wherever they are, will be their sanctuary. It will also be a just, humane and good society.

Through the call, I kept wondering, why did he call me? He answered without my asking. '*Rakhte hain phone, sir, aapko daudna hoga. Lagaa aapko chintaa ho rahi hogi, iss liye phone kar diya.*' (Let me end the call now, you may have to run. I felt you must be worrying about us, so I called.)

After walking for fourteen days in the Indian summer, expelled from a city you thought of as home, to think about what a stranger would be feeling merely because he stopped and chatted with you. Give us a drop from this ocean of empathy in you, Hindustani, and we will all be better people.

18 June 2020

Hum Hindustani

It was the dark before dawn on Labour Day. The highway was empty for miles. Other than the steadily moving silhouettes in a single file ahead of me. Five young men, each with a backpack. I hate slowing down or pausing during a run. But where will I run to, if I run away from a lone little girl searching for food, or two kids pushing a cartful of red chillies or a silent procession fleeing my city. So, I started walking with them.

They were walking home. One to Chhattisgarh, one to Odisha, two to Jharkhand and one to Bihar. These are long walks, from the outskirts of Bengaluru. Hearing of the changed lockdown conditions allowing migrant workers to return home, they started. Not waiting for special trains to start, nor for their states to send buses or for confirmation that the interstate borders were indeed open. Waiting, anymore, was unbearable. '*Mazdoor hain, bhikhaari nahin, sir; bhookh se ladna hai toh gaon me ladenge, apnon ke saath, iss ajab shehar mein nahin.*' (We are labourers, not beggars, sir; if we must battle hunger, we will do it in our village, along with our own people, not in this strange city.)

All of twenty-three or twenty-four, they have not been back home for three to four years. But this city is not theirs. Living on alms, begging, going hungry, all forced upon them in turn, has clarified where they belong. '*Aisa kyon kiya hamaare saath, sir?*' (Why was this done to us, sir?) There is no answer to that, since it cuts to the core of our systemic ineptitude and collective moral failure.

So, I asked for their names. Waman, William, Mohabbat, Harold and Hindustani. A paean to India, those names together; the last—a conclusion—which I asked him to repeat. '*Hindustani,*

hum Hindustani hain, sir.' (Hindustani, I am Hindustani, sir.)
With first light, we parted ways. They walked home, and I ran
with their questions.

Questions that have been asked many times every day of me
for the past few weeks. Not that those asking expected an answer.
But they had to ask, finding me amid them, because clearly, I was
not battling hunger.

In early April, we estimated that there were 14 lakh people
in Bengaluru driven to the verge of hunger by the lockdown. All
daily wage earners of some kind, with no savings, and no access
to the public distribution system. We started supporting food for
these people from the first week of April. Over the past forty-five
days, the numbers we are supporting have grown to over 7 lakh.
Some directly from our own large campus kitchens, and the rest
through financial support from over thirty non-governmental
organisations (NGOs) and citizen groups. We estimate that other
organisations and the state government have been supporting
another 4 lakh people.

Till I started going out to see how all this was happening,
my imagination fell short of the complexity. The enormity of the
supply chain is unsurprising, given the scale of the operation.
Including the daily sourcing of tonnes of rice, dal, salt, oil and
more. Unloading, sorting, cooking or repacking them in kits,
and then onwards for distribution. All this has been developed on
the fly, by the ingenuity and teamwork of hundreds of members
of NGOs and volunteers. Schools, colleges, marriage halls and
office spaces have been converted into warehouses and 'ration-kit'
factories.

Distribution is a different order of challenge. Merely delivering
tonnes of material to the shanties and blue-tarp huts, whose
existence this Silicon Valley, Bengaluru, is unaware of, is the
first hurdle. How does one know how many ration-kits to take

to a place, with not even a hint of any enumeration of residents? When the consignment reaches there, how can the crowd be controlled? These are people who haven't had a square meal for days, and dread the uncertain immediate future. All this enacted in slushy narrow lanes, on garbage heaps or sinking construction sites. And then the lockdown is extended, so we start all over again.

Enforced loss of livelihoods, stranded with chronic hunger and no end in sight, is the sure-fire formula to eviscerate the sense of agency amongst people and demolish their identity. Exacerbated by discrimination on the giving of aid and delivery of healthcare services—on every conceivable dimension of prejudice possible—by too many local politicians and some NGOs. People from outside the state, Muslims, those from the Northeast, Dalits, transgender people, voters-of-other-parties and others, have all borne the brunt, though many NGOs, government officers and even politicians have done everything possible to stop this criminal misconduct and compensate for it.

The numbers confronting starvation have risen every day. The initial 14 lakh were mostly construction workers, ragpickers, cobblers and others already in or near poverty. With no income for over forty days, the self-employed with small businesses, or informally employed, many of whom would be firmly in the lower-middle class, have been dragged into virtual poverty: from the plumber, maid and security guard to the barber, shoe-shop owner and auto driver. I have encountered more such people each passing day, understandably ashamed of hunting for food. The number on the verge of hunger in Bengaluru may well have risen to twice our initial estimate. The rest of the country is in no different state.

There are stories aplenty of heroism and sacrifice, both individual and collective, on all fronts, all deserving of this nation's gratitude. These are but a thin veil on the failure of our democracy and society. We have brazenly extracted the life and liberty of the weakest and poorest as the price for combating the pandemic. And we are yet only at the beginning of our battle with the scourge.

'How did you get your name?' I asked him. 'My great-grandfather named me; he and many people of my village went to jail in 1942. He wanted us to remember what they fought for.'

It is time we remember.

7 May 2020

Pandemic in Farmland

Ripe papayas hung on each tree, with squishy rotting ones at the base of many. We sat on the mud in a big circle under the trees, shielded partially from the summer sun. The farm's owner explained the details of his 75 per cent loss on the crop during the lockdown. His market is Hyderabad. With no transportation across states available to the average person, he could only sell locally in the nearby towns of Surpur and Yadgir. The offtake was a tiny fraction of what it would have been in a big city. Prices kept dropping each day. Till it made no sense to spend on labour to pick the papayas and transport them across 20 km to either town. So, he was letting the crop rot.

The man next to me looked more ragged than the other farmers there. He sat outside the circle on his haunches. I asked him to join the circle; he refused. The others narrated their own stories of helplessness. All of them grow fruits, vegetables or flowers. Each had problems and losses, like the papaya farmer. The man on the haunches didn't speak, till we coaxed him to. He was not there to participate in the discussion, but was looking for work. He had returned from Bengaluru ten days earlier, where he worked at a construction site. From being a provider of money to his family in the village, he had become dependent on them, which was fine by him. But they were running out of food other than rice, and needed money quickly. He went away disappointed as we left.

About 100 m from the farm, where the mud track joined the road, another farmer stopped us. He was trying to sell us papaya, our car marking us as people with some resources. It didn't matter that he had seen us leave a farm full of ripe and rotting papaya; what's the harm in trying your luck when there isn't much else to try?

All of last week I spent in north-east Karnataka, in the districts of Bellary, Yadgir and Gulbarga. India's first COVID-19 death was in Gulbarga. Now, Yadgir and Gulbarga districts are among the three districts with the highest infection count in Karnataka. The population of each of these districts has increased by 8–12 per cent in the past few weeks, with migrants returning from across the country. They are expecting much more, as the influx continues unabated.

The ragged man next to me was one of them, and like him, most of these people were remitting money to their homes in the villages. That money flow has vanished, populations have surged and local livelihoods are devastated. Estimates are that more than twice the current numbers would eventually be back. The local population could rise by about 20 per cent in a matter of weeks.

Those who grow crops like paddy and dal, which are not as perishable, are in no better state. That region grows both in plenty. With transportation and market disruptions, prices have fallen by 30–40 per cent. Even at those prices, the demand is meagre. There is no place to store harvested crops and wait for prices to pick up. If farmers do find storage, they have no money to pay its rent. Livestock farmers are in a similar situation. Bank loans are beyond the grasp of farmer; they are not even allowed to enter banks, as we heard often in many places. These banks seem not to have even heard of the economic package announced by the Prime Minister.

Weavers and other artisans are in worse condition, since their businesses have been completely shut. Almost all other small businesses, ranging from marriage-party caterers and construction contractors to traditional drama and dance troupes, have come to a standstill. Consequently, those employed by these businesses are jobless. Daily wage labourers have had no work. Transgender people, ragpickers and sex workers have zero income. The pandemic's economic effect is amplified by pre-existing levels of disadvantage and social exclusion.

None of this is hearsay; I met these people in their own milieus. Similar pictures of severe economic distress and human misery are what we have from almost 400 districts, where we have ground-level presence; I will travel to many of those places soon. There won't be any rapid improvement as the lockdown is eased. The crisis of today has a cascading effect. Working capital, resources for investment and other inputs available are all a fraction of what is needed for the next agrarian cycle, without even accounting from the looming debt trap, because of the last cycle's loans.

Current projections of 1–4 per cent growth in the rural farm sector in 2020–21, with a normal monsoon, seem as disconnected from reality as were the projections made by the same people about thirty days ago of the overall Indian economy growing 1–4 per cent this fiscal year. Some of these analysts and economists seem to have an inveterate faith in miracles.

The people and the economy are in deep distress, and the pandemic is swiftly worsening. To act effectively, we need to listen to those at the storm front and also in the storm. Dismissing them or attacking them as 'prophets of doom' or 'vultures' is a self-defeating tactic. The most important lesson from the Spanish Flu that crushed the world in 1918 was not an epidemiological one. It was to speak the truth and to have the courage to listen to the truth.

4 June 2020

Zara Mulk ke Rahbaron
Ko Bulaao …

It was dawn. She was swinging her hands shoulder-high, getting an empty jhola (cloth bag) in each hand to flutter like a flag in the wind. Her long strides were like spot jumps. Not a soul or vehicle was in sight for miles visible on that stretch of the highway. It was the twelfth day of the lockdown. Even as we neared each other, she did not interrupt her routine. She was no older than ten, perhaps eleven.

I called out thrice before she stopped and looked at me. I tried Hindi, *'Kahaan jaa rahi ho?'* (Where are you going?)

'Khaana, subzi lene,' (To get food and vegetables) she responded, as an equal.

'Akeli kyon jaa rahi ho?' (Why are you going alone?) I asked.

'Didi ghar mein hai, woh baahar nahi nikal sakti,' (My elder sister is at home and cannot come out) she said. Her parents are among the lakhs of migrant labour stuck in nowhere land. They had been able to call and convey that. The elder sister is actually an elderly lady; the word 'didi' is used with deep affection. The conversation was a flash, with my mind focused only on what to do. Leaving her to her own means on that vast desolate stretch was not an option. I turned to walk with her.

A policeman crossed us on his bike. We were a curious sight, the little girl with swinging bags, and sweat-laden me in shorts and running shoes. He turned the bike and came to us. Hearing the story, he asked the child to hop on to the bike. Her calm visage cracked for the first time as she said 'bye' with a smile, and they were off.

A little girl alone on a desolate road at dawn, in search of food. It's a measure of what we have made of ourselves—a people with hundreds of millions of our own on the precipice of existence, with the deepest chasms of discrimination and prejudice. All exacerbated and revealed by the pandemic, if it needed any revealing. When we get to the other side of this once-in-a-century-storm, we must rebuild a society such that no little girl ever has to be out on a desolate road alone. Never, ever. Everything else will fall in place.

But for that, we must get to the other side first, to safety. We seem to be underestimating or appear unaware of what all may await us within the raging ocean of contagion before we reach any kind of safety.

Safety lies in a vaccine and some form of 'herd immunity'. The lockdown is merely a mechanism to avert an immediate escalation of cases. The best estimates for the introduction of a vaccine are eighteen months from now. We must live with and manage the scourge till then. This will require profound changes in our social life, including our culture and economy. Even more critically, it will require a nationwide, robust healthcare system to tackle inevitable new outbreaks of COVID-19 during these eighteen months, or longer, since we don't fully understand the virus and its behaviour.

Physical distancing will change our social life. Large congregations of people must stop. Great Indian weddings will have to take a pause, Dussehra and Eid will go private, cricket stadiums will remain empty or seat one person to five seats. Trains, airlines, theatres and restaurants may have to drop their capacity to a third, mandis and bazaars will be re-laid, construction sites will reduce labour concentration. How we come together for anything will have to be modified, with a cascading effect on lives, the economy and livelihoods.

Our moribund and iniquitous health system will have to be brought to life. That too with the infrastructure and human capacity to identify the infected very quickly, trace their contacts rapidly, isolate the clusters and provide treatment. This will have to be everywhere in the country, absolutely everywhere. Any uncontained cluster, or any breach anywhere, could demolish the whole country's defence.

If we do a good job of all this, we will reach safety, scarred and scathed. We will all share in the misery, with most of the burden borne by those in poverty, even if we miraculously transform our public systems for social security and safety, by universalising them, which we must, as our first duty.

If we do a shoddy job of all this, a catastrophic nightmare awaits us. Repeated and expanding outbreaks of the pandemic will undermine everything in the country. The economy will be in tatters. The world will put us in quarantine, isolating us to protect themselves. The human tragedy, directly from the disease and from a devastated economy, will have no parallel.

Where we end up in the arc between good and shoddy will be determined by our actions, some more important than others. First, by the speed, quality and universality of the response by the healthcare system. Second, by the fiscal and public-system support we give to lives, livelihoods and businesses. Third, by the quality and empathy of leadership—political, administrative, civil society and business.

Each one of us must contribute; this is that time. Hope will delude and despair will misguide us. Good science, resolve and wisdom are what we need. We don't have it all individually, but can muster it collectively. Everything and everybody we care for, or should care for, is at stake in some way. How is she now? And her didi? I don't know. But what I know is that I must do the best of what I can, and more, to try and make a difference to their lives.

PS: Perhaps there has been no deeper a cry of anguish in Indian films than that song from *Pyaasa* quoted in the title. But Sahir turns it on its head in the last stanza, into a challenge and an invocation, 'call, call out the leaders of this realm'. In Rafi's voice, set to the music of Sachin-da, only as could have envisioned it and V.K. Murthy could have shot all brought together by the master—Guru Dutt.

23 April 2020

Zindagi Ki Lau Unchi Kar Chalo

A decade is a long time in one life. But each decade hasn't left as deep an imprint. The tumult of the 1980s in India, when I grew up from a boy to a young man, was formative. Some of those days seem to be around even now. The 2010s, with their great unravelling of the inevitability of human progress, will similarly be with me till the end of my days. There is no contradiction in that, that during this unravelling, my already blessed life became even more so. The opportunity to do what I do, the experiences that come along and the people of my life have blessed me doubly. Even as the world has frayed.

Those who have lived through the 2010s will know what to expect in the 2020s. Work ceaselessly for the good and the true to come true. Impermanent and imperfect, as it will be. So, keep at it. Some of the deepest imprints of the 2010s will be with me in 2020s, to help fare forward, and perhaps fare well, too. Embossed in my heart are sentences spoken by fellow voyagers offering an essence of their lives. Which, when I compare to mine, leave me astonished by my privileges and their grace under pressure. They live those realities, and that is enough for me to find an anchor in these uncharted times. I have written their words (and stories) before in the past ten years in this column. Now I write them as beacons for the next ten.

She said, '*Yahaan sab kuchh chalne lagtaa hai.*' (Everything works here.) Up and down the mountains, and then again, and again and again and higher each time. Then across the river on foot. That was as far as you could go in this country. She had no sight for what she didn't have.

And anything she had, she could make it work. Stubs of chalk, waste rusted wire, the lives of hard labour—all were learning tools. Her students loved it and learnt. The minor miracles that she created every day for those children were invisible to her; she was 'just doing her job'.

He said, '*Mushkilen ginaane se kum nahin hoti.*' (Problems are not solved by recounting them.) He said that with a smile, after cycling 7 km in the blazing desert of November, teaching all three subjects to fifty-six kids across five classes, all alone. The blaze in March or July could be imagined by the one in November. The fire of his life was in full blaze all the time, burning down problems that could burn most others out.

She said, '*Har koi jogi to nahin ho saktaa.*' (Not everyone can be a jogi.) A term with no single-word equivalent in English: a seeker, monk and/or warrior for a cause to which an entire life is given. Her words ricochet from a lifetime of relentless patriarchy. A jogi she was, breaking chains and dragging others along the way, much like the Bhagirathi on the banks of which I heard this, educating children who had little else. She had borne the cost of being a jogi, which she knew not every kindred spirit could bear. That doesn't make them smaller, just more worthy of her support. Empathy leads the fire in her.

He said, '*Yeh lo aur beti ke paas jao.*' (Take this and go back home to your daughter.) He was six, looked like four, poverty having stunted his growth and limited his life. But his generosity was unlimited. From the pocket of his torn shirt, he gave me ₹5. He could not bear the thousand miles between me and my daughter, and wanted to help. My hoard is full of the generosity of little children.

She said, 'Don't be so sure'—that there is a categorical difference between dogs and cats and humans. So, cruelty to animals is just as reprehensible. And much else. the poignant image of Jacob Bronowski, standing ankle deep in slush with the ashes of four million people in Auschwitz, warning against certainty, 'I beseech you, in the bowels of Christ, think it possible that you may be mistaken' was conjured from the lockers of my memory. In time, as I lived for a time with six cats, made friends with dogs and read research studies on animal behaviour, I was not so sure.

About much else.

He said, '*Kuch to kariye iss desh ke liye.*' (Do something for this country.) Up and up another set of mountains. As far as one could be from any privilege or power. Gently and continually trying to heal every cleavage and fight every act of discrimination, till wherever he could reach. Through his students, whom he was helping grow every day. And in that sparse setting, when the time came, all he asked was for the country—giving me the privilege of his solidarity.

He said, '*Pyaar to karke dekho.*' (Try love.) In a jungle clearing so deep that it held the winter mist at noon, he was imploring and challenging. To have empathy, to care and to love. And to change, through that, first yourself and then others. Even the weary bunch of teachers and officers who were challenged could not remain unmoved. It was a full echo of what I had heard my father say many years ago, 'The heart of the matter is that it is a matter of the heart.'

She said, '*Kya faydaa?*' (What is the point?) I wrote about her in my year-end piece for 2019. I thought there was no further room, but it strengthened my belief in being ziddi, stubborn, in the good fight and for her. Together we can make it matter. Work at it, bit by bit. For the arc of history to bend towards the good and the true in the 2020s. And, in trying, our infinitesimal lives will have more meaning. That is the faydaa.

2 January 2020

Baat Nikli To Har Ek Baat Pe ...

Over twenty-five days, we have realigned our entire organisation of 1,700 people across 200 locations to help battle the COVID-19 pandemic and the humanitarian crisis emerging in its wake. Many of our 300 partners across the country, which we support with financial grants, are also going through a similar shift. They have over 30,000 team members and community workers. We are, for the most part, an educational organisation built over twenty years and this change has been massive. The scale of this crisis demands it. Without this transformation, we cannot respond adequately. We are trying hard not to lose momentum on regular work, but most of our energy is focused on responding to the havoc wreaked by the pandemic.

This crisis must be tackled where the people of this country are. On-the-ground presence through our field team, the teachers we are engaged with and our partners with similarly strong teams, have become key to this work. We have assigned dedicated teams to tackle crushing supply chain constraints, such as on personal protective equipment (PPE) for frontline healthcare workers, and to build delivery capability for the last mile. We are supported by Wipro's large sourcing and distribution network, and its technology expertise.

A systematic response is urgent on both the humanitarian and healthcare fronts. The livelihoods of hundreds of millions of people have been disrupted, with the earnings of daily wage earners and most small businesses vanishing. The most disadvantaged are hit the hardest and struggle to survive. Bare necessities like food, water, soap and sanitary napkins are not accessible. A tragedy not seen since the days of Partition appears to be unfolding. We are delivering such basic life necessities to over 7,50,000 people across seventeen states. These numbers are growing by the day, and it is not clear how long such support will be required.

And this is but a tiny fraction of what the country needs. On healthcare, one part is medical care for the usual diseases. Clinics and small hospitals are shut, so people with 'normal' ailments are finding treatment elusive. Most avoid hospitals, but when forced by the severity of their condition, they don't find one to treat them. The great urgency is for the health system to contain the pandemic. It is a race against the virus's spread, and it takes rigorous micro-planning to create capacity for testing, quarantines, isolation and intensive care in every geographical unit, like a district. The actual capacity and protocol of each of these four elements has to be based on medical and epidemiological modelling of the pandemic. Healthcare workers are to be trained on these protocols. Also, communities must be involved and educated.

Clearly, all this is the business of the government. We provide a range of support to these efforts, along with our partners. We collaborate with local officials and other organisations on planning and execution, on community education, supplying PPE and other critical equipment, even financially supporting public-service-oriented private hospitals to supplement the public system, and more. All this work is at the front lines, so the safety of our teams is paramount. To systematise our response, along with our partners, we have developed an integrated district response plan for civil society.

The news is not good from any front. We are struggling. Our country, that is, not merely us. Governments are not solely to blame; we are all complicit. We the people have built this state and its public systems with the capacity they have, and these are having to deal with an unprecedented crisis. Even countries with the most effective states are besieged. A time for rumination and reckoning will come, but that time is not now. Today, it is all hands on deck.

We do not know when this tsunami will recede. The debris that will be left behind cannot be put back together soon, and we do not exactly know how. Particularly for the millions in poverty, and in the informal sector. The pandemic itself will not be tamed till there is a vaccine and treatment, and some form of 'herd immunity'. Life will be even more uncertain for people in the informal sector, and those on the edge of poverty. We must brace ourselves for this darker new world. We need wisdom to see us through. The wisdom of courage, thoughtful judgement and empathy. Many individuals seem to have all that in abundance, but collectively we seem to be coming up short.

This morning, I saw a beautiful black dog framed against the bright blue sky looking down lovingly from atop a building. And I remembered that people have been throwing out their dogs, driven by unfounded fears of dogs being carriers of the virus. In February this year, when I wrote about what we do with our old horses as a metaphor for our society, I did not anticipate that the evisceration of empathy from our core as a people would be revealed so soon by a pandemic. We have created a society where hundreds of millions are a hair's breadth away from oblivion, and we seem to have let them go over the precipice. No amount of individual sacrifice and heroism can wash away this original collective sin. Redemption lies only in rebuilding ourselves as a people on the foundation of empathy.

PS: The title for this chapter is a line from a song. *Baat nikli to har ek baat pe rona aaya* ... is Sahir's quiet, still, cry of anguish for where we find ourselves. In Mohd Rafi's voice, to the tune of the vastly underrated genius of Jaidev, from the movie *Hum Dono*. A few weeks before passing away, Dev Anand listed this as one of his three favourite songs.

9 April 2020

The Importance of Being Stubborn

As the year ends, there is a need to be stubborn and be committed to a shared moral purpose in action, in order to strengthen the fight for the good.

One thing that we take for granted about years is that all of them come to an end. Each one of them is a tragedy for some and a glowing triumph for others. But for most, each year is a continuation of their lives' arc with mild or minimal changes.

Why then think in years? Perhaps because we need to organise time, to make sense of our lives, to mark our journeys. And then there is a year that upends our worlds, not only individually but collectively. What is unleashed has been gathering perhaps for years before, but it comes out all at once, then. There is no end to such a year. It shapes the future, gnaws at all years to come.

For most of us Indians, who lived through that year, 1984 was one such. Especially, like me, if you were in Bhopal on the night of 2 December, or were in Delhi in November, or were in Punjab any time. It was a state of siege, a country at war with itself. No institution or faith came out unscathed. And it has not ended yet, it continues to gnaw at us.

I suspect 2016, too, is not going to end soon for the world. The political upheavals are on the surface, the forces are deep in the core. Gathering for decades. An elected leader who has no hesitation publicly promoting 'death to the drug dealers', justice and the rule of law be damned. Or calling another elected president a bastard. When German chancellor Angela Merkel is compelled to say, 'When a free-trade agreement with the US drives hundreds of thousands of people to the streets, but such horrible bombings as in Aleppo do not trigger any protest, then something is not right,'—something is certainly not right.

Unprecedented changes in climate just bring even stronger denials and untruth. Such is the tapestry of today's world. We could stop by in almost any country across the world in 2016, and watch these ruptures in the arc of humanity. Years in the making but bursting and hurting together this year. Only now do we have the clarity to ask, 'What have we done?', like after Smaug the Dragon is awakened and flying. These are ruptures in the most fundamental notions that make us human. We are in the fight of our lives, for the good, the right and the truth. I am sure it has happened before, and it will happen again, but that doesn't make it less epochal. Answers to troubling questions, like where do we go from here, how long will 2016 gnaw and will these ruptures heal, depend on what we do now.

I still believe Martin Luther King, Jr when he said, 'The arc of the moral universe is long, but it bends towards justice.' But having lived through 1984 in Bhopal, I would rather back up that belief with King's own statement: 'Human progress is neither automatic nor inevitable … Every step toward the goal of justice requires sacrifice, suffering, and struggle; the tireless exertions and passionate concern of dedicated individuals.'

The privilege of my job is that I meet and work with so many of these dedicated individuals, that the long insidious unfolding of 2016 only fills me with fight and not despair. Because I know that they are there, not as abstractions or inspirational stories on social media, but real people of flesh and blood. Willing to shed their blood for the good fight. I met the woman who reveals, in its most intimate detail, her struggle for justice which continues to be denied to her because of her gender. Not only does she not let go of her struggle, but her courage to share energises everyone around her. Then there is the young man who has learnt to report stories from the jungles in English, else no one files stories from there that are real in the media. That he lives on the edge of survival, threatened by violence and debilitating disease, doesn't even give him pause.

The man who runs a shelter for every kind of 'the other'— of caste, gender, religion or region, none turned away. He is a lightning rod for the bigoted, and he just takes it with a nod of the head. The principal of a school of a community in the midst of a virtual civil war, who gets the warring groups together after two generations. The principal secretary of education who continues to drive through the miasma of corruption, resistance and sloth, for real improvements in the fundamentals. The young woman who demolishes all barriers of caste and creed between her students within her school, and then uses the school to undermine discrimination in the village. I could go on.

Hope or despair is ours for the making. If we stand away, even if admiring, we let in despair and weakness. If we commit to a shared moral purpose in action, then we strengthen the fight for the good. All these people are ziddi (stubborn), as was King. That word captures what all these people have in common. They are ziddi and empathetic, they are ziddi and courageous, and they are ziddi and intellectual. The core of their identity is being ziddi. It is not surprising, because when the good, the right and the truth are all unanchored and untethered, being ziddi, unrelenting under all circumstances, counts more than anything else. But being so alone is insufficient. We all must be ziddi together, with a shared moral purpose, to put an end to 2016 and not let another year like this arise.

22 December 2016

Glossary

Anganwadis: Meaning the 'courtyard shelter', these are rural childcare centres started in 1975 as part of the Integrated Child Development Scheme of the Ministry of Women and Child Development of the Government of India to combat child hunger and malnutrition by providing supplementary nutrition to children in the age group of three to six years. Preschool activities and non-formal preschool education are also provided.

Block Resource Centre (BRC): Established in each block of every district in the country under the Sarva Shiksha Abhiyan to conduct in-service teacher training; provide academic support to teachers and schools on a regular basis, and to help in community mobilisation activities.

Cluster Resource Centre (CRC): There are several in each block covering a small number of schools within easy reach. Each CRC has a Cluster Resource Person/Cluster Resource Coordinator whose role is to provide academic support to teachers and schools on a regular basis and help in community mobilisation activities.

Continuous and Comprehensive Evaluation (CCE): A process of assessment, mandated by the Right to Education Act, 2009. The main aim is to evaluate every aspect of each child in school with the aim to decrease the workload on the student by means of continuous evaluation through a number of small tests throughout the year in place of a single test at the end of an academic programme. As part of this system, students' marks are replaced by grades which are evaluated through a series of curricular and extra-curricular evaluations along with academics.

District Institute for Education and Training (DIET): Established in each district of the country by the Government of India as a centre of guidance for educational institutes and schools of a district. As part of their mandate, these institutes offer a pre-service teacher-education diploma and provide academic and resource support at the grassroot level for in-service training of teachers.

Department of State Educational Research and Training (DSERT, also known as SCERT or SIERT in some states): Established at the state level to provide overall academic leadership in school education and for improving the quality of education provided in primary and secondary schools in the states.

Learning Resource Centre (LRC): An Azim Premji Foundation-initiated centre in the districts where its field institutes are established. These are located in towns where the larger number of teachers have their residences and serve as venues for teachers to gather, discuss academic issues and access necessary teaching material. Launched with the intent to improve the quality in educational development at all stages of education, this centre is called the LRC in Rajasthan and the Teacher Learning Centre (TLC) in other states.

Nali-Kali: An initiative of the Government of Karnataka, launched in 2001, it was first piloted as a small UNICEF-assisted pilot project in H.D. Kote, Mysore district. Meaning joyful learning, it is a multigrade, multi-level (MGML) activity-based learning programme for primary classes based on the methodology developed by the Rishi Valley Institute for Educational Resources (RIVER). It was expanded to cover nearly 14,000 schools by 2009 and the state education department is considering significant modifications to the programme.

Sarva Shiksha Abhiyan (SSA): A programme aimed at universalisation of elementary education as mandated by the 86th Amendment to the Constitution of India making free and compulsory education for all children between the ages of six to fourteen years a fundamental right. It is implemented by the central government in partnership with state governments through a district-level decentralised management framework involving local bodies.

School Development and Monitoring Committee (SDMC) or School Management Committee (SMC): Committee consisting of parents and teachers to encourage community participation and ownership for the effective management of government schools. The head teacher is the secretary and one parent, the president of the committee. The members and president are elected by the parents of students of the school.

School Leadership Development Programme (SLDP): Government of Karnataka and the Azim Premji Foundation conceptualised and implemented this programme to build and enhance the capacity of school heads on a long-term and continuous basis. The same was also implemented with necessary modifications for head teachers of primary and upper-primary schools in Uttarakhand.

School Head Teachers Programme: The ten-day training programme for head teachers of Surpur Block was conducted in 2004 jointly by the education department and the Azim Premji Foundation as a part of the Child-Friendly School Initiative.

Teaching Learning Centre (TLC): See Learning Resource Centres (LRC).

Teacher Certificate Higher (TCH): Two-year teacher diploma course after PUC/Class XII in Karnataka till 2002; subsequently replaced by the equivalent two-year D. Ed. (Diploma in Education).

Voluntary Teacher Forums (VTF): A self- and peer-learning platform for continued professional development of teachers from government schools organised and run by the Azim Premji Foundation. It is a network of teachers that has been formed through voluntary participation. The informal group meets periodically on its own initiative and not as a part of any department directive.

Acknowledgements

Writing the 'acknowledgments' for this book seemed impossible. Till it occurred to me, what made it so difficult.

This book is a chronicle of my experiences over the last twelve years, and so is a result of interactions with too many people to name. From those that have been with me always, to those with whom I have spent but a fleeting hour on a school visit, and the many people in-between—all have shaped this book. I am deeply grateful to them all.

And then there is another angle.

Looking back at these years, it is clear, what a privilege my life has been. Those who have made it such—with their unconditional love and unstinting support, have really made me and made this book. My gratitude to them is such that it cannot be expressed in the 'acknowledgement' section of a book, even when it happens to be my first book. There will be a time and place for that. But you know, what I feel. Thank you.